T0293895

TRUSTING GOD

GOD
WHEN YOUR
WORLD IS
FALLING APART

DR. ALPHONSO SCOTT

Published by: HigherLife Publishing & Marketing

PO Box 623307
Oviedo, FL 32762
AHigherLife.com

Content: Chris Maxwell; Editor: Ashley Niro; Design: Janet Robbins

ISBN: 978-1-954533-00-4 Hardcover
ISBN: 978-1-954533-02-8 eBook
Printed in the United States of America.
10 9 8 7 6 5 4 3 2 1

Contents

Foreword

AFTER READING THROUGH the draft of *Trusting God When Your World Is Falling Apart*. I am thoroughly convinced that the devotionals shared in this volume are ordained of God. Rarely have I seen so many answers to life's recurring questions presented as if they were the sole experiences of this author. But, having known Dr. Alphonso Scott since my early childhood, I saw many of the qualifying experiences that rendered him extraordinarily capable of dealing with life's curves and dips to the degree that he was able to extract the many lessons he shares with us in this volume.

Devotional after devotional speaks to the real feelings and aspirations of the average reader who finds himself passively forced to live with a disengaged society that often fails to sense the hurt caused by careless, and often callous, disregard for others. Dr. Scott captures the heart of both the struggling pessimist, whose life is frequently sidetracked by the unexpected, and the enthusiastic optimist, whose reach is never quite as far as his ambitions.

The hope portrayed in Week 2,"No One Is Hopeless Whose Hope Is in God" and pragmatically actualized in Week 32, "Lord, Be with Me in All the Changes in My Life", is uniquely tailored for all of us by a writer who has experienced the dichotomy of both the highs and lows of life; he has learned to navigate as if all things were equal! *Trusting God When Your World is Falling Apart* speaks to every station of life.

I highly recommend this series of devotionals to all persons whose life demands the interactions of an authority greater than him or herself. Benjamin Franklin advised that we seek not only to live by our own experiences, but rather, that we learn to take advantage of the lessons to be gained from other people's experiences. In his own inimitable way, Dr. Scott suggests that we not attempt to live our life without the ever-present assistance of an active relationship with God. He makes that suggestion in realtime, as he captures life as most of us know it and live it!

—Bishop Jesse Battle, July 2021

Introduction:
The World Seems to Be Falling Apart

BAD NEWS JUST KEEPS FOLLOWING BAD NEWS. We get tired of hearing it, but we keep on listening. We feel weary and worn, but we keep on paying attention to all the division, all the hate, all the lies, all the deception, and all the negative stories.

But, my friends, while everything makes it seem like this world is falling apart, I have news for you. I have good news to tell you.

We can put our trust in God.

The reason we can trust God is because of who He is, not because of who we are. This book is going to remind you about who God is. These devotions will fill your mind with truth about God being the one we can trust.

Let me tell you about this God. He is the God of love. Real love. True love. No matter what another person has done, God loves them anyhow. No matter what you have done, God loves you anyhow. God loves everybody every day and in every way.

Don't you want to receive what God has for you? It is a gift of love. His love for every kindred, every tribe, every nationality on the face of the earth. For God so loved the world that He gave His Son. And He gave His Son so the people He loves might have eternal life with Him (John 3:16). The Bible does not say that God loves a particular segment of humanity, but the whole world.

Though this whole world seems to be falling apart, I am inviting you to believe it is time for us all to be falling in love with the God who already loves us.

Spend a few moments each day to read and reflect on my thoughts and on God's Word. Hear His voice. Receive His love. If you do, you just might begin trusting in Him like you never have before. If you do, you will place yourself in His strong and loving arms even when the world seems to be falling apart.

That is where I want you to be. That is where God wants you to be. So, let us join together right there, held in the arms of the God who loves us completely.

We Are Blessed to Be in Another Year

Sunday: Let There Be Light

And God said, "Let there be light," and there was light. God saw that the light was good, and he separated the light from the darkness. God called the light "day," and the darkness he called "night." And there was evening, and there was morning—the first day. (GENESIS 1:3–5)

LET'S BEGIN THE NEW YEAR WITH THESE THREE WORDS: We are blessed. Yes, there have been many struggles and challenges. Yes, much uncertainty surrounds us.

But the best way to starting a year is to go all the way back to the beginning. What did God say? Let there be light! Hear Him saying that again today. Hear His voice declaring blessings of light amid all the sadness and questions.

Though these days feel so dark, we are blessed. "Let there be light," God said, and there was light. "Let there be light for you today," God is saying, and there is light. Like God did on that first day of His design, God is doing that on this first day of a new year. Evening, morning, a day: God is bringing new light and His light is good.

See His light today. Refuse to let any darkness diminish His light. It is a new year, a new start, a new beginning for a new life. Welcome it. Let there be light in your life today. This day begins your year of light.

Monday: The Light of the World

When Jesus spoke again to the people, he said, "I am the light of the world. Whoever follows me will never walk in darkness, but will have the light of life." (JOHN 8:12)

NOTICE THE LIGHT EARLY IN THE MORNING when the sun rises. Notice the light in the afternoon when the sun shines brightly. Notice the light in the evening as the sun sets. The light allows us to notice the beauty around us. It provides safety as we walk and travel. It brings warmth during these times of cold weather. It helps us see what is all around us.

Not only did Genesis begin with God creating all things and bringing light, Jesus reminded people that He is the light. That illustrates the safety, direction, and warmth Jesus brings. He said, "I am the light of the world."

He followed that revelation by saying those who follow Him will have the light of life.

You are blessed to be in another year, so be mindful of who Christ is. John 8:12 gives us the answer for a life of victory this year: Jesus is the light of the world. Because of His light and because we walk not in darkness but have the light of life, this year can be a bright year.

Because of that, this year will be a blessing to all.

Tuesday: Living in the Light

This is the message we have heard from him and declare to you: God is light; in him there is no darkness at all. If we claim to have fellowship with him and yet walk in the darkness, we lie and do not live out the truth. But if we walk in the light, as he is in the light, we have fellowship with one another, and the blood of Jesus, his Son, purifies us from all sin. (1 JOHN 1:5–7)

CAN'T IT ENCOURAGE YOU TODAY that the light of Jesus shines our way? Can't it encourage you today that the light of Jesus shines through our lives to others?

Even when clouds cover the sun, light is still there. Even when clouds of life hide the light of Jesus, that brilliance is still there. It is within us, His people.

Live today aware of the light. Live today thankful for the light. Live today giving that shining light to others.

In 1 John we read how in God there is no darkness at all.

Think about that. Dwell on that. Believe that. While hearing all the darkness in the news, believe that in God there is no darkness at all. None at all!

Our calling is to walk in the light, fellowshipping with one another. Washed clean and purified from all sin, we shine like the light.

What are you doing this new year? You are living in the light!

Wednesday: His Light in Our Hearts

For God, who said, "Let light shine out of darkness," made his light shine in our hearts to give us the light of the knowledge of God's glory displayed in the face of Christ. (2 CORINTHIANS 4:6)

WE DON'T WANT TO DRIVE OR WALK THROUGH THE DARK. We need to be able to see where we are going.

So, we reach for a light.

In 2 Corinthians, Paul reveals the place for God's light to shine. To walk through the dark and to see where we are going, we need to identify a source of light. Where is it? His light is in our hearts.

What a wonderful truth that is. God isn't just a distant being. He has made His light shine in the hearts of those who serve Him. And think about what His light is like. Paul said it is the light of the knowledge of God's glory displayed in the face of Jesus.

What an honor we must not forget. The light and love of Jesus shines through the hearts of His people.

Let us grasp what we can do today. A shine of His love to go through us to someone else. A shine of His hope to flow through us to this sad world.

Rather than relying on other sources to bring us the light of God, we can receive that light and reveal it to the world around us.

Thursday: Good Words as a Shining Light

You are the light of the world. A town built on a hill cannot be hidden. Neither do people light a lamp and put it under a bowl. Instead they put it on its stand, and it gives light to everyone in the house. In the same way, let your light shine before others, that they may see your good deeds and glorify your Father in heaven. (MATTHEW 5:14–16)

TO REVEAL HOW WE ARE SHINING LIGHTS, Jesus used a wonderful illustration in what many refer to as the Sermon on the Mount. "You are the light of the world," Jesus said.

He then made interesting statements:

- A town on a hill cannot be hidden.
- People do not hide light but place it where it can light up the house.
- Live as a shining light so others see your good deeds and give God the glory.

Think about how the world would be a different place if we accepted that assignment from Jesus.

One way we can begin today is by speaking kind words. Speak words of light. Communicate with a tone of God's light. Declare shining words.

And please remember, the words of light will be coming into this world through people like us. We are the voices God has chosen.

I know, we often do not feel confident. But Jesus said we are the light of the world. That is who we are! Realize that is your identity and your assignment. His light will shine through us as our words change the world.

Friday: My Light and My Salvation

The Lord is my light and my salvation—whom shall I fear? The Lord is the stronghold of my life—of whom shall I be afraid? (PSALM 27:1)

THERE IS SO MUCH FEAR IN THE WORLD TODAY, isn't there? Think about your own fears. What have you been the most afraid of? As this new year begins, what fears frighten you each day?

The psalmist David knew about fear and about light. He was a shepherd. He had spent time in the darkness and watched the sun come up. He knew how fear could attack quickly. He also knew the power of God to bring light into darkness, to bring victory into what appears to be defeat, and to bring peace when everyone else is afraid.

Protect his sheep? David chose faith instead of fear.

Kill a giant? David chose faith instead of fear.

How? How did David make that choice? Because he knew the Lord was his light and his salvation and his stronghold. Reflect on those words today:

- Light
- Salvation
- Stronghold

Confess today that God is your light, that He is your salvation, that He is your stronghold.

Because of who God is, there is no reason to fear.

Saturday: Children of Light

For you were once darkness, but now you are light in the Lord. Live as children of light (for the fruit of the light consists in all goodness, righteousness and truth) and find out what pleases the Lord. (EPHESIANS 5:8–10)

FOR THOSE WHO MADE IT THROUGH LAST YEAR, please know this: you are blessed. You are blessed to endure. You are blessed to face another year. You are blessed by the God of blessings.

In Ephesians, Paul wrote a specific way he wanted his readers to know they were blessed. Though they formerly were living in darkness, Jesus brought them to light. They were now children of light in the Lord. What a true blessing to them. What a true blessing to us. What a true blessing to all who follow Jesus.

Because of their role as children of light, Paul instructed them to live like it. It isn't enough to preach it or to sing it. It isn't enough to just say it. The truth of being children of light must be lived out.

Paul revealed that the fruit of the light includes all:

- Goodness
- Righteousness
- Truth

That not only brings light through our lives but also is pleasing to the Lord.

Isn't that the way to begin and endure a new year? Living as the light and pleasing God? Yes, that is the way.

No One Is Hopeless Whose Hope Is in God

Sunday: When Feeling Hopeless

Create in me a pure heart, O God, and renew a steadfast spirit within me. (PSALM 51:10)

MUCH OF TODAY'S NEWS reports sound hopeless. Money problems. Medical problems. Marriage problems. Conflict among families and businesses and churches and nations. Disagreements lead to hate. Bitterness flavors conversations.

Those are often reactions to internal issues. Fear displays itself in an argument or a harsh tone of voice. Worry shows itself with anxiety and lack of sleep. People feel like there is not hope for the future—even next week.

Let me remind you that no one is hopeless whose hope is in God.

David, one of our Old Testament heroes, knew both victory and defeat. He made wonderful decisions and poor decisions—just like we do.

In his prayer of Psalm 51, David finally knew what to do when he felt hopeless. Instead of placing hope anywhere else, he turned to the God he loved.

Pray that prayer of David today. If you feel hopeless, ask God for these two blessings:

- Create in me a pure heart.
- Renew a steadfast spirit within me.

When feeling hopeless, don't attack others or remain defeated. Refuse to rely on help coming from your own effort or the applause of people. Cry out to God, requesting a pure heart and steadfast spirit. God can create and renew today.

Monday: Calling on God

Do not cast me from your presence or take your Holy Spirit from me.
(Psalm 51:11)

Sometimes we pray, asking to be given something. We have hopes that our desires will come our way. Provision. Peace. Joy. Hope. Good health.

Other times we pray, asking for a thing to be kept distant from us. We have hopes that what we dread will stay far away. War. Hate. Sickness. Harm. Bad days.

And other times we call on God to be sure He never leaves us. When we view ourselves unworthy to be in His presence. When we feel like complete failures. When we think there should be no way God stays with us.

Those prayers are vital to our endurance. Have you been there? Are you there now? What should you do?

Call on God.

In the prayer of Psalm 51, David called on God not only for things to come his way. He pleaded for God not to cast him away from God's presence. He requested for God never to take the Holy Spirit from him.

If you feel unworthy today, if you feel rejected today, if you feel defeated today, pray. Pray the way David prayed: he let his worries be released in prayer to God.

Calling on God might not be asking for an abundance of riches today. It might not be asking for a huge revival in your church. Your prayer today might need to say: "Dear God, stay with me."

Call on God with that prayer. He will hear you and never leave you.

Tuesday: Desiring Restoration

Restore to me the joy of your salvation and grant me a willing spirit, to sustain me. (Psalm 51:12)

HAVE YOU LOST SOMETHING important to you?

You thought you'd always keep that gift nearby. But somehow you misplaced it.

You thought you'd drive that new vehicle for a long time. But someone crashed into you on the highway.

You thought that money would stay in the bank. But those hospital bills were higher than you expected.

You thought that friend would always be around to talk to. But a small disagreement became something they refused to let go.

David was feeling like he had lost his closeness to God. His joy was gone. His willingness was gone. And he wanted them again. He desired restoration so he pleaded with God to bring back what felt like was gone.

If you feel that way, join David in praying these requests right now:

· Restore to me the joy of your salvation.
· Grant me a willing spirit.
· Sustain me.

Pray those words to God. The ancient prayer can become real in your heart today. Pray it in faith, believing God will answer—no matter what your emotions might be telling you. Trust God, not your feelings. Trust God, not your doubt. Trust God, not your own ability.

Even though you lost something very important, today is your day of restoration.

Wednesday: Hoping for a Future

Then I will teach transgressors your ways, so that sinners will turn back to you. (Psalm 51:13)

WE HAVE ALL HAD TIMES WHEN WE PLEADED WITH GOD to provide something. We prayed over and over for that same request to be answered. Not much else would come to our minds. Just that one prayer.

Then? God answered. He did what we had hoped, and He did it better than we hoped or imagined.

That, my friends, cannot be the end of the story. We should rejoice and thank God for His answers, yes. We should celebrate with humble hearts of gratefulness, yes. But we should also glance into the future—realizing God wants us to take what He has given to us and give it away to others.

David wanted his past washed away from him. David also was the type of leader who wanted to see something good come out of something bad. He had hope for the future. This was what he hoped to do:

- Teach transgressors God's ways.

He also had a wonderful reason for such a goal:

- So that sinners would turn to God.

Grab on to those hopes for you future. You have received God's forgiveness, now hear His calling to teach others the ways of the Kingdom so that others will turn to God.

Pray that prayer. God will answer.

Thursday: Believing Again

Deliver me from the guilt of bloodshed, O God, you who are God my Savior, and my tongue will sing of your righteousness. Open my lips, Lord, and my mouth will declare your praise. (PSALM 51:14–15)

THIS STORY OF DAVID IS CRUCIAL for our own stories. It reminds us that sin isn't the end of the story. Confession and repentance lead to forgiveness. Accepting God's forgiveness can move a person toward believing again. No longer controlled by doubt. No longer held back by defeat. No longer stepping to the side.

Now it is time to believe again. Now it is time to stand up again.

Pray for deliverance from evil, then sing to God for His righteousness. Let praise to God come from your mouth every time you open it. Believing again helps us give praise again. Believing again helps us live in righteousness again.

On this day, will you believe that is happening? Look at today's date and mark it. Admit again that this is the month, that this is the week, that this is the day, that this is the moment when you choose to believe again.

You are delivered from evil. You declare God's praise. Look up today. Although so much fell apart, you have trusted God.

Friday: Praying with a Broken Heart

You do not delight in sacrifice, or I would bring it; you do not take pleasure in burnt offerings. My sacrifice, O God, is a broken spirit; a broken and contrite heart you, God, will not despise.
(PSALM 51:16–17)

THE BIBLE SPEAKS OF THREE SACRIFICES that are to be offered:

1. **The sacrifice of a broken spirit**—"The sacrifices of God are a broken spirit: a broken and contrite heart, O God, thou wilt not despise" (Psalm 51:17). God sometimes despised the sacrifices the people took to the altar because they were blemished, but He never despised the sacrifice of a broken spirit and a contrite heart.

2. **The sacrifice of praise**—"By him therefore let us offer the sacrifice of praise to God continually, that is, the fruit of our lips giving thanks to his name" (Hebrews 13:15). That is another sacrifice that always pleases God.

3. **The sacrifice of dedicated lives**—"I beseech you therefore, brethren, by the mercies of God, that ye present your bodies a living sacrifice, holy, acceptable unto God, which is your reasonable [spiritual] service" (Romans 12:1, addition mine). *(The New Testament Speaks)*

Reflect on each of those three areas. As you pray with a shattered heart, offer your broken spirt. Offer your praise. Offer your sacrifice.

Rejoice in God's response. He has forgiven you. He has received you. He has restored you.

Receive His healing of your broken heart.

Saturday: Living with Hope

May it please you to prosper Zion, to build up the walls of Jerusa-
lem. Then you will delight in the sacrifices of the righteous, in burnt
offerings offered whole; then bulls will be offered on your altar.
(PSALM 51:18–19)

ALL THOSE YEARS I PREACHED I wanted to see people who
would truly hear the Word of the Lord. Why? I knew what it could
do to them. I knew what it had done to me.

With so many people hopeless in this world, we must hear God's
Word of hope. He restores cities and nations. He reunites families.
He revives churches. He rescues sinners. He reveals truth.

Those areas in your life where walls are broken down and you
feel fearful, God is rebuilding walls of His protection over you. He
will not let you be defeated or destroyed. He will not let the enemy
win over you. He will not let your life be of no value.

That is the Word of the Lord for you today. That is the Hope of
the Lord for you today.

Stop dwelling on all those negative words. Stop obsessing over
situations distant from God's plan.

God will take delight in you as you give your life to Him. He can
take your broken life and build up new walls for you. Do not resist
His hope. Believe and receive His hope today.

Nothing Is Too Big for God

Sunday: God Is So Big

Great is the Lord, and most worthy of praise, in the city of our God, his holy mountain. Beautiful in its loftiness, the joy of the whole earth, like the heights of Zaphon is Mount Zion, the city of the Great King. God is in her citadels; he has shown himself to be her fortress. (PSALM 48:1–3)

BEGIN YOUR WEEK by comparing situations to God. Whatever you are facing is tiny compared to how big God is.

It helps us if we confess this truth:

· Great is the Lord!

Concentrate on the various ways God is great. Think about His character and His miracles. Think about what He did in Scripture and what He has done in your life. Start your sentence with these words, then finish it with a list of how you see God being great:

· I have seen the greatness of the Lord in …

That collection can remind you that God is big.

The psalm also said that the Lord is:

· Most worthy of praise.

It then gave examples of places and traits for which God could be praised:

· In the city of our God, His holy mountain.
· Beautiful in its loftiness,
· the joy of the whole earth,
· like the heights of Zaphon is Mount Zion,
· the city of the Great King.
· God is in her citadels;
· He has shown himself to be Her fortress.

Nothing is too big for God to accomplish. Nothing is too little for Him to use you in accomplishing His goals.

God is so big. Your problems are so small. And you are a big part of the solution.

17

Monday: Everything Else Is So Small

When the kings joined forces, when they advanced together, they saw her and were astounded; they fled in terror. (PSALM 48:4–5)

REMEMBER, NOTHING IS TOO BIG FOR YOUR GOD. He can accomplish what He chooses.

Remember also that nothing is too tiny for Him to use in accomplishing His plans.

Those huge situations? God sees them as just more opportunities to do His will. God sees them as circumstances for His character to come forth. God sees them as occasions to triumph.

The enemy who seeks to destroy you today will see God's work and be astonished. He will see God's favor in your life and flee in terror. He will see God's shield and comprehend he has no chance in seeking your destruction.

However situations look through our human eyes, each one is so small from God's view. He is big and strong and victorious. Everything is so small when compared to God's capability of bringing victory.

All through the Bible we see God turning big problems into big miracles. Goliath does not seem as big if David looks at him through God's eyes. A storm on the water while in a boat does not feel as frightening if disciples could see it through the eyes of Jesus. Five thousand hungry people might not look as large if disciples could see a miracle of Jesus waiting.

See God's victory already happening. The final results might be a little bit away but remember everything else is so small when compared to how big God is.

Tuesday: God Brings Victory

Trembling seized them there, pain like that of a woman in labor.
You destroyed them like ships of Tarshish shattered by an east wind.
(PSALM 48:6–7)

THE WRITER OF PSALM 48 GAVE EXAMPLES of what it was like for the enemy when God did His big work.

This is what happened to the people who attacked God's chosen people:

· Trembling seized them there.

The prayer next reveals an illustration of what it felt like for the foe:

· Pain like that of a woman in labor.

The rivals were not comfortable. They were in excessive anguish. Discomfort propelled their direction. Agony pillaged their world. They were no competition for God.

Notice the next phrase in this ancient prayer:

· You destroyed them.

That war was finished by God. He completed His work on the enemy. The evil nation had been defeated and destroyed.

Then, the psalm offers an image of how the defeat felt for the foes:

· Like ships of Tarshish shattered by an east wind.

When God brings victory, the enemy is destroyed. His remains appear to look like ships shattered at sea by winds and waves of a storm.

View your situation that way. God is on your side. You are on God's side. He brings victory. The enemy is defeated. Their remains are removed from your life. Can you see that today? Can you believe that today? Pray it! See it! Believe it!

Wednesday: God Brings Security

As we have heard, so we have seen in the city of the Lord Almighty, in the city of our God: God makes her secure forever. (PSALM 48:8)

GOD NOT ONLY BRINGS VICTORY. God also provides security.

The prayer from Psalm 48 offers a confession. They prayed, "As we have heard, so we have seen. God keeps us secure forever."

Many of us might say, "But I have faced many struggles. Why wasn't God there to protect me?"

Yes, there are many situations where God didn't seem to be there. Why didn't He stop that abusive person? Why didn't He bring the miracle before a house was taken away? Why didn't He heal that child before death came her way?

This life on earth will continue bringing sadness and disappointment. We live in a fallen world and death awaits us. Pain comes. Grief comes. Storms come. Difficult days come.

But, through it all, we can dwell on potential negatives or ultimate positives. Our minds must choose to realize nothing is too big for God. Our thoughts must dwell on learning to trust God when the world seems to be falling apart.

One way to help redirect our thinking is to pray prayers like Psalm 48. Confess promises like this one:

- God makes her secure forever.
- God makes us secure forever.
- God makes me secure forever.

Even with all the stuff happening around you, believe today in the security of God.

Thursday: God's Unfailing Love

Within your temple, O God, we meditate on your unfailing love.
Like your name, O God, your praise reaches to the ends of the
earth; your right hand is filled with righteousness. (PSALM 48:9–10)

THERE ARE DAYS LIKE TODAY when we have a choice. What voice will we hear? What words will dwell in our minds? What will be our focus? Where will we invest our inner energy?

Psalm 48 gives us a glimpse at what we should do in those moments of questioning.

Look at the steps we can make to have our attention take residence in God's unfailing love:

- Within Your temple,
- O God,
- We meditate on Your unfailing love.
- Like your name,
- O God,
- Your praise reaches to the ends of the earth;
- Your right hand is filled with righteousness.

Placing our attention on those traits can redirect our thoughts and correctly guide our choices. Why should we let our minds go any other direction? God's unfailing love is what keeps us safe and secure.

Live within God's temple today—wherever you are. Cry out to God over and over: O God, O God, O God. Meditate on His unfailing love. Remember His name of power and strength and holiness and reverence. Let praise reach the ends of your earth: your house, your room, your office, your vehicle, your desk, your bed, your kitchen, your neighborhood, your town, your state, your city, your world. Believe again that God's right hand—that place of power and authority—is covered in righteousness.

And let these words be the words you choose to dwell on today: God's unfailing love.

Friday: Telling the Next Generation What God Can Do

Mount Zion rejoices, the villages of Judah are glad because of your judgments. Walk about Zion, go around her, count her towers, consider well her ramparts, view her citadels, that you may tell of them to the next generation. (PSALM 48:11–13)

ONCE WE GRASP GOD'S UNFAILING LOVE, what next? Once we realize nothing is too big for God, what next? Once we trust God even when the world is falling apart, what next? Once we choose to look up, what next?

In our Scripture for this week, we now see that the nation began to celebrate. They had a party of rejoicing. They toured with festivity. They delighted in God and hoped the younger ones would hear:

· That You may tell of them to the next generation.

On this day, pray for those who are young. Contact people in the next generation and tell them about God's unfailing love. Reach out to them, telling them stories which prove how big God is. Spend time with them, offering examples of ways to endure when the world is falling apart.

Your voice is the one they need to hear today.

Your influence is the one they are waiting on.

You might be the mentor who can lead them to Mount Zion.

You might be the chaperone who can guide them toward the towers of God.

Tell them. Tell the children and grandchildren and great grandchildren what God can do. Tell them today.

Saturday: God Is Our Guide

For this God is our God for ever and ever; he will be our guide even to the end. (PSALM 48:14)

OUR BIG GOD is also our guide.

When we try to assist others, we don't need to rely on our own capabilities. Remember these words:

• God is our God.

And notice the timing placed on this passage. God is our God for ever and ever. He is our God forever. There is no end. He is our eternal God. Forever is just that: forever!

Even to the end—another way of writing about eternity—God is directing us:

• God is our Guide.

If we remember today that our God is our guide, how might that impact our energy? Possibly, we just might pay more attention to what really matters instead of what isn't such a big deal after all.

Remember what we learned this week:

• Nothing is too big for God to accomplish.
• Nothing is too little for Him to use you in accomplishing His goals.

Thank Him for those facts. Ask for His guidance. Let Him be your God.

Read through Psalm 48 over and over. Those words were not only for them. Those words are for you. Those words are for the next generation. God is so big. Everything else is so small. God brings victory, security, and unfailing love. God is our guide as we let the world know nothing is too big for Him—or too big for us.

When You Have Nothing Left but God, You Learn That God Is Enough

Sunday: Nothing Left

At this, Job got up and tore his robe and shaved his head. Then he fell to the ground in worship and said: "Naked I came from my mother's womb, and naked I will depart. The Lord gave and the Lord has taken away; may the name of the Lord be praised." (JOB 1:20–21)

"THE LORD GIVES AND THE LORD TAKES AWAY," Job said. "Naked I came from my mother's womb, and naked I will depart," he said.

Job had lost just about everything. He got up, tore his robe, and shaved his head. He then fell to the ground in worship and voiced those statements.

Think about entering a time of worship when you have nothing left. When all is gone except your own life, how can a person worship God? That seems impossible.

But when we have nothing left but God, we begin to learn that God is enough.

Job can teach us that, as we read his story.

"May the name of the Lord be praised," Job said.

We might have responded by saying, "I thought God loved me. I thought God has promised His protection and provision. What did I do wrong? Why is God doing this to me? Why is He allowing this to happen?"

You know how we feel those emotions and contemplate those thoughts when all seems to go wrong. But, even when we have nothing left, we have God. Even when we have nothing left, God has us.

Remind yourself today: even with nothing else today, God is enough. I will praise Him.

Monday: Nothing Left but God

In all this, Job did not sin by charging God with wrongdoing.
(JOB 1:22)

IN SITUATIONS WHEN ALL GOES WRONG, how do you respond?

If you ask those questions as mentioned in yesterday's devotion, do you move on or stay in that place of resentment?

Read today's verse:

"In all this, Job did not sin by charging God with wrongdoing" (Job 1:22).

Remember that Job was upright and blameless, living in a righteous way. God bragged to Satan about Job's virtue, but Satan argued that Job was only righteous because of God's favor. God allowed Satan to attack Job, but not to take Job's life. Job began receiving reports about sheep, servants, and children all dying.

The story goes on. Conversations between God and Satan. Conversations between Job and his wife. Conversations between Job and men claiming to be his friends.

If we put ourselves in Job's place, how would we have responded? He had nothing left but God.

We might say "God is enough," but do we believe it the way Job had to believe it?

Take a moment to mentally remove all your personal belongings. What if they were all gone? What if they were all gone today? Would God be enough for you?

If you have nothing left but God, would that be enough?

Tuesday: God Wins in the End

After Job had prayed for his friends, the Lord restored his fortunes and gave him twice as much as he had before. (JOB 42:10)

READING THROUGH THE BOOK OF JOB allows us to see many different moods. Those conversations between Job and the other men disclose a variety of attitudes.

Even with a mixture of questions, Job chose to let the story end well. He refused to turn away from God. He prayed for his friends and the Lord restored Job's fortunes—giving Job twice as much as he owned before this disaster.

What is the lesson for us when the world is falling apart? Is there a way to keep looking up and trusting God when we feel like everything has gone wrong?

We must never forget: God wins in the end.

Those words should be our theme for today, for this year. God wins. So much else might be gone today, but we still have God and that is what really matters. Friends come and go. Money is saved, and money is lost. Material possessions arrive, and they leave. People appear, and people depart. Through it all, God is enough. Through it all, God wins in the end.

Can't we decide today to live like we believe God wins? Can't we think better thoughts today, dwelling on the truth that God is enough?

Yes, we can. Yes, we must.

God wins, and He is enough.

Wednesday: A Reason to Endure

For to me, to live is Christ and to die is gain. (Philippians 1:21)

Philippians is an epistle of joy. Paul's words inspire us to live in Christ's joy no matter what we are going through.

Paul certainly endured hardships. He battled persecution, disagreement, and division. But he did not quit. He chose to endure. And he had joy along the way.

Why? Why did he stay on course and endure the race? Paul did not see death as the end of a story. He saw his eternal home as a positive outcome.

So, he was stable, firm, unchanging. If there has ever been a time that was needed on earth, now is that time. We need followers of Christ to stand up and shout: "I am living for Jesus. If I die for Him, that is fine. Nothing can stop me, detour me, defeat me, or trap me. I am finishing the race. I am called to endure. God wins in the end. If I am with God, I also win. When it feels like we have nothing left but God, we begin to learn that God is enough. God is enough!"

That outlook can bring joy during trials, celebration during persecution, stamina during conflict, endurance during harassment. May the assurance be that what you have left in your life is God, and nothing else really matters.

To live is Christ. To die is gain. What a reason to endure!

Thursday: The Best Perspective During Pain

But whatever were gains to me I now consider loss for the sake of Christ. What is more, I consider everything a loss because of the surpassing worth of knowing Christ Jesus my Lord, for whose sake I have lost all things. I consider them garbage, that I may gain Christ. (PHILIPPIANS 3:7–8)

HOW BAD WAS IT FOR PAUL? Didn't he see miracles and revival at the beginning of our New Testament Church? Didn't his letters become our biblical epistles? Were things that bad for him?

Oh, my friends, there were many times when Paul wasn't sure if he would last any longer. Those trials brought deep pain, but Paul refused to quit.

The way Paul endured when so much was falling apart was to have the best perspective. His view helped him tolerate the trials. He wrote to the church that he had decided to count anything that might be gains as losses for the sake of Christ—and the things that might be considered losses as only rubbish so that he might gain Christ.

The best perspective during difficult times is to count all things to be loss in view of the surpassing values of knowing Jesus.

Look through Paul's perspective today. Perceive circumstances the way he chose to see them.

Friday: Treasures in Heaven

Jesus answered, "If you want to be perfect, go, sell your possessions and give to the poor, and you will have treasure in heaven. Then come, follow me." (MATTHEW 19:21)

JESUS RARELY ANSWERED QUESTIONS the way people assumed He would.

Once a young man approached Jesus and asked, "What good thing must I do to obtain eternal life?"

Jesus, as He often did, responded to the question with His own question: "Why do you ask me about what is good?" Then Jesus said, "There is only One who is good. If you want to enter life, keep the commandments."

Those remarks brought more uncertainty to the man. He didn't know for sure what commandments Jesus was talking about. "Which ones?" he asked.

Jesus answered, "You shall not murder, you shall not commit adultery, you shall not steal, you shall not give false testimony, honor your father and mother, and love your neighbor as yourself."

"I have kept all of those," the man answered. "Is there anything else I still lack?"

Jesus replied with an answer that has been talked about for many centuries in many languages. It has left people confused.

Jesus said to him, "If you wish to be complete, go and sell your possessions and give to the poor, and you will have treasure in heaven; and come, follow Me."

That might not be what you would have said or what I would have said. But it is what Jesus said. The man went away sad, because he had much wealth.

Today, ponder these two questions: Are you planting treasures in heaven or only on earth? Is God enough?

Saturday: God Is Enough

And everyone who has left houses or brothers or sisters or father or mother or wife or children or fields for my sake will receive a hundred times as much and will inherit eternal life. (MATTHEW 19:29)

GOD REALLY IS ENOUGH.

Think about those who have left all to follow Jesus. People are being persecuted around the world because they have chosen to follow Jesus. They had to realize that, no matter what happens, God is enough.

Do you believe that today? Is God enough for you today?

I could not have made it through the ministry all these years if God had not been enough for me. I have faced many seasons where God was all I could depend on. He was all I could trust. He was the one holding me up and holding me together. And, you know what? God was enough.

If you feel like you have nothing left today, God is with you. He will not leave you. He will not forsake you. He will not abandon you.

People might. Pleasure might. Prosperity might. But God and His promises are always with you. He is not just here to help us feel better; He is here to help us live better. We do that by choosing to see God as enough.

Through the love of Jesus we can live eternal life. Job would tell us God is enough. Paul would tell us God is enough. Can you believe that today? Can you receive that today?

When you have nothing left but God, you begin to learn that God is enough.

The Strength of the Church
Is in Its People

Sunday: The Church and People

Here there is no Gentile or Jew, circumcised or uncircumcised, barbarian, Scythian, slave or free, but Christ is all, and is in all. (COLOSSIANS 3:11)

"I WOULD LOVE CHURCH if it wasn't for the people." Have you heard someone say that? Have you said it yourself? Or maybe you thought it but resisted saying it?

Think about what Paul wrote in Colossians. Remember that God is speaking those words for us to apply today. The people in the church are all made in the image of God. The people in the church are God's people. All people are loved by God. All people are so loved by God that He gave His Son for them.

Not Gentile or Jew. Not old or young. Not tall or short. "Christ is all and is in all."

The church is people. The church is people who choose to see Christ as all. The church is people who choose to see Christ as in all.

Paul wanted that original audience to stop the division between circumcised or uncircumcised, slave or free. He wanted to bring a new form of life, a new understanding of being the people of God, a new understanding of Christ being among all the people.

So, look around the next time you're in church. Or the next time you're walking through your neighborhood. Glance at the faces. Listen to the voices. And choose to let Christ be all and in all.

Monday: God's People

Therefore, as God's chosen people, holy and dearly loved, clothe yourselves with compassion, kindness, humility, gentleness and patience. (COLOSSIANS 3:12)

THOUGH SOME SAY the problem of the church is the people, God sees things differently. To Him, the strength of the church is in the people.

People—those made in the image of God. People—those offered forgiveness by the blood of Jesus. The chosen. The holy and dearly loved.

As the holy and dearly loved people, as the strength of the church, how can we be sure to live in such a way that others can see those realities? Paul makes it clear, instructing us what to wear. He wasn't writing about the colors of our clothes or the styles of our suits. He wasn't writing about whether we wore new or old, or if our outfits are expensive or thrilling. He was talking about how the strength of the church is people who are clothed in the character of Christ.

God gives a list of ways that character is displayed:

- Compassion
- Kindness
- Humility
- Gentleness
- Patience

So, today, ask yourself these questions. Am I acting with compassion? Am I displaying kindness? Am I living with humility? Am I revealing gentleness? Am I showing patience?

Those traits come from God, into God's people, then to those around us. Let us show God's strength through our compassion, kindness, humility, gentleness, and patience.

Tuesday: People Living as the Church

Bear with each other and forgive one another if any of you has a grievance against someone. Forgive as the Lord forgave you. (COLOSSIANS 3:13)

FOCUS AGAIN ON THOSE CHARACTER TRAITS from Colossians: compassion, kindness, humility, gentleness, and patience. Wonderful qualities of life. Godly behaviors. Christlike attitudes and actions.

But Paul wrote a few specific examples of how those are displayed in real life. If the strength of the church is in its people rather than buildings or property or performance, members must be sure to live this way. Think about how these words are so needed in these days.

- Bear with each other.
- Forgive one another.

Those two actions can change families and churches. They can change cities and cultures. They can begin seeing God's work in action.

To bear with each other indicates not giving up or running away. Stay there with one another. Don't skip church. Don't avoid church because you have been hurt by people. Bear with each other as God has chosen to bear with us.

And forgive. Even if you have a grievance—and we all have those—forgive just as you have been forgiven.

What if those two goals became the descriptions of our lives? Bearing with others and forgiving others. That would be the people truly living as the church.

Wednesday: The People of Love

And over all these virtues put on love, which binds them all together in perfect unity. (COLOSSIANS 3:14)

HOW DO PEOPLE DESCRIBE your church? Do they talk about how many people come or how good the preaching is? Do they discuss the style of music or the design of the sanctuary?

God wants the church described as the people of love. Above any other virtue, Paul wrote, must be love. That love binds people together. That love brings perfect unity.

In these days of separation and division, we need people of love. In these times of hurt and hate, we need people of love. In these days of anger and anxiety, we need people of love.

Think about it this way. What if people leave a church service and—before they say anything about lights, sound, sermon, or temperature in the building—say, "I felt loved by those folks"? What if people said that about your church? What if people said that because of how you welcomed them?

That love binds people together. It holds people in perfect unity.

Oh, yes, it is simple to think about this in theology and in theory. But, I'm talking about it related to how we treat other people. Talking to them in loving ways. Speaking to them with that virtue of love flavoring everything we say and how we say it.

Unity can come from that kind of church. A church of love.

Thursday: The People of Peace

Let the peace of Christ rule in your hearts, since as members of one body you were called to peace. And be thankful. (COLOSSIANS 3:15)

LET US REMEMBER THIS AGAIN: the strength of the church is in its people. The church is not powerful by properties, wealth, or endowments, but by its membership. It must therefore convert and conserve people. It must evangelize and educate followers of Christ. It must receive and retain members.

Today we read a verse reinforcing the importance of God's people "as members of one body." Paul wrote to that early church. In these days our churches need to hear that. In these seasons of conflict and confusion our people need to believe that. Members of one body—not people hating and harming one another.

But how is that possible? How can unity be significant during these uncertain times? The verse for this day reminds us how. It must be the peace of Christ ruling our hearts, not manmade power trying to control the hearts of people. It is the peace that comes through Jesus.

We are members of one body. Though of various ages and nationalities and backgrounds, we must be one in Christ. That invitation brings us to the spiritual climate of peace. In homes. In hearts. In churches. In communities. Peace of God is what we must allow to rule and reign in our true selves.

Receive that peace today as you pause and give God thanks.

Friday: The Message of Christ

Let the message of Christ dwell among you richly as you teach and admonish one another with all wisdom through psalms, hymns, and songs from the Spirit, singing to God with gratitude in your hearts. (COLOSSIANS 3:16)

AS PEOPLE OF PEACE we can dwell together in a variety of ways. We can worship together. We can study and hear God's Word together. We can pray together and eat together and laugh together and cry together.

But, whatever we are doing when together, everything should be centered around the message of Christ. That is what is to dwell among us. That is what is to live among us.

Like a peaceful fragrance in the air brings a calmness when we breathe it in, so the message of Jesus—His life and death and resurrection—can change our atmosphere. Paul said we should let it dwell in us richly. As we teach. As we admonish. As we sing psalms and hymns and spiritual songs with gratitude in our hearts. Let the message of Jesus be a part of everything we do.

Try it today. Look at your schedule and think: How is the message of Christ a part of that? Then, include Jesus in all you do and say.

People will notice the gratitude. People will notice Jesus through your life.

Saturday: In All We Do

And whatever you do, whether in word or deed, do it all in the name of the Lord Jesus, giving thanks to God the Father through him.
(COLOSSIANS 3:17)

SOMETIMES PEOPLE SAY, "Whatever."

They use the word to mean, "I don't really care," or "It doesn't matter."

Think about it differently today. Read Colossians 3:17 and pay attention to that word, "whatever." We are instructed, invited, and inspired to have one way of doing "whatever" we do. When we talk. When we listen. When we act. When we wait. There is one way we must do "whatever" it is we do.

We must do all in the name of the Lord Jesus. We must do that with thankful hearts.

Imagine how such motives and behavior can change us. Imagine how such motives and behavior can change our homes and schools. Imagine how such motives and behavior can change our churches and cities. Imagine how such motives and behavior can change our nation and world.

Don't wait until Thanksgiving. Don't wait until everything is just how you want it to be. Believe today that God is at work in your life and bring His blessings to you. Choose—in whatever you say and do—to bring a spirit of thankfulness. Change the world one word and one deed at a time through a thankful heart.

God Often Knocks Out the Props before We Settle Down

Sunday: A Cry for Mercy

*Have mercy on me, O God, according to your unfailing love;
according to your great compassion blot out my transgressions.*
(PSALM 51:1)

GOD OFTEN HAS TO KNOCK OUT the props before we settle down to work for Him instead of ourselves.

Hasn't that happened to you? Haven't we all made poor decisions? We look back through the calendars and notice those years, those months, those weeks, those days when we see how our choices brought huge impacts on our lives. And on the lives of others.

That is why God gives us commands. Those directions are not to earn His love. God loves us no matter what. Those instructions are to keep us from harming ourselves and other people.

David, like many of us, loved God. David, like many of us, prayed regularly. David, like many of us, could tell story after story of God's amazing works. But David, like us, also chose to do what he should not do.

He let lustful desires determine his choices. Adultery, death, deception: how would this poetic prayer warrior talk to God after he committed such terrible sins?

He cried for mercy. His prayer of Psalm 51 desperately pleads to God to blot out his transgressions. He knew the only way God would do that was because of unfailing love and great compassion. Today, confess your sins. Today, repent of those sins. Today, cry for mercy. Today, remember God's unfailing love. Today, reflect on God's great compassion. Today, believe God will forgive you.

Monday: Made Clean

Wash away all my iniquity and cleanse me from my sin. For I know my transgressions, and my sin is always before me. (PSALM 51:2–3)

NO ONE IS HOPELESS whose hope is in God.

Do you believe that today? Even when you feel hopeless, do you believe that you can still have hope in God?

David had a heart after God. He prayed. He led a nation. He fought battles. He saw impossibilities become realities. But he failed.

Haven't you seen victories before? Haven't you been successful? Haven't you also sinned?

Yes, you have. We all have. Today God is reminding us all there is a way to be made clean. God is declaring into our spirits that today is the day to be made new.

What must we do to see that happen? Confess as David did. Request as David did. With hope in God, ask Him to wash away all your iniquity and cleanse you from all sin. You know your transgressions and God does too. You know that sin which is always before you but hope God moves it away through His forgiveness. Let it happen today. Ask God to make you clean.

Let your hope be in God today. You will never be hopeless again.

Tuesday: Understanding God's Judgment

Against you, you only, have I sinned and done what is evil in your sight; so you are right in your verdict and justified when you judge. (PSALM 51:4)

IF WE REALLY BELIEVE that no one is hopeless whose hope is in God, we must also understand the results of refusing to truly put our trust in God. It isn't God's fault if we have failed. Why should we blame Him? It isn't God's will for us to turn away from Him. Why can't we accept responsibility?

Understanding God's judgment means that we come to view Him correctly. His goal isn't to destroy us. It is the devil who is out to steal, kill, and destroy us. God wants to guide us in the right way to keep us from evil.

When you are driving and see a stop sign, what do you do? I hope you stop. When the traffic light is red, what do you do? I hope you stop. If you choose to keep driving when you shouldn't, who is at fault? You are. Who is responsible for the consequences? You are.

David was close enough to God that he could understand God's judgment. Against God had David sinned. God's guilty verdict was justified.

By confessing his understanding of God's decision, David was able to find hope again. The hope that was gone had returned because of God's grace and forgiveness.

What about you? Did you drive through when you should have stopped? Are you suffering from a poor decision? Pray today to the judge who has found you guilty. Confess your sins. Believe He will bring His grace and forgiveness your way, just as He did for David.

Wednesday: Why We Sin

Surely I was sinful at birth, sinful from the time my mother conceived me. Yet you desired faithfulness even in the womb; you taught me wisdom in that secret place. (PSALM 51:5–6)

DO YOU LIKE TO LISTEN in to someone else praying? Hearing them talk to God can disclose much about their hearts and their hurts. It can also reveal their hope. Again, no one is hopeless whose hope is in God.

David had his hope placed firmly in God. David knew his sinfulness came from birth. Some folks might see this as a negative perspective of humanity. But it is reality. We can see all the hate and sin around us. Anger, bitterness, war. Harsh words stated. Hateful lives lived. So, our hope cannot be based on humanity's ability to do what is right. Like David, our hope must come from God.

We sin because of our inherited sinful nature. For all have sinned and fall short of God's glory. There is none righteous, no not one. That is why we sin. That is why David sinned.

The God who despises our sins is also the God who desires wisdom. He is also the God who can teach us wisdom. Though He loathes and detests our wicked decisions, God sees a way to bring us to that secret place.

Today, understand why you sin. Today, choose to bring your sinful self to God—just like David did.

Thursday: Whiter Than Snow

Cleanse me with hyssop, and I will be clean; wash me, and I will be whiter than snow. (PSALM 51:7)

DO YOU LIKE TO SEE THE SNOW? Do you like to play in the snow?

David mentioned the good news in his honest prayer to God. He asked God to make him clean—he asked for God to cleanse him with hyssop. He declared a statement of faith that if God washed him, he would be whiter than snow.

Think about the snow. How clean it looks. How stunning it feels. How transformed it is. That is how David illustrated God's power of forgiveness.

This keeps us from living hopeless lives. This keeps our hope in God. He is God the Father, God the Forgiver, God the Redeemer, God the Cleaner. He washed us so we become whiter than the snowflakes falling on a winter evening.

Stare at our face in the mirror. See yourself the way God sees you now. You've repented of your sins and asked Him to forgive you. He has! God has forgiven you and washed you whiter than snow.

Thank God for His forgiveness. Sing a song of praise. Celebrate—not because of a winter snow fall but because of God washing you clean. Rejoice that you are clean today.

Friday: A Time to Rejoice

Let me hear joy and gladness; let the bones you have crushed rejoice. (PSALM 51:8)

NO ONE IS HOPELESS whose hope is in God. That is what we emphasize throughout this book.

Have you been willing to take that new perspective? Have you chosen to let go of old things and pursue new things? Have you decided to repent of your sins and surrender totally to God? Have you entered a time of rejoicing?

David's prayer made a transition from repentance to rejoicing. The regret, the sorrow, the remorse was genuine. He released his sadness to God.

And what did God do? God forgave David.

What does God do for us when we repent? God forgives us.

What should we do then? We should do what David did:

- Repent of our sins and pursue God.
- Receive His forgiveness and begin this new journey with Him.
- Initiate a time of rejoicing.
- Hear joy and gladness!
- Let the crushed bones rejoice!

Something happens to us when we take time to truly rejoice. This isn't something fake. This isn't a show. This is the forgiven ones singing to our Forgiver. This is the healed ones thanking our Healer. This is the formerly hopeless ones now being filled with hope as we acknowledge our Giver of Hope.

Let us rejoice.

Saturday: Sin Removed

Hide your face from my sins and blot out all my iniquity. (PSALM 51:9)

WE SOMETIMES FORGET THINGS. We schedule something and expect to remember it. If we don't write it down, we just might forget it. If we don't have someone reminding us, we just might forget it.

Think about the prayer David prayed. Think about the thoughts we have been dwelling on this week. David didn't forget his sin. He remembered it and repented of it.

What did God do? God forgave David. God has now chosen to forget in a new way—He no longer holds David's sin against him.

That is what we need. We need our sins removed, taken away, forgiven, forgotten by God.

If you have prayed as David prayed, please remember: your sin is removed. If you have repented as David repented, God hides His face from your sins and blots out all your iniquity.

Please remember this also: no one is hopeless whose hope is in God. You might feel hopeless, like there is no way out of your own mess. Others might treat you like you're worth nothing. God, though, is offering you hope—as long as you put your hope in Him.

Let the Forgiving God remove your sin today. Let the Forgiving God forget your sin forever.

Life Is Our Most Precious Possession

Sunday: God Is Whole

As obedient children, do not conform to the evil desires you had when you lived in ignorance. But just as he who called you is holy, so be holy in all you do; for it is written: "Be holy, because I am holy." (1 PETER 1:14–16)

LIFE IS OUR MOST PRECIOUS POSSESSION. Christ is our highest Rewarder. Therefore, a life devoted to Him is the greatest investment one can make.

Many people have created their own god(s).

As I observe them, I realize that the god they've molded is not the God of the Bible. They only want a god in a certain part of life. They do not want to live entirely through Him. They make a god that fits their life, afraid to trust Him wholly.

Scripture reveals that we need all of God; we cannot live with pieces of Him. His nature is perfect, removed from evil, and untainted. Holy is His will, mind, council, protection, and wisdom.

God is Holy.

I love the Holiness of God! It expresses His glory. Everything about God is glorious. When people go their own way they miss God's wonderful plan for their life.

Do not be as those who choose their own devices. I plead with you to make sure that your god lines up with the Holy One of Scripture. We cannot shape our own god; we need Him to shape us.

Who are we to play games with God? Christ is no Burger King; we can't have it our way.

It is all about God. All power is in His hands. We overcome the world through Him. God doesn't change because of circumstances; circumstances change after meeting God's power.

Trust God in his wholeness.

Monday: Two Tactics to Give Your Children a Good Foundation

Start children off on the way they should go, and even when they are old they will not turn from it. (PROVERBS 22:6)

OUR CHILDREN are our most precious commodities. They are the Lord God Almighty's gift to us. Our job as parents is to give them a solid foundation upon which to build the rest of their lives. It is my charge as a parent to see His fingerprints expanded on the lives of my family.

My wife and I worked hard to give our children a solid biblical foundation. The question we repeatedly faced was how to develop positive morals, values, and a biblical worldview in our children when they were surrounded daily by negative outside influences.

Based on my life experience and the Word of God, here are ways to give children a good foundation:

1.) Ask God for Help

Raising children can be terrifying. There were times when my boys found themselves in situations that I did not know how to handle. But I trusted God to show my wife and me what to do—even if the children didn't agree. Also, I stayed in the Word, walking in the footsteps of the parables. If we really want to help our kids, we need to ask God to give us strength and wisdom at the right time.

2.) Start Early

Engage with your children on their level about matters that they care about early in life. Their first ten years is the period of time when our children are the most malleable due to their dependency. This is the time when you can help to shape who they are and who they will become.

With age the parent's influence diminishes and the "friend" influence increases so we must create positive exposure early.

Tuesday: Two More Tactics to Give Your Children a Good Foundation

Fathers, do not exasperate your children; instead, bring them up in the training and instruction of the Lord. (EPHESIANS 6:4)

LET'S CONTINUE from yesterday's thoughts. Today, here are two more tactics to give our children a good foundation.

3.) Be a Watchman

We need to monitor what our children view through the media. Believe me, if you have filth on your television or other devices, your children will find it. Our children are exposed to too much junk that teaches them how to be disrespectful, rebellious, and use profanity. As parents we must be the watchmen for our children and limit their exposure to the grime of the world.

4.) Get to Know Their Friends

The voices of your children's friends become important. So, become the friends of your children's friends. Take the extra time to be with your son or daughter when they are with their friends. See who is influencing them. You will maximize your influence while having enlightening conversations.

We must take measures to make sure we give our kids' biblical foundation top priority. Ask God for help. Take time right now as you are reading this to pause and pray for them. Begin early. Make this time the right time. Be a watchman and a friend to their friends.

That is God's calling in your life.

Wednesday: Furthering God's Kingdom

Therefore go and make disciples of all nations, baptizing them in the name of the Father and of the Son and of the Holy Spirit, and teaching them to obey everything I have commanded you. And surely I am with you always, to the very end of the age.
(MATTHEW 28:19–20)

I REMEMBER RETURNING from an incredible mission trip to Nairobi. We spoke about expansion, new schools, youth programs, camps, etc. Our investment there allows Christ's work to grow. Fellowships will multiply as news of the good work spreads.

Jesus Christ is the light of the world; He died for our sins. He defeated death to bring life. We must share this message. The Body of Christ must agree on the importance of spreading the good news globally.

We are followers of the Apostles Doctrine. This truth is steadfast, and we must continue our commitment to it. Jesus said in the Gospels, "I come in my Father's name." Therefore, we call on the name of Jesus. We are in partnership to further the Gospel.

We do all things in the name of Christ, because we are His followers. There is power to heal, to baptize, and to *save* in the name of Jesus.

African ministries and the needs they serve grow in tandem. We are all the family of Christ and must assist our fellow Christians.

The Lord will aid us in addressing all our issues. When God gives a vision, He will supply provision.

Will you join in furthering God's Kingdom?

Thursday: God's Path to Financial Victory

And my God will meet all your needs according to the riches of his glory in Christ Jesus. (PHILIPPIANS 4:19)

THAT VERSE IS TRUTH.

The world tries to weigh us down, tries to convince us God isn't enough. *This is a lie.* God is faithful to His promises; He will always supply our needs. We need to tell the world there is nothing God can't do.

Folks like to make excuses. They always have a reason for their financial struggles. People fail to remember that everyone has God-given abilities. Let me ask you this, "Are you holding on to some things tighter than God?"

Jesus said that we must not lay up for ourselves treasures on earth but in heaven (Matthew 6:19–21). Stuff on earth is taken away, but what is in heaven remains. If our treasure is in heaven, that is where our hearts will be.

We must be obedient to the Lord. If God requires us to release something and we do not, how can we expect Him to bless us?

All I have belongs to the Lord. He has entrusted me with a loan. All I have is His to take and I will praise Him for whatever He leaves me.

Ask God to give you a dream, and test yourself so your faith will increase immeasurably. He wants His people to rise up. He gave us His Word so we have the secret to success; He does not want us to fail.

We must trust in His eternal Word. That is the path to financial victory.

Friday: How to Handle Financial Crises

Now to him who is able to do immeasurably more than all we ask or imagine, according to his power that is at work within us, to him be glory in the church and in Christ Jesus throughout all generations, for ever and ever! Amen. (EPHESIANS 3:20–21)

MANY PEOPLE ARE FACING FINANCIAL SITUATIONS that are impossibly heavy: upside down mortgages, maxed out credit cards, unemployment, living pay check to pay check.

When we are going through challenging times, we can't look at our financial circumstances. Don't look to the bigness of your need but look to the bigness of your God.

Remember, God spoke everything into existence and we can never fall out of His grace. He has a plan for us. But, the devil doesn't want us to hold onto God's Word. He wants us to look at our troubles and be diminished by our circumstances.

As we go through our financial difficulties we can't be discouraged by our need; we need to look to the bigness of our God and listen to His command, *"Follow My Word."* We can't allow the devil to influence us.

Where I served at Lively Stone Church in St. Louis we knew how to get out of financial crises. We followed the biblical principle of sowing and reaping. For us to reap a harvest we must first sow seed. Why would we do that? We placed our trust in God.

Trust Him today!

Saturday: The Bigness of God

Give, and it will be given to you. A good measure, pressed down, shaken together and running over, will be poured into your lap. For with the measure you use, it will be measured to you. (LUKE 6:38)

YES, AS WE FOCUSED ON YESTERDAY, giving to God is proof that our true trust is in God. Don't hold on. Let go. Give to God. This is how we know that we believe in the bigness of God.

If you want the blessings of God in your life, open up and give. Plant your seed. When it seems like you can't, God can. Give your way out of debt. The seed you sow is not your harvest but a pathway to your harvest.

Place your faith in God; you will see some miraculous things happen. Give and those blessings will come. Can't we truly trust God and give?

God wants to bless you in *good measure, pressed down, shaken together, and running over*! God wants it *poured into your lap*.

Your needs might be large today, but God is larger.

Your troubles might be heavy today, but God is heavier.

Your debt might be strong today, but God is stronger.

Don't just say you believe. Give like you really do believe!

Don't look to the bigness of your need but look to the **bigness of your God.**

Letting Disappointments Reinforce My Confidence in the One Who Is Enough

Sunday: Confidence in God

In you, Lord my God, I put my trust. (PSALM 25:1)

THIS WEEK, WORK ON SEEING all of your disappointments from God's point of view. That will reinforce your confidence in the One who is enough.

Placing confidence in God must include time in God's Word. Each day we offer Scripture for you to read, study, and reflect on. Each day we provide words to help shift the way you might normally view life's situations.

Psalm 25 is our prayer for this week. David wrote that prayer long ago, but it is fitting for us today. These three components from verse one guide us toward reinforcing our confidence in the One who is enough:

- In You
- Lord my God
- I put my trust.

We could place trust in a variety of locations or situations. We often make the mistake of misplacing our trust.

David confessed his direction for confidence in God: "In You." Join with David in that today. Let all your confidence be in God.

David then identified the One he placed his trust in: "Lord my God." He believed God was the Lord over all. He called out to the God who was above all.

It was in such a God and Lord that David could place his trust. And for us? That must be the route we take today. Our confidence must be placed in no other area or person or situation. Only in God.

Monday: Trusting God during Times of Disappointment

I trust in you; do not let me be put to shame, nor let my enemies triumph over me. (PSALM 25:2)

AS YOU REFLECT ON THESE VERSES from the Psalms, please remember the history. David wrote these poetic journal entries as he prayed to God.

Have you written any notes to God lately? Maybe you should. David did. His prayers were with words in rhythm and flow. The words of prayer were important to David. He would cry them out to God. He would sing them out to God.

Those poetry prayers then became hymns for the nation of Israel to sing. Now, so many years later, they are prayer examples for us. They are songs for us.

And Psalm 25:2 is just what we need today. Even during seasons of disappointments, even during such difficult years, even during times when we feel defeated, we can plead to God as David did. "Do not let me be put to shame," David cried. "Do not let my enemies overthrow me," David shouted.

Do you want to pray that way today? Go ahead. During times of disappointments we can release feelings in healthy ways to God. And this is why—because of David's first phrase: I trust in You.

Let God hear your blunt requests but let Him also know you place your trust in Him. Around all those disappointments, you choose today to place your trust in God.

He is enough.

Tuesday: My Hope Is in God

No one who hopes in you will ever be put to shame, but shame will come on those who are treacherous without cause. (Psalm 25:3)

Psalm 25:3 shows a contrast. For those who place hope in God, things will turn out one way. For those who are away from God, things will turn out another way.

Make a list of issues you are presently worried about. Money? Health? Relationships? Spiritual growth? Revival? Forgiveness? Abundance?

Beside each of the words on your list, write this phrase: "My hope is in God."

Oh, my friends, when we place our hope in God we will never be put to shame. We will never be without. We will never be defeated. We will never be forsaken. We will never be shaken.

Placing hope in God is a choice we make.

Can you make that choice today?

Now, whatever you are facing and whatever is on your list, let those five words bring confidence and hope and courage and joy to you today:

- My
- Hope
- Is
- In
- God!

Decide to place your hope in Him. Refuse to let any other person or any other situation be your source of hope. Let it come from the Giver of Hope.

Wednesday: Learning during the Journey

Show me your ways, Lord, teach me your paths. (PSALM 25:4)

How can our God of Hope help us trust in Him when everything around us seems to be falling apart? How can we "look up" when our world is telling us to look down? How can this year be better than last year? How can a new relationship endure the troubles that destroyed other relationships?

Friends, we must learn through this journey. Turning to God is a decision we make but it is an ongoing process. It is a relationship. It involves communicating with our Creator.

David did that. And He asked God, the Lord, for two specific things which can help David—and you—endure the journey:

- Show me Your ways.
- Teach me Your paths.

Step aside for a moment and pray that prayer with David. You are asking God for His revelation and His instruction. You are asking God to expose His ways. You are asking God to teach you His routes.

Let God be your teacher. Let God be your coach. Let God be your doctor. Let God be your professor. Let God be your parent. Let God be your shepherd. Let God be your leader.

Even with all your questions, trust the Lord today. Place your confidence in Him—He is enough.

Thursday: All Day Long

Guide me in your truth and teach me, for you are God my Savior, and my hope is in you all day long. (PSALM 25:5)

YOU KNOW THOSE DAYS that start out good but seem to suddenly go bad? What about those days which begin terribly but eventually become delightful?

A fun conversation can turn into a harsh argument. A time of anger can merge into hours of fun.

Why is that? Why can't we have God's heart all day long?

You know why. Sometimes we push truth aside and begin believing lies. When we do, we go in many dangerous directions.

David prayed a prayer that would be good for us to pray. He asked God—the One David viewed as his Rescuer and Savior—to:

- Guide me in Your truth.
- Teach me.

How much that would help us if we let God be our Guide and our Teacher all day long. In the morning when we wake. During the day when we experience a mixture of moods and experiences. In the evening when our bodies are tired, and our minds can hardly think any more. All day long our hope can be in one place and only one place: in our Guide and our Teacher.

Let God guide you today, all day long.

Let God teach you today, all day long.

That will be enough!

Friday: The Lord's Great Mercy and Love

Remember, Lord, your great mercy and love, for they are from of old. (PSALM 25:6)

SOMETIMES WE TALK ABOUT the old days. Songs we sang. Ballgames we played. Favorite meals. Preferred places. A church service we will never forget. A time of laughter that just won't leave our minds.

David knew the importance of remembering things from the old days. He knew this about it: God is the same God of mercy and love today and He has always been.

David prayed in a way to remind himself about two parts of God's character:

· God's great mercy.
· God's great love.

Mercy from God might be old, but it is also new. It is needed today.

Love from God might be old, but it is also new. It is needed today.

What about letting God's love and mercy be your main areas of attention? What if, instead of all the other feelings and thoughts which come to you today, you dwell your mind on love and mercy?

It might not change the weather, but it might make that weather not matter as much. It might not put money in your bank account, but it might make that money not matter as much. It might just let what matters most to God become the very same things which matter most to you.

God, and His great love and mercy, is about to show you today what matters most. Receive it.

Saturday: God Is Enough

Do not remember the sins of my youth and my rebellious ways; according to your love remember me, for you, Lord, are good. (PSALM 25:7)

I LOVE TO HEAR A TESTIMONY of someone who has surrendered all to the Lord. Don't you?

They tell of years wasted, but transition to stories about a total life transformation. They once hated church, but now they just can't get enough of church. They never wanted to sing to the Lord, but now they worship with excitement. They had a past of pursuing all those things which harmed them, but now they live in pursuit of God and His plan for their lives. They once lived like those who never cared about others, but now they seek ways to show God's love to the world around them. They formerly acted just like the devil, but now the Spirit of the Lord shows God's light through their lives.

What made the difference? How did they transition from one type of person to a totally different one?

They stopped looking for other things to make them happy.

They realized God is enough.

And, oh, how that changed so much. God forgave them of their past. God gave them more than enough in the present. God promised to guide them in their future.

Though the world was falling apart, they decided they weren't going to fall with it. Now, every day, they reinforce their confidence that God is enough.

Those are the stories I love to hear. Don't you?

Isn't that the story you want to live? Yes, it is. Start living it today. God is enough.

If at First You Don't Succeed, Keep Trying. You Are Above Average

Sunday: Trying Hard with a Thankful Heart

I thank my God every time I remember you. (PHILIPPIANS 1:3)

MY FRIEND, IF AT FIRST YOU DON'T SUCCEED, you are running above average. Keep trying.

The Apostle Paul was someone who kept trying. He refused to quit. When people turned against him, Paul kept on keeping on. During persecution, Paul finished the race. Quitting was not an option for him. Quitting shouldn't be an option for us, either.

But what can help us endure? What can overthrow those tendencies to resign? What can defeat desires to leave?

We must try hard in all we do. As we try hard, we can rely on strength from God instead of our own capabilities.

Over our efforts, though, arise our attitudes. We should try hard with a thankful heart.

Paul thanked God for those fellow believers every time they came to his mind. Yes, they had conflict in churches. Yes, they had disagreements. But Paul viewed the situation through the lens of thankfulness. His attitude of gratitude motivated him to keep on trying when others might want to give up. His heart of appreciation inspired him from deep within.

Begin this new week with a new strength. The muscle of thankfulness. You'll be inspired to take the next step, then the next step, then the next step. You'll soon be surprised to see how far you have gone.

Monday: Adding a Little Joy to Our Prayers

*In all my prayers for all of you, I always pray with joy because
of your partnership in the gospel from the first day until now.*
(PHILIPPIANS 1:4–5)

I SURE DO BELIEVE in the power of prayer. I cannot make it without those times when I call on God. There are moments when I weep in prayer, crying out to the Father in desperation. There are experiences when sorrow joins in the intercession and petitions, pleading on behalf of myself and many others.

But there are those additional times when joy comes in the morning. It is joy unspeakable and full of glory. Paul said it was in "all" his prayers for "all" of them that he "always" prayed with joy.

Oh, I want to live like Paul and believe like Paul. Don't you? If so, we need to pray like Paul. Let us pray often and pray with joy.

It is good to choose those moments when you pray with a big smile on your face. When you begin rejoicing and celebrating before you can even complete your prayer. When you shout a hallelujah to the Lord.

Paul had joy because those reading his epistle were his partners. He rejoiced because of the fellowship, the partnership, the family, the community, the unity.

Choose to rejoice and be glad today. Be above average; be someone who rejoices in the Lord as a lifestyle.

Tuesday: The Story Isn't Over

being confident of this, that he who began a good work in you
will carry it on to completion until the day of Christ Jesus.
(Philippians 1:6)

Our friend Paul was not only rejoicing, he was also confident. I didn't say he was cocky. I didn't say he was prideful. No, Paul was humble and gentle and kind. But he was also courageous and bold and confident.

What about you? Are you confident today?

Paul believed that the same God who started writing the story of Paul's life would complete that story. God, the author, knew where to take the story. He knew how to get the story to its conclusion.

State your confession today this way:

He who started a work in me will be faithful to complete it!

Say those words over and over. Pray them and believe them and sing them.

He who started a work in me will be faithful to complete it!

Your story isn't over. The best is yet to come. God's best is yet to come. So, keep on praying and obeying. Keep on believing and receiving. Don't give up. Keep on.

The story isn't over.

Wednesday: Memories of the Past

It is right for me to feel this way about all of you, since I have you in my heart and, whether I am in chains or defending and confirming the gospel, all of you share in God's grace with me. (PHILIPPIANS 1:7)

PEOPLE WERE IMPORTANT to Paul. People are important to God. People should be important to us.

Look at the heart of Paul revealed in Philippians 1:7:

- It is right for me to feel this way about all of you,
- since I have you in my heart and,
- whether I am in chains or defending and confirming the gospel,
- all of you share in God's grace with me.

Paul remembered his past. He wasn't always living for God. He wasn't always a follower of Jesus. God rescued Paul from religion and turned his life in a different direction. After that, Paul wanted to see that same transformation happen to others.

Even when chained and in prison, Paul would remember the past, so he would do what was right in the present. Even when people argued in opposition, he stayed true to the gospel.

Those are the memories which should guide our decisions. Remembering what the Lord has done. Refusing to forget the price paid so God would forget our sins.

Such memories can motivate us to be more like Paul and more like Jesus. Sharing in God's grace even when the world seems to be falling apart, we realize God has made us more than average people. We are His children, called by Him to change the world.

Thursday: Hope in the Present

God can testify how I long for all of you with the affection of Christ Jesus. (PHILIPPIANS 1:8)

DID YOU FORGET to make that phone call you promised? Stop right now before you read any further and make that call.

Did you forget to send that note you felt you should? Stop right now before you read any further and write that note.

Did you forget that prayer God invited you to pray? Stop right now before you read any further and pray that prayer for your friend.

Paul had hope in the present as he longed for other people. But it wasn't just a natural friendship. He called it the "affection of Christ Jesus."

Do you realize what God does with that affection? It isn't just fondness or liking someone. It is more than a superficial friendship or a romantic attraction. We are reading about spiritual connection.

God connects us with others in His family to become prayer warriors with them. It is hope in the present through those relationships which remind us of the deeper hope for all eternity. It is the affection of Jesus Christ—the love with a hope which believes in the best for others; the love with a commitment which sacrifices for others; the love that helps us keep on trying.

Friday: Love May Abound

And this is my prayer: that your love may abound more and more in knowledge and depth of insight. (PHILIPPIANS 1:9)

PAUL REVEALED HIS PRAYER to the Philippian believers:

- That your love may abound
- more and more
- in the knowledge and depth of insight.

He didn't pray for them that their talent would abound or that their success would abound or that their popularity would abound. He prayed that their love might abound.

Paul hoped those Christians would love like Jesus and live like Jesus. He wanted them to have so much love it was overflowing.

Think of those times you hear a song and you want to keep on hearing it. Or those times you eat some food and you just can't stop eating it. Or those times a sermon has you so inspired you can't get to that altar quick enough.

Things like that just have you wanting more and more.

That is what Paul wanted the early Christians' love to be like. He wanted it to abound. More and more and more. Never running out. Never becoming empty.

What a testimony that would be to the world today if our love for one another would abound. This world would be a changed place if we loved each other rather than treating people the way we often do. Let the love abound!

And Paul described how he specifically wanted their love to abound more and more: in the knowledge and depth of insight.

Knowing God well. Loving God's people. That must become our prayer too.

Saturday: Way Above Average

So that you may be able to discern what is best and may be pure and blameless for the day of Christ, filled with the fruit of righteousness that comes through Jesus Christ—to the glory and praise of God. (PHILIPPIANS 1:10–11)

THE SENTENCE FROM FRIDAY'S devotion continues in today's study. Paul revealed what he was praying for and he continued by giving the reason:

- So that you may be able to discern what is best
- and may be pure
- and blameless
- for the day of Christ,
- filled with the fruit of righteousness
- that comes through Jesus Christ—
- to the glory and praise of God.

What if similar phrases became our prayer every day? What if those words describe who we are in Christ?

Able to discern what is best. Pure. Blameless. Filled with righteousness. I see those traits as way above average. I see those qualities revealing Jesus Christ through our everyday lives.

As this week's studies end, this is how I want you to end. End in prayer. Go through the names of people you know—family, friends, strangers, missionaries, pastors, neighbors—and pray Paul's prayer over them. Believe each of them can become way above average.

Then, end the prayer by praying it for yourself. Believe God is making you pure and blameless, filled with the fruit of righteousness through Jesus. And believe God is going to get all the glory for your above average life.

Faith Is a Way of Walking, Not a Way of Talking. Be Mindful

Sunday: The Walk of Faith

Therefore, since we are surrounded by such a great cloud of witnesses, let us throw off everything that hinders and the sin that so easily entangles. And let us run with perseverance the race marked out for us. (HEBREWS 12:1)

THOUGH FAITH IS ALL THROUGH SCRIPTURE, Hebrews chapter 11 is that portion of the Bible specifically about faith. The pages define and defend faith. The stories tell us about people of faith. Their hardships, their waiting, their enduring, their attitudes. They chose to still believe, no matter what happened. They chose to walk in faith, whatever stared them in their faces.

But what is faith? How can we truly be people of faith?

Faith is a way of walking, not a way of talking. We must become mindful of that.

Some folks just want to talk about faith and preach about faith and sing about faith. Some folks want to teach on how to have faith. Some folks want to just say that word "faith." But those views limit the large truth about faith.

Our faith—trusting totally in God—should be about who we are and everything we do. Each day of the week. Every single conversation. The way we live. The attitude we carry. Those are all revelations about what faith is, and if we are truly people of faith.

More folks need to stop talking so much about faith and start walking by faith. If you want to be mindful of faith as a lifestyle, ask yourself this question today: Am I throwing off everything which could hold me back and hinder me, so I can run this marathon of faith?

Monday: Fixing Our Eyes on Jesus

Fixing our eyes on Jesus, the pioneer and perfecter of faith. For the joy set before him he endured the cross, scorning its shame, and sat down at the right hand of the throne of God. Consider him who endured such opposition from sinners, so that you will not grow weary and lose heart. (HEBREWS 12:2–3)

FOR US TO CHOOSE THAT MARATHON of faith, we must be sure to glance in the right direction. The writer of Hebrews says we must fix our eyes on Jesus.

You know what it's like to fix your eyes on something. When we do that, we choose to look no other direction. We focus, and we stay focused. We avoid the distractions. We resist what could lure us off course.

That is what the heroes of faith from Hebrews 11 did. That is what people of the church have done through good times and difficult times. That is what we are called to do today.

Fix our eyes on Jesus. Don't let our look waver. Don't allow our view to wander.

It helps to know who this Jesus is. The King James Version describes the One that we are fixing our eyes on as the:

· Author of our faith.
· Finisher of our faith.

What did this Author and Finisher do? For the joy set before Him, Jesus:

· Endured the cross,
· Scorning its shame,
· Sat down at the right hand of the throne of God.

How do we choose to complete the marathon? How do we fix our eyes on Jesus? We must consider Him who endured hardship so that we will not grow weary and lose heart.

That is our assignment for today. Let us fix our eyes on Jesus.

Tuesday: Faith during Hardship

Endure hardship as discipline; God is treating you as his children. For what children are not disciplined by their father? If you are not disciplined—and everyone undergoes discipline—then you are not legitimate, not true sons and daughters at all. (HEBREWS 12:7–8)

FOR A TIME, UNBELIEF encamped on the outside of the church and hurled its weapons of ridicule against it. But, failing there, unbelief sneaked into the church and began its deadly work.

Paul found unbelief at work in the churches he established: "I marvel that ye are so soon removed from him that called you into the grace of Christ unto another gospel: Which is not another; but there be some that trouble you, and would pervert the gospel of Christ" (GALATIANS 1:6–7).

Similarly Peter warned those to whom he wrote, "But there were false prophets also among the people, even as there shall be false teachers among you, who privily shall bring in damnable heresies, even denying the Lord that bought them" (2 PETER 2:1).

Unbelief is still at work in the churches: unbelief concerning the very fundamentals of our faith, unbelief concerning the truth and authority of the Scriptures, unbelief concerning the person and work of Christ, unbelief that would pluck the diadem of deity from His brow and present Him to the world as a mere man, unbelief that would tear the cross from the heart of the gospel and leave the world without a Savior, unbelief concerning the resurrection of Christ, unbelief that would leave His body in the grave and leave us with a dead Christ instead of a living Savior, unbelief concerning sin and salvation and the world to come. (BLUEPRINT)

We must endure hardship with faith.

68

Wednesday: Walking with Our Heavenly Father

Moreover, we have all had human fathers who disciplined us and we respected them for it. How much more should we submit to the Father of spirits and live! (HEBREWS 12:9)

THERE ARE MANY OF US who from time to time have overwhelming surges of doubt. Some people question God's desire to bring His blessings to us. Some people are unsure about the Kingdom life being for our wellbeing. Some go so far as to question their own salvation. Some ask, "Am I really on the Lord's side?"

As those questions and doubts come, we must remember this: The Lord came. He is the One who came to rescue us. He is the One who invited us and enabled us to walk with the Father.

Never forget that Jesus came. God so loved the world in its pitiful state. In its lost condition, God so loved. We all are like filthy rags to our Holy God. But He loved us, and He loves us today. Right now, He loves us.

So how did that Heavenly Father discipline us? He sent Jesus to make a way to transform us. That is the Father we must submit to, the Father we must trust today, the Father we are to walk with.

No, He is not against us. He is for us. Even as you doubt a little bit today, just shove that doubt out of your way.

Stand up and choose to believe. By faith, walk with your Heavenly Father.

Thursday: Sharing in God's Holiness

They disciplined us for a little while as they thought best; but God disciplines us for our good, in order that we may share in his holiness. (HEBREWS 12:10)

OUR PARENTS DISCIPLINED US a little bit, just as they thought was best. You remember those days, don't you? Some maybe didn't discipline just right, and we have had to work through those things. But God's discipline is just right. He has the correct motives. He knows exactly what to do and how to do it.

Notice the goal mentioned in Hebrews 12:10—in order that we may share in His holiness.

God isn't turning us away from Himself. God is recreating us more like Him. God is inviting us to be people of holiness, sharing in His character. Time with God gives us the opportunity to become more like God.

Today, please grasp the fullness of what God is saying. This isn't just another story. God has done this for us. God continues doing His work within us.

God thought of us even when we were too low down to think about ourselves. He pursued us and rescued us and redeemed us even when we were like disobedient little kids. He is still thinking about us and inviting us to share in His holiness.

Welcome His discipline and guidance. Share in His holiness.

Friday: Producing a Harvest of Righteousness

No discipline seems pleasant at the time, but painful. Later on, however, it produces a harvest of righteousness and peace for those who have been trained by it. (HEBREWS 12:11)

Every Christian is to be a soul winner. This is not work for a few to do, but for all Christians. And each one should prepare him or herself to be the best soul winner possible. In the early church, all the members were witnesses for Christ: "Therefore they that were scattered abroad went everywhere preaching the word" (ACTS 8:4). If Christians all through the centuries had maintained the zeal of the early Christians, there would not be millions of people in the world who have never heard the gospel.

There are several ways in which the individual Christian can witness for Christ. Exemplary living comes first. Christians are to live so that others will "take knowledge of them, that they have been with Jesus." Then, there is the testimony of the lips. If one is a real Christian, he or she has something to tell, and God expects him or her to tell it. Letters and gospel tracts can be used in winning others to the Savior. People who have the passion in their souls will find a way to witness for Christ. (BLUEPRINT)

Even in times of struggle and correction, even in those times when God redirects us, we can be producing harvests of righteousness. We can be people of faith, bringing God's peace to others.

Let us live in that zeal and that faith today, producing a harvest to change the world.

Saturday: Paths for Our Feet

Therefore, strengthen your feeble arms and weak knees. "Make level paths for your feet," so that the lame may not be disabled, but rather healed. (HEBREWS 12:12–13)

BECAUSE OF MANKIND'S SINFUL nature after the fall of Adam and Eve, humans still tend to stray away from God.

What did God do about that? He sent Jesus on earth to endure crucifixion in order to save the souls of people.

That is what God did. Remember what He has done for you. Yes, you. Realize He has done this for you. And remember because of that, God has new plans for your life. He has new paths for your feet. He has new hope for your future.

So, as the writer of Hebrews says, strengthen your feeble arms and your weak knees. These are the days to step out. These are the days to stand tall. These are the days to race onward. These are the days to stay on course. These are the days to be healed.

Look at your schedule. Review your goals. Evaluate your plans. Receive His strength. Let Him set up straight those weak knees. Know that this day is the day for God's plans to be done.

Be sure that all you do is in fulfillment of God's goals in your life. Let God lead the paths for your feet. Even when the world is falling apart, God knows where to take you.

Action Is Necessary for the Job at Hand

Sunday: Faith Brings Confidence

Now faith is confidence in what we hope for and assurance about what we do not see. This is what the ancients were commended for. (HEBREWS 11:1–2)

MY FRIEND, ACTION IS NECESSARY for the job at hand. "No farmer ever plowed a field by turning it over in his mind." Even in the mess we all face, if we have faith we shall be blessed. Hebrews 11 makes that clear to us.

We see all kinds of examples in the Bible, in history, and in our contemporary culture. We need faith to believe God will see us through. Unemployed? Have faith that all is not lost. Told by your spouse you are no longer loved? It is not the end of the story. Have faith. God will take care of you. Even if that person doesn't want you, God wants you.

Jesus loves me, this I know. For the Bible has told me and the Bible doesn't lie. If we based our beliefs and behavior on the Bible, we could have the faith desperately needed today.

We need faith in the real world. Your children, your job, your happiness—no, take it to Jesus. The economy, the wars, the society—just take it to Jesus. Take it all to Jesus. He knows how to take care of it.

What can calm our nerves and have us say thank you Lord, is when we notice God knows what we need and how to provide what we need.

We need faith that God will help us rise above all our personal guilts. Some of us are living with guilt that should have been gone long ago. There is therefore now no condemnation: have faith and believe that today.

Monday: Faith Brings Vision

By faith we understand that the universe was formed at God's com-
mand, so that what is seen was not made out of what was visible.
(HEBREWS 11:3)

WE CANNOT HAVE FAITH in this real world if we continue carrying around guilt. A child of God should not carry around guilt.
If you have done wrong, get on your knees and confess to God.
Repent, and then get up and get going. You are forgiven. The past is
gone. Stop letting it control you. Your thoughts. Your feelings. Your
decisions. You are running from God when all you need to do is run
toward God. He will forgive you. Have faith. Have faith today.

Let faith bring a new vision to you—a view that grasps through
the failures and the small expectations, a view that refuses to be
held back.

Live today with faith. And, if tomorrow comes, we have faith
that God will carry us through.

If you don't have faith, fear will paralyze you. You won't do what
you can do because you are scared. If you stop doing things because
you might have a heart attack, you are being controlled by fear. You
could have a heart attack just sitting around doing nothing. Fear
must not stop us from rising up and stepping out in faith.

The world is feeding us fear. The enemy wants us crippled with
fear. We are afraid to look out the window. Fear can control what we
do, what we think, what we buy, what we say. It must be faith rather
than fear that directs our decisions.

Tuesday: Faith to the Finish

All these people were still living by faith when they died. They did not receive the things promised; they only saw them and welcomed them from a distance, admitting that they were foreigners and strangers on earth. (HEBREWS 11:13)

IN HEBREWS 11 WE READ about the people who chose to ride faith to the finish line. That was the action necessary for the calling God has on them.

Abraham had a certain uniqueness about him. Even to the point of God calling him His friend. You must have a unique quality for God to call you His friend. The quality that Abraham acquired was a faith quality. That quality was so important he became the father of faith.

We really need to hear about the quality of life we need in the real world. The realities of life did not always look hopeful for Abraham. Yes, he was a man. He had feelings and desires and aspirations. Things did not always go the way he had hoped. But the quality God had given him kept coming forth. He had to face the realities of life. When things didn't go well even after God had promised him he would be a father of faith and that a seed would come, things didn't look very good.

We get upset when God promises something, and it doesn't happen when we think it should. It seems like something comes along and washes our faith away. When the perils of life come before us we let that get us down instead of letting our faith stand strong.

That is when we choose to believe. That is when we have faith to the finish.

Wednesday: Faith and the Job at Hand

People who say such things show that they are looking for a country of their own. If they had been thinking of the country they had left, they would have had opportunity to return. (HEBREWS 11:14–15)

ARE YOU A BELIEVER? Faith is what will carry you and keep you standing.

But, you might ask how. Begin to pray right now. That is what will help you and what will help the world. That is having faith for the job at hand. Being scared isn't what will change us or change the world. Having faith can. Having faith will. People are waiting and watching to see our faith. Our faith will get them to follow Jesus.

To be here is Jesus. To live is Jesus. To step forward is Jesus. To minister is Jesus. To give is Jesus. To love is Jesus. What we do for Christ is what counts. Not what we did before, but what we are doing now. It is not time to sit down. It is time to stand up.

At times I have had to tell myself, "I'll not let my own mind be my mind. But I will let the mind of Christ be my mind." It is still day, so have faith. Ask God to help you and bless you and bring you out of your darkness. He can do it. Just have faith. God gives strength to do what He calls you to do.

Thursday: Living by Faith for What God Has Prepared

Instead, they were longing for a better country—a heavenly one. Therefore God is not ashamed to be called their God, for he has prepared a city for them. (HEBREWS 11:16)

WE ALL NEED FAITH for the real world. Those mentioned in Hebrews 11 lived in faith.

Faith was reversed when God showed up. How many of us would get in a hurry when we see a bush burning? God knows how to move us. How many of us, if we ever get in the belly of a fish, would get up running? God knows how to give us the faith for what is happening. God knew that Jonah would meet opposition. He knew he would sit under a tree. God knew that Jeremiah would be just like fire all down in our bones. God knows how to give you faith.

When that little boy met Goliath, faith came alive. David had already taken down a lion. We have already met great obstacles. Give God all you have, and God can turn it into what He wants it to be. Have faith in what God already has prepared for you.

God knows how to refresh you by showing what happens to the disciples in the middle of a storm. They could end up in the bottom of the deep. Somewhere along the line they saw a little hope in the middle of that body of water. That wasn't just anything or anyone coming their way.

They saw Jesus showing up.

Friday: An Action of Faith Is Necessary
No Matter the Outcome

These were all commended for their faith, yet none of them received what had been promised. (HEBREWS 11:39)

JESUS CAME TO THOSE PEOPLE of faith. Jesus came for those people of faith. Would they believe? Would they have faith and believe?

Will we live by faith for what God has prepared even when the world is falling apart? Yes, let us have faith today!

We are always wanting and wanting and wanting. What about just believing that God is who He says He is? What about taking actions of faith which are necessary no matter the original outlook or the long-term outcome. Faith in God. And acting on that faith.

Those people of faith had not all received what was promised. But they believed. They knew all would come at the right time and in the right way. They were worshiping God for who He was, and not what He might do for them. They knew they were in trouble out there. Sometimes we know we are in trouble right here. They wondered what they should do. Sometimes we wonder what we should do.

But they had faith in Jesus. Jesus showed up. Will we have faith in Jesus to show up? Will we? Do we?

Saturday: God's Plans Are Better for Us

Since God had planned something better for us so that only together with us would they be made perfect. (HEBREWS 11:40)

MY FRIEND, LET'S END AS WE STARTED. Please remember that action is necessary for the job at hand. "No farmer ever plowed a field by turning it over in his mind."

We have four seasons. Sometimes within each of those seasons it might act like another season. It is like a season within a season. It might get hot one day in the winter, but it is still winter. It might get cool one day in the summer, but it is still summer. A temporary change doesn't totally change the season.

But that is what the enemy is trying to do with many of us. He wants us to react on something temporary and forget what season God really has us in. We must have faith in God and His season. Without faith it is impossible to please God. Show forth faith.

The people of faith choose to be sold out to God. Completely dedicated to God. Content with our commitment to God. Refusing to waver from God. Choosing to walk with God.

God has plans for each of the people of faith. God has plans for us. We can have faith. We can look up and trust God even when the world is falling apart. Action based on faith is necessary today. The harvest will come. Believe it!

It Is Better to Be Despised for the Right Than Praised for the Wrong

Sunday: Living with Wisdom

The proverbs of Solomon: A wise son brings joy to his father, but a foolish son brings grief to his mother. (PROVERBS 10:1)

REFRESH YOUR MEMORY. Since the fall of man, our world functions abnormally. Since the fall of man, things have been going downhill. Even though man has come up with various inventions, even when God has stepped in and given man a certain amount of reprieve, human beings have constantly messed up.

Have you seen the mess ups? Have you messed up? Look at what these behaviors have done to our societies through the ages. Civilization is in chaos. Relationships are at war. Minds are dwelling on unhealthy methods of thinking.

Seems as though that is where we are now. We are constantly being bombarded by the thought that we could be done away with at any time. We are hearing so much intensity. Visit your local supermarket. Get three days of supplies. Get some snacks. Get extra water. The world seems to be just falling apart all around us. We are panicking as we sit back watching the news.

Like that old saying, "When I take one step forward it looks like I have taken two steps back." Well, it is better to be despised for doing what is right than praised for doing what is wrong.

Be wise children today. Refuse to be among the foolish ones. Even when the world seems to be falling apart, this is our time to live with wisdom. Let's not miss it.

Monday: Bad Decisions Bring Bad Results

Ill-gotten treasures have no lasting value, but righteousness delivers from death. (PROVERBS 10:2)

WHEN WE MAKE BAD DECISIONS, we shouldn't be surprised when we face bad results. That is how it goes. That is what the Proverbs teach us.

We can also see that in how people responded to Jesus. People pursued ill-gotten treasures instead of listening to the Voice of God. Those folks saw what Jesus had done. They knew Jesus was a mighty healer. They saw Jesus talk to dead people who came alive. They saw Jesus call on people who could not see or hear or walk. They saw Jesus doing His mighty deeds. Jesus showed up in their midst.

Some made bad decisions. Some made right decisions. The results were revealed. When Jesus called Peter, Peter—though he has previously made bad decisions—stepped out and made the right decisions. That is having faith in the real world. You will step out. When danger is all around, you will step out. When all has gone wrong, you will step out. When everything seems like it is not good, you will step out.

Jesus said it this way: "My sheep hear my voice."

The enemy has a way of trying to frighten us out of our wits. He has a way of trying to tell us we aren't going to make it. He has a way of letting us know that we are in a losing battle.

But today let us choose to do right. The wrong way is just that— it is the wrong way. We refuse to go there today. We will be among the righteous.

Tuesday: The Lord Provides for the Righteous

The Lord does not let the righteous go hungry, but he thwarts the craving of the wicked. (PROVERBS 10:3)

GOD WILL BLESS YOU, today. Don't let your own cravings override God's will for your life. Live with the zeal of God within you to empower you to do the will of God through you.

Ask yourself today, "Where is my trust in God?" Sometimes, we just need a little faith. Just a little leap of faith. A risk. A chance for change. We don't need outward signs, do we? Can't we just have faith in what already is before us?

Think back. What has God provided for you? Make a list here:

-
-
-
-
-
-
-

Next, think ahead. What has God promised for you? Make a list here:

-
-
-
-
-
-
-

Be among the righteous. God has promised. He will provide. Even when you feel despised, the Lord will provide more than enough.

Wednesday: Choosing to Be Diligent Rather Than Lazy

Lazy hands make for poverty, but diligent hands bring wealth.
(Proverbs 10:4)

Not all are called to preach, but they can help in the support of those who are called. Not all can go out as missionaries, but they can contribute their means to make it possible for others to go. And each one is to contribute according to his or her means: "Let every one of you lay by him in store, as God hath prospered him" (1 Corinthians 16:2). Every Christian is a steward of God, and "it is required in stewards, that a man be found faithful" (1 Corinthians 4:2). The people of Israel were required to take their tithes to the Lord: "The tenth shall be holy unto the Lord" (Leviticus 27:32). Certainly, no less than the tenth would be expected of Christians. Not only that, but as we are stewards of God, all we have is to be held in trust for God and used for His glory. (Blueprint)

How do we accomplish those things for God? We choose to be diligent rather than lazy. We choose to do what is right no matter how we feel or what others might think. We remember how much better it is to be despised for the right than praised for the wrong.

How can you apply that today? Think back at those people of faith we read about last week. They didn't have results yet, but they walked in faith. They had to put their trust in God, even when the risk seemed large.

Be one of the people of faith today. Be diligent. Be stewards of God. The wealth will come your way.

Thursday: Being Prudent or Disgraceful?

He who gathers crops in summer is a prudent son, but he who sleeps during harvest is a disgraceful son. (PROVERBS 10:5)

WOULD YOU RATHER BE PRUDENT or disgraceful? I think I know what you would prefer to be.

Those old people of faith knew how to plant seeds and wait a long time for harvests to arrive. They were prudent.

Abraham had to face reality after a lengthy period of waiting. The promised seed had not yet come. He had to face the reality for him and his wife. "If God would give me a promise like that He should have made it happen by now," we would say. Think about him hearing a promise to bear a child. "And I am 100 years old? My wife cannot have a child now! God is too late."

But God wasn't too late. Faith makes the impossible happen for those who believe and continue planting seeds regularly.

It takes faith when reality sets in. More assurance that what is mine will come to past. Even after reaching a certain point, it seems like past time. We have some unbelief and need help to go farther in faith for what God has promised. We feel hopeless instead of hopeful.

Faith might look bizarre at times. But we keep our eye on the daily tasks. Each seed to be planted. Each step to be taken.

Be prudent by faith. Change is on the way. It will soon be time to gather the crops.

Friday: Blessings for the Righteous

Blessings crown the head of the righteous, but violence overwhelms the mouth of the wicked. (PROVERBS 10:5)

RESEARCHERS TELL YOU that if the world comes apart it will take three days for them to find out where you are. You need some supplies to carry over. Like junk food, of course. Get a flashlight and a bunch of batteries. No radio or television? Don't forget blankets and pillows. Put those things in your bunker. Get what you need to help you live for those three days.

When we hear stories about the world falling apart people respond differently. Some are panicking and over reacting. But not everyone. Some are saying, "I'm not worrying about anything." They act like nothing is wrong and they keep doing the same old stuff.

Sadly, that is what often happens when it comes down to receiving Christ. Why stop doing what I'm doing? I like it like this. I plan to keep doing this. It is not my time yet.

If God would come and stop your clock, you won't be able to keep going.

Now is the time to look at, to really look at, where we are. We must not wait any longer. We must look now and ask, "Where am I? Is this where I should be?" Be among the righteous today and await the blessings of God—no matter what others say might happen next.

We don't just need three days and some food. We need Jesus. With Jesus come blessings for the righteous.

Saturday: Names to Forget

The name of the righteous is used in blessings, but the name of the wicked will rot. (PROVERBS 10:7)

PEOPLE OFTEN SAY, "So now you are in that mess." Well, maybe things are not going well. But the Lord provides for the righteous ones. You have chosen to do what is right rather than pursuing what is wrong.

God has said to you, "I will deliver you. I heard your cry."

While God's people were locked up in bondage under the Egyptians, what was happening? God was putting things in place. God was getting everything and everyone ready for His miracles.

How can we hold on to anything for 400 years? Or 40 years? Or 40 weeks? We can hold on because God is holding on to us.

People might say, "Just forget it." There are names and situations and feelings maybe we need to forget. But we cannot forget what God promises to do. The Bible says, "God has heard the cries and supplications."

That is the reason we let this just roll by us. That was the reason we forget the names of those doubters. But we remember Moses. God told Moses, "Tell them I am that I am. I will let them know that I am. I am the one. I am the only one no matter how many years you have waited."

You might be counting the wrong things. You are counting the years when you should be counting the blessings.

You might be remembering the names you need to forget and forgetting what God has instructed you to remember.

The Pessimist May Be Proved Right, but the Optimist Has a Better Time

Sunday: What We Have Seen and Testify

And we have seen and testify that the Father has sent his Son to be the Savior of the world. (1 JOHN 4:14)

IN THE LONG RUN the pessimist may be proved right, but the optimist has a better time on the trip.

Jesus performed many healings. During those occurrences, multitudes of people were amazed. Some of the Pharisees, though, found those miracles as more reasons to create disturbance and division. Those religious leaders were not very optimistic, though miracles were all around them.

John wrote about what he had seen Jesus do. He continued testifying to others what he had experienced himself. Remember when Christ's followers wondered who had committed sin which would cause such a situation? Jesus redirected their thinking, indicating it all happened so God might be displayed in that man. Jesus did a few rather odd things—He spit on the ground, made mud with the saliva, and put that spit in the man's eyes. Jesus told the man to go and wash in the Pool of Siloam. That was not, and is not, a normal response to a difficult situation. But that is what Jesus did.

The man was healed. Jesus met him again, and of course, the religious leaders did too. They investigated what people said had occurred. Those leaders eventually threw the man out—what a sad story. But Jesus found him and asked, "Do you believe?"

That is what we are being asked today? "Do we believe?"

Monday: God Living in Us and Us in God

If anyone acknowledges that Jesus is the Son of God, God lives in them and they in God. (1 JOHN 4:15)

HAVE YOU SEEN JESUS? Do you want to see Jesus today?

He is speaking to you. Do not miss Him. This is what He is wanting: To live in your life. Not at a distance. Not far away. Here with you today. Right where you are at this very moment.

Let me ask you again, have you seen Jesus? Do you want to see Jesus today?

God living in us. Us in God. What a wonderful way to live. Be sure that today you are living the life with God.

My friends, that experience allows us to be more that optimistic. It assures us of eternal life. It holds us a place in a heavenly home. It grants us abundant life.

Acknowledge Jesus today as the Son of God. Admit He is the way toward salvation. His life and His death opened the door for us to gain eternal life.

Believe in Him. Receive Him. Talk to Him regularly about your struggles, your desires, your needs, your plans. Trust Him to guide you. Trust Him to provide your every need.

Knowing Jesus allows us to be the greatest optimistic people around. God is with us! We are never, ever alone! And our future is better than anything we can hope for!

Tuesday: God Is Love

And so we know and rely on the love God has for us. God is love. Whoever lives in love lives in God, and God in them. (1 JOHN 4:16)

What if today we can join with the healed man and choose to believe?

What if today we can battle our own reluctance and choose to believe?

What if today we can fight back normal doubt and choose to believe?

What if today we can step away from the haters and choose to believe?

What if today we can silence the skeptics and choose to believe?

What if today we can live by faith and choose to believe?

What if today we can read this Scripture over and over and choose to believe?

What if today we can remember what God has done for us and choose to believe?

What if today we can recall what God has done for others and choose to believe?

What if today we can overthrow the enemy and choose to believe?

What if today we can resist temptations and choose to believe?

What if today we can walk away from our foe and choose to believe?

What if today we can look up and choose to believe?

What if today we can believe God is love and invites us to live in His love?

What if today we can hear God created us in His image and choose to believe?

What if today we realize God has given us sight to see His love and choose to believe?

Wednesday: In This World We Are Like Jesus

This is how love is made complete among us so that we will have confidence on the day of judgment: In this world we are like Jesus. (1 JOHN 4:17)

One may worship God alone or with his or her fellow Christians. A person may worship in the home, in the field, in the forest, or in the house of the Lord. A person may worship at any time or at an appointed time. People who do not worship God in private are not likely to worship Him in the church.

This does not mean that private worship can take the place of public worship. Some professing Christians give as an excuse for not attending the services of God's house that they can worship God at home or out in the field just as well as they can at the place of public worship. But the truth is, they do not. There is something to be gained, and something to be given, in public worship that cannot be gained or given anywhere else. God has appointed worship in all of His churches as a means by which His people may grow in the grace and knowledge of the Lord Jesus Christ and may impart spiritual benefits to others. He warns against neglect of this sacred privilege and responsibility: "And let us consider one another to provoke unto love and to good works: not forsaking the assembling of ourselves together, as the manner of some is: but exhorting one another; and so much the more, as ye see the day approaching" (HEBREWS 10:24–25). (BLUEPRINT)

Thursday: Choosing Love Instead of Fear

There is no fear in love. But perfect love drives out fear, because fear has to do with punishment. The one who fears is not made perfect in love. (1 JOHN 4:18)

"THERE IS NO FEAR IN LOVE." That is a powerful statement. It follows with another declaration:

· Perfect love drives out fear.

Read and reflect on the entire verse again:

"There is no fear in love. But perfect love drives out fear, because fear has to do with punishment. The one who fears is not made perfect in love" (1 JOHN 4:18).

What does that mean to us today? It should have a significant meaning. Those people who struggle to sleep at night because of fear might find a deep peace that gives them good rest. Those couples who are always mad at each other might choose love and kindness instead. Those people who might not always fit in church could be the very ones who come to Jesus because they have found perfect love through Him. Those people who might be trying to run the church could be the very ones who cannot see Jesus as who He is, and they might miss His perfect love all together because fear is a basis for all they do.

What are you choosing? Love or fear?

Friday: Why We Can Be Optimistic

We love because he first loved us. (1 JOHN 4:19)

SOME OF THE PHARISEES REFUSED to go out on a limb. John knew that. He knew them. He knew their behavior and their beliefs.

They were too afraid of change, of taking a risk, of believing the promised King had arrived. They just would not accept Jesus as the Messiah. He was too weak and poor and normal. But the real problem? They were afraid. They would not be optimistic.

Remember the story of Jesus healing the blind man? "What is wrong with you," they seemed to ask Jesus. "Are you indicating that we are blind?"

Those blind ones couldn't see the world is falling apart. They couldn't see how to truly trust God when those things happen. They couldn't see what looking up really means.

They were too busy looking at their own accomplishments to see God had loved us first.

Shouldn't that concern us these days? I say so. I believe their behavior should warn us of how not to live. They stared at their own laws and couldn't see Jesus for who He really was. Their rules rejected His love. Their demands vetoed His acceptance.

Why? They had to be afraid of Jesus. If He was the Messiah what would that mean to them and to their positions?

For us, being optimistic and loving can be healthy. We can choose to be afraid the right way instead of the wrong way. We can choose today to fear God, knowing that through Jesus we are now finally able to see the truth.

Saturday: Love Is the Answer

Whoever claims to love God yet hates a brother or sister is a liar. For whoever does not love their brother and sister, whom they have seen, cannot love God, whom they have not seen. And he has given us this command: Anyone who loves God must also love their brother and sister. (1 JOHN 4:20–21)

REMEMBER, DON'T BE AFRAID to go out on a limb for that is where the fruit is. And also remember: In the long run the pessimist may be proved right, but the optimist has a better time on the trip.

What is it that God has said to you this week? What has He wanted you to learn? How can those truths change your life? What steps should you now take to see such transformation occur?

You know where you must start. Love is the answer. Think of all the places Jesus is wanting to take you, and how Jesus is wanting you to love those often rejected.

Fruit of love and joy and peace is there. Forgiveness of guilt. True pardon from the Lord. Acceptance into God's family. Finally able to see through the eyes of Jesus after living with spiritual blindness for so long.

Go today, choosing optimism through God's Word. Open your eyes and see through faith. You are no longer blind to God's will. You are no longer only seeing the bad, but God is revealing to you His good—what a wonderful future awaits.

So much fruit is now growing. Get out there in the field. The harvest shall come.

Think Seldom of Enemies, Often of Friends, and Every Day of Christ

Sunday: A New Way to Think

Dear friends, let us love one another, for love comes from God. Everyone who loves has been born of God and knows God. (1 JOHN 4:7)

LAST WEEK WE STUDIED 1 John 4. We will continue in that chapter this week but meditate on a few of the earlier verses.

It helps to remember this epistle was written by John, one of the closest friends of Jesus. His heart comes out on these pages. He reinforces over and over the importance of thinking often about friends and thinking every day of Christ.

Why do we dwell on our foes? Why should we let the views of our enemies defeat us in our minds? John offered a better way—a new way to think.

He called his readers "dear friends." Isn't that how we should see one another in the body of Christ? The church of Jesus must be a place of family relationships developed by similar beliefs and godly behavior. We must be followers of Christ who consider other Christians as true friends.

It isn't enough to call them friends, though. The new way to think is to love one another. John knew about love. He had witnessed it in Jesus. He wanted to carry on that heritage. "Love one another," he wrote, "because love comes from God." "Everyone who loves has been born of God and knows God," John said.

Begin this week with that as your focus. Think seldom of your enemies, often of friends, and every day of Christ.

Monday: What Is God Really Like?

Whoever does not love does not know God, because God is love.
(1 John 4:8)

THERE CAN BE NO BETTER WAY to think, really, than loving one another as Christ loves us. Even when the world is falling apart, love can be that which directs our decisions. God's love. The love seen in the life of Jesus. The love implanted in us through the Holy Spirit.

And, honestly, that is the best way to describe God. So many people ask me, "What is God really like?" I tell them He is the exposure of love. He is the specimen of love. He is the catalyst of love. To know God truly is to receive and reveal His love. To grow in that knowledge of God is to cultivate in His love.

What about those who do not love other people? John tells us. He wrote, "Whoever does not love does not know God." Then he wrote the reason. "Because God is love," he said.

What is God really like? He is what love really is.

Love is often misunderstood in our culture. We use that word love when we should select other words. It is more than a desire or lust or pleasure or enjoyment. Love is commitment and dedication. It is sacrifice—even martyrdom, if necessary.

We see that in how God loved us so much that He offered His Son Jesus as a sacrifice to set us free. What an example of love!

That, my friends, is what God is really like.

Tuesday: This Is How God Loves

This is how God showed his love among us: He sent his one and only Son into the world that we might live through him. (1 JOHN 4:9)

PEOPLE LIKE TO HEAR ABOUT LOVE and sing about love. People like to read about love and talk about love. Movies and books emphasize love. Commercials and songs accentuate love.

But do we know what love is?

Have we misunderstood love?

To truly trust God and to think every day of God, let us remember His example of what love really is. I want you to know how God loves. I want you to know that is what love is all about. We cannot let this culture control our perception of love. We must let God guide our interpretation of love.

1 John 4:9 reveals to us how God sees love:

· This is how God showed his love among us: He sent his one and only Son into the world that we might live through him.

We need to see love as He does. We need to realize this world uses that same word "love" when they are talking about such different things. We need to know God's love is the type of love that should be directing who we are and what we do.

We might just live through Him with such a love. We might just change the world with that kind of love.

Wednesday: Thinking about God's Love

This is love: not that we loved God, but that he loved us and sent his Son as an atoning sacrifice for our sins. (1 JOHN 4:10)

WHAT HAS BEEN ON YOUR MIND THIS WEEK? It is Wednesday, so take a few moments to look back on what you have focused on the last few days.

Have you dwelled on negative thoughts? Have you placed your mind on positive thoughts?

As John wrote to his original readers he continued stressing the importance of one thing: God's love. When the world is falling apart what do we need to remember? God's love. When bad news hits us so hard that we can't figure out the best way to respond, what can we dwell on? God's love.

John reminded them that it wasn't because they loved God. The meaning of love was all because God loved them:

- This is love:
- not that we loved God,
- but that he loved us
- and sent his Son
- as an atoning sacrifice
- for our sins.

Thinking about God's love reminds us of the price Jesus paid for us. That is what should come to our minds when we receive communion. The cup and the bread are physical prompts—they are symbols of Christ's atonement. Jesus displayed love by being the sacrifice for our sins.

Think about God's love that way. Remember it. Believe it. Receive it. And think every day of Christ.

Thursday: How We Ought to Live and Love

Dear friends, since God so loved us, we also ought to love one another. (1 JOHN 4:11)

JOHN WROTE TO HIS READERS as friend to friend. His tone was kind, but firm. His mood was revealing. His emphasis was the love of God.

As he called them in chapter 4, verse 7, John again addresses his audiences this way: "Dear friends."

He cared deeply with the love of Jesus. He wrote to them with the hope of guiding them toward experiencing the love of Jesus.

Who are your dear friends? Do they know your opinion about how we should love and live?

John explained the reasons we should:

- Since God loved us,
- we also ought to love one another.

Why do we love others? Because we are loved by God.

How should we treat others? The way we are treated by God.

What thoughts should be in our minds as we think about others? The same thoughts God would have us think.

God loved us. We must never forget that. We must also let that truth influence everything we say and do.

And it should influence us this way: We must love one another.

Dear friends, love God by receiving His love. Dear friends, show God's love by loving others. Dear friends, we must love our friends and our enemies just as we are loved.

Friday: Love Is Made Complete

No one has ever seen God; but if we love one another, God lives in us and his love is made complete in us. (1 JOHN 4:12)

THROUGHOUT SCRIPTURE we read many miraculous encounters. God creating all. Moses hearing God's voice. David letting God empower him to defeat Goliath. Jonah hearing from God but trying to disobey the God he heard. Prophets stating God's warnings and His promises. Psalmists singing and dancing before the Lord. An angel speaking to Mary and to Joseph. Jesus healing the sick and raising the dead. Jesus dying but coming back to life.

But, even with all those miracles and fascinating stories, John says in today's verse that no one has ever seen God. He then follows by declaring how love is revealed and made complete:

- If we love one another
- God lives in us
- And His love is made complete in us.

So where should we see God and His love? In the life of someone who has chosen to love others. In the lives of many people who have decided to follow Jesus by being those who love one another.

It isn't just "liking" someone. It is choosing to be dedicated to seeing God's reflection in the face of someone. It is deciding to do what is best for them, instead of ourselves.

Let love be made complete today. That is the way someone will see God at work: through your kindness.

Saturday: A Life in the Spirit of Love Every Day

This is how we know that we live in him and he in us: He has given us of his Spirit. (1 JOHN 4:13)

YESTERDAY WE FOCUSED on how—because God lives in us and makes His love complete in us—we can love one another. What a wonderful truth that is! What an honor to believe God lives in us and loves through us!

That type of love will help us think seldom of our enemies, think often of our friends, and think every day and every moment of Christ. Placing Jesus at the center of our minds influences how we see and treat others. Looking through the eyes of Christ gives us a love we cannot make in our own abilities.

That, my friends, is life in the Spirit. Loving others every day is what the Holy Ghost can do in us.

And, that is the only way we can truly love others. That love of Christ comes to us through the Spirit which dwells within us. Such love then arises into relationships because He has given us His Spirit.

Conclude this week by grasping what that really means. God's Spirit within you is how He chooses to love others through you. Isn't that remarkable?

God speaking through you. God listening through you. God serving through you. His Spirit at work loving others every day through you even when the world is falling apart.

God Cannot Move Us to the Next Level until We Joyfully Accept the Present

Sunday: Accepting the Present

Who is wise and understanding among you? Let them show it by their good life, by deeds done in the humility that comes from wisdom. (JAMES 3:13)

WE ALL WANT TO WORK with wise people. We also want to be wise in our decisions and relationships.

In God's Kingdom, we must accept the present situations God places us in. Those who do that are wise and understanding. Instead of trying to rush to another position, a higher ranking, a more popular role, James declared that deeds must be done in humility.

Here are a few ways to accept our present situation with humble attitudes:

· *By the Spirit of humility, the way up is down.*

Human pride is crucified. Godly servants are not to think too highly of themselves, but rather to think soberly of self. Jesus spent much of his time equipping his disciples, and that began by teaching them how to view themselves. The true servant leader does not promote self, but promotes, exalts and glorifies the name of Christ (COLOSSIANS 3:17). Every work, every program and every deed is to exalt the name of Jesus.

· *By the attitude of submission.*

When the will of the servant and the will of the Master clash, the Master must win. That is how we grow although such growth is painful. Submissiveness means carrying out a duty even when we may feel reluctant. Following Jesus is not always easy: it may require doing some things we do not want to do. But in time, our duty becomes our desire! That is the essence of growth.
(WISDOM CONVERSATIONS)

Monday: Releasing the Past

But if you harbor bitter envy and selfish ambition in your hearts, do not boast about it or deny the truth. (JAMES 3:14)

ANOTHER WAY TO FOLLOW that leadership role is this:

· *By the grit of faithfulness.*

A good servant may not be outstanding, but they are faithful. Jesus said, "Well done, good and faithful servant" (MATTHEW 25:21). A faithful servant is dependable and perseveres. They endure to the end. Our prayer is: help me, Father, to have a servant heart. May my gratitude for salvation motivate me to serve, to spend and be spent. In Jesus' name, amen. (WISDOM CONVERSATIONS)

Living in the grit of faithfulness means looking up when everything might be falling apart. We choose to endure. We choose to let go of past situations which might hold us back.

We all know people who refuse to let go of the past. They harbor bitterness and selfish ambition. They boast. They deny the truth.

James wrote his epistle fitting for times like our days. God wrote those words so we could choose gratitude and faithfulness, as leaders.

Pray the prayer included above. End your day with that prayer.

Tuesday: Wisdom from God

Such "wisdom" does not come down from heaven but is earthly, unspiritual, demonic. (JAMES 3:15)

GOD CANNOT MOVE US to the next level until we joyfully accept the present situation as part of that plan.

To make that more likely, we must notice the difference in wisdom from God and wisdom from the enemy. As we have studied, God's wisdom includes us walking in humility.

In James 3:15 we can read of three descriptive words revealing what wisdom is like when it is not from God:

- It is earthly.
- It is unspiritual.
- It is demonic.

We see much of that sort of "wisdom" these days. I don't even like to call it wisdom. People might act like they are wise, but they are fools when basing decisions on earthly, unspiritual, and demonic components.

As you make decisions, check these motives:

- Where is your heart?
  - o   Think about what is motivating you to do this.
  - o   Ask yourself, "Why am I pursuing this?"

- What do you hope to achieve?
  - o   Think about preferred outcomes.
  - o   Ask yourself, "What do I hope to accomplish?"

- How will God's Kingdom be affected?
  - o   Think about how more people will know Jesus.
  - o   Ask yourself, "Is this what Jesus would do?"

You want to walk in the wisdom of God. Talk to Him. Reflect on these thoughts. He will guide your steps.

Wednesday: The Life of Envy, Bitterness, and Selfishness

For where you have envy and selfish ambition, there you find disorder and every evil practice. (JAMES 3:16)

LOOK AROUND YOU. Check the news. Read the latest reports. They are troubling. People are turning against one another. People make ongoing comments with hateful statements in harsh tones. People write about it, talk about it, fight about it.

Wouldn't it be nice if people just got along? Wouldn't it be nice if people found joy in the present rather than pushing so hard to move to another level? Those kinds of folks won't make it to another level until they realize how to live better life right where they already are.

We need to keep these three words out:

- Envy
- Bitterness
- Selfishness

Envy is living a jealous life. It is living with comparisons. It is about ranking and grading. It is not about love. We must avoid such a life.

Bitterness is carrying a grudge. It is allowing hurts from the past to keep us mad. It holds on to resentment instead of letting it go correctly. We must avoid such a life.

Selfishness is getting what we want no matter the cost. It is placing one's self in the center of attention. It is full of greed and self-interest. We must avoid such a life.

Trusting God lets go of those tendencies. Looking up is better than always looking in the mirror and thinking only of ourselves.

Thursday: Pure Wisdom

But the wisdom that comes from heaven is first of all pure; then peace-loving, considerate, submissive.... (JAMES 3:17A)

SO, IF WE SEE NEGATIVE TRAITS like envy, bitterness, and self-ishness as qualities of wisdom from the enemy, what does God's wisdom look like? How can we be sure the wisdom we seek to obtain is from heaven?

James lists several characteristics. He wrote that wisdom which comes from heaven is:

- Pure
- Peace-loving
- Considerate
- Submissive

Look at each of those four words. We will add more tomorrow but focus on those today. Ask yourself these questions:

When you hear the word *pure*, what thoughts come to your mind? What biblical stories do you remember? What events in your life can you remember when you knew God's will because it revealed purity?

When you hear the word *peace-loving*, what thoughts come to your mind? What biblical stories do you remember? What events in your life can you remember when you knew God's will because it revealed a love for peace?

When you hear the word *considerate*, what thoughts come to your mind? What biblical stories do you remember? What events in your life can you remember when you knew God's will because it revealed being considerate?

When you hear the word *submissive*, what thoughts come to your mind? What biblical stories do you remember? What events in your life can you remember when you knew God's will because it revealed submission?

Friday: Full of Mercy and Good Fruit

... full of mercy and good fruit, impartial and sincere. (JAMES 3:17b)

YESTERDAY WE FOCUSED on four words to help us understand the will of God. Today, we will put our attention on four more. Again, please remember that all the qualities listed help indicate when we are discerning the will of God.

Meditate on these words:

- Mercy
- Good fruit
- Impartial
- Sincere

When you hear the word *mercy*, what thoughts come to your mind? What biblical stories do you remember? What events in your life can you remember when you knew God's will because it revealed mercy?

When you hear the words *good fruit*, what thoughts come to your mind? What biblical stories do you remember? What events in your life can you remember when you knew God's will because it brought good fruit?

When you hear the word *impartial*, what thoughts come to your mind? What biblical stories do you remember? What events in your life can you remember when you knew God's will because it was impartial?

When you hear the word *sincere*, what thoughts come to your mind? What biblical stories do you remember? What events in your life can you remember when you knew God's will because it revealed sincerity?

Glance again at all eight words, and let these be your list of discernment:

- Pure
- Considerate
- Mercy
- Impartial

- Peace-loving
- Submissive
- Good fruit
- Sincere

Saturday: Peacemakers in the Present

Peacemakers who sow in peace reap a harvest of righteousness.
(JAMES 3:18)

JAMES CONTINUED making his point by including this sentence: "Peacemakers who sow in peace reap a harvest of righteousness." The seeds must be planted. The field must be worked. The ground must be fixed. The timing must be right. The goals must be clear. The labor must be precise. The effort must be meticulous.

And for his illustration to fit how we can be successful in the present, we must seek success right where we are placed.

If we expect God to move us to the next level, we must joyfully accept our present place of vocation and ministry. We can't just look out the window without cleaning the floor we are standing on. We can't just stare into space without mowing the yard we are standing on. We can't try to become friends with someone famous without seeing the people we already know as famous in the eyes of God.

The way we are to be faithful is with hearts of peace. Momentous world changers are peacemakers. Historic world shakers begin by planting this seed over and over and over: peace.

Can you plant seeds of peace today? I believe you can. I believe you can sow in peace on a day just like today.

Begin now. A seed at a time. One seed of peace at a time.

An Imperfect Conscience
Needs a Perfect Guide

Sunday: Imperfect People

As for you, you were dead in your transgressions and sins, in which you used to live when you followed the ways of this world and of the ruler of the kingdom of the air, the spirit who is now at work in those who are disobedient. (EPHESIANS 2:1–2)

WHAT DO YOU HOPE will be said about you after you leave earth and go to heaven? We all hope there are good reports about us. We desire positive remarks from family and friends. We pray that we leave heritages pleasing to God.

In Ephesians 2, Paul gave his readers a look at who they were—he didn't wait until their funeral services. He wanted them to know right then. God wanted them to be aware of truth in those moments.

Paul revealed the contrast between living with Jesus and living without Jesus. Those people had, as many of today's people often do, forgotten the big story. They were not good enough in themselves to earn salvation. They could not work their way there. They were dead in their transgressions and sins. Paul said they had previously followed the ways of the world and the enemy.

They were, like us, imperfect people. That is what he wanted them to remember. That is what God wants us to remember. Not as the end of our story. But, so our story can begin where it should. So we can be imperfect people seeking to be guided by God.

Monday: Lacking Conscience

All of us also lived among them at one time, gratifying the cravings of our flesh and following its desires and thoughts. Like the rest, we were by nature deserving of wrath. (EPHESIANS 2:3)

PAUL CONTINUED CLARIFYING his point in Ephesians 2. Don't let this come across as a negative devotion. Let it remind you of the large truth. Allow these verses and thoughts to prompt you to return to the truth so often missed in our demanding world.

Here is why it is so important. We are all prone to do wrong. We are all among the wicked who are only saved by God's grace.

The early readers lacked a conscience. Don't we see that in our days? We wonder why people can do what they do. And then we begin to sometimes wonder why we do what we do.

Our human nature—wicked and corrupt—deserved the wrath and rejection of God. No guilt. No conscience. No repentance. No remorse. But, yet, the Lord has saved and rescued us from ourselves. The Spirit and the Word bring a conscience to us.

Take a little time now to pray, giving thanks to God for your salvation. And, if you have not yet repented from your wrongs, do that at this very instant. Confess your sins to God. He will forgive you. He will rescue you. This can be your day.

Tuesday: By Grace We Have Been Saved

But because of his great love for us, God, who is rich in mercy, made us alive with Christ even when we were dead in transgressions—it is by grace you have been saved. (EPHESIANS 2:4–5)

PAUL HAD MADE CLEAR TO his readers that there was a problem. It was an immense problem—one they could not solve in their own energy.

He next revealed the greatest news of all. By grace they had been saved:

- Because of His great love for us,
- God,
- who is rich in mercy,
- made us alive with Christ
- even when we were dead in transgressions—
- it is by grace you have been saved.

Oh, my friends, we must never forget we are saved by grace. Because of His great love for us—that is how God made this happen. God is rich in mercy. God made us alive in Christ. Though we were dead in transgressions, it is by grace we have been saved.

We should rejoice in that. We should celebrate in that.

In fact, take a few minutes—or a few hours—to rejoice and celebrate right now. Revel in the sensation of what God has done.

Repeat this line over and over: "Because of His great love," "because of His great love," "because of His great love." Now, repeat this line over and over: "It is by grace I have been saved," "it is by grace I have been saved," "it is by grace I have been saved."

Rejoice and be glad today. Look at what the Lord has done.

Wednesday: Seated with Christ

And God raised us up with Christ and seated us with him in the heavenly realms in Christ Jesus, in order that in the coming ages he might show the incomparable riches of his grace, expressed in his kindness to us in Christ Jesus. (EPHESIANS 2:6–7)

IN THE NEXT TWO VERSES of Ephesians 2, we read biblical truth from which we must never depart. As you hear this day's news reports and as you try to fight your way through your own battles, meditate on these statements Paul made. They can change our way of thinking. They remind us where our home really is.

There is so much more to life than what we spend most of our time fretting about. Those battles might not be as large as we let them be if we see beyond the now and notice eternity.

Remember we are seated with Christ!

Remember what really matters in this world that seems to be falling apart!

Remember to look up and see our eternal home!

Remember the perfect guide has won a victory over our imperfect conscience!

These verses help us remember:

- God raised us up with Christ
- and seated us with Him
- in the heavenly realms
- in Christ Jesus,
- in order that in the coming ages He might show the incomparable riches of His grace,
- expressed in His kindness to us in Christ Jesus.

Once again, on a day like today, dwell on God's Word. Those verses can change how you view life today and every day. Have a seat with Christ!

Thursday: Faith in the Perfect Guide

For it is by grace you have been saved, through faith—and this is not from yourselves, it is the gift of God. (EPHESIANS 2:8)

WHEN PEOPLE ASK ME HOW I GOT SAVED, I can use this verse to explain it. By grace and through faith. And, it is good to include Paul's other reminder: we did not do this ourselves, but it only came as a gift from God.

To have faith in God to guide us in the future, to have faith to look up during difficult times, to have faith to truly trust God, we must begin here. We absolutely must begin here.

Saved by grace through faith. That is how. There is no other way. That is the only way.

And what a wonderful way it is. We cannot take credit. We cannot brag on ourselves. We cannot rely on our own strength.

Paul had already informed them of their tendencies to do wrong. We know about that, don't we? We have experienced that, haven't we?

To have faith in God to guide our steps, this is where we must begin and where we must end. Everything must take us back to this. By grace. Through faith. By grace. Through faith. By grace. Through faith.

It is God's gift to us. Our job is to believe in that gift and to receive that gift. What a wonderful story this is. Pray for those who have not yet received this gift. As we mentioned earlier this week, if you haven't, please do. The gift is waiting. Do not reject it. Receive the gift—by grace through faith.

Friday: Nothing to Brag About

Not by works, so that no one can boast. (EPHESIANS 2:19)

WE CAN ALL LOOK FOR THINGS to brag about. Duties and tasks and accomplishments. Those great achievements. The times we heard applause. The situations which brought approval.

None of those things take us to God, though. None of our personal accomplishments draw us closer to Jesus. Some of them might get in the way.

Since all of that is true, what do we have? We can have salvation through Jesus. What else really matters? Isn't that more important that anything else?

Since we are saved by the grace of God through Jesus instead of by our own efforts, we have nothing to brag about. Though we are reflections of God, though we bear His image, we cannot brag on ourselves. As we study and learn, as we work out our own salvation with fear and trembling, as we choose righteousness, we have nothing to brag about.

God is our perfect guide. Let Him direct your steps.

Saturday: God's Handiwork

For we are God's handiwork, created in Christ Jesus to do good works, which God prepared in advance for us to do.
(EPHESIANS 2:10)

WE NEED TO STUDY to put forth the effort needed to learn and grow. We need to reveal our trust in God through our actions. We are here today to change this world. We must not miss a moment in time.

It helps to remember that God is the one who is at work in us and through us. Our actions are His actions. Our words can be His words.

God is choosing to change the world through us. Yes, through us.

But how? How do we accept that and live like we truly believe it?

By remembering we are God's handiwork. God is designing and crafting us through His Spirit. He is working His will through our lives as He continues transforming us to Christlikeness.

This is all God's idea. It is His plan.

Will you welcome His plan today? Will you trust His ability to finish His plans in your life?

Our Guide has prepared responsibilities for us to do and He has prepared us to do those tasks today through Christ. You are God's handiwork. He will work through you today.

Prayer Is Striking the Winning Blow

Sunday: Beginning Our Prayer with Praise

How lovely is your dwelling place, Lord Almighty! (PSALM 84:1)

WE ALL WANT TO WIN, don't we? We have all seen people getting close to victory but never finishing what they seek to accomplish, haven't we?

Victories in life involve striking the winning blow. We need to find that blow that leads us to triumph. We need to gain the confidence to complete any task we are facing.

Our faith tells us that prayer is hammering that final punch. Refusing to quit, we endure by God's grace as we pray. We continue toward a victorious ending of each struggle by praying.

But we end in victory if we remember how we started. And we must begin our battles by giving praise to God.

Thank Him. Worship Him. Celebrate Him. Rejoice in Him.

Psalm 84 is an ancient prayer. We can see it as a praise song declaring victory. How does it start? By calling out to the Lord Almighty. By confessing how lovely is His dwelling place.

Can't we begin there? As we look at obstacles around us, as we begin a conversation with God and plead for His victory, as we seek assurance, can't we begin there?

Yes, we can. So, let us start with praise to God. Today, tell Him that you see His creation as lovely. Tell Him that you see Him as your Lord who is almighty. Worship Him. Praise Him. Begin your prayer by giving Him praise.

Monday: Our Yearning for God

My soul yearns, even faints, for the courts of the Lord; my heart and my flesh cry out for the living God. Even the sparrow has found a home, and the swallow a nest for herself, where she may have her young—a place near your altar, Lord Almighty, my King and my God. (Psalm 84:2–4)

What can follow our worship of God? As we start a prayerful conversation with praise and thanksgiving, what should we voice next to strike a winning blow through prayer?

One way is to follow Psalm 84 as an example. We can confess our needs. The psalmist admitted a soul yearning for God, almost fainting in desperation for God, with a heart and body crying out for the living God.

The writer used a sparrow as an example. The sparrow found a home—a swallow a nest where she could have her young. Like our altar where we can rely on God, the sparrow found a place to stay.

We don't need to continue flying around from one place to another. We don't need to frantically attempt to force our plans into realities. We wait with God. We confess, and we bow. We worship, and we surrender.

It helps to remember who God is as we wait on Him. The psalmist titled God as the Lord Almighty, my King, and my God. That is who we yearn for.

Rest in His presence today. He is your Lord and your King and your God. He is what you truly crave. Be still in His presence.

Tuesday: Dwelling with God

Blessed are those who dwell in your house; they are ever praising you. (PSALM 84:4)

BY STILLING OURSELVES in the nest of God's presence, we released the luggage we might too often carry in our own strength. That will not work. We are too weak for that. The weights are too heavy for that. So, we choose instead to stay in that place and bless the Lord.

Can you bless the Lord today? Think about what He has done for you. Give Him thanks.

Write a list of all the many good things the Lord has done. Then look at that list. Stare at it. Give God thanks for each blessing He has brought your way.

Blessed are those who dwell in His house. Don't come in for a quick visit then hurry away. Stay there. With God, stay and rest and rejoice. Ever praising Him. Always praising Him.

How long should the worship and praise last? Ever praising Him indicates an ongoing attitude of praise. Choose to do that today. No matter how you feel. No matter what hurts you deep inside. No matter what else comes your way. Continue dwelling with God—declaring His goodness to yourself and to Him.

Let wherever you are be like the house of God. Let now be your time of praise. Dwell with God and rejoice in His goodness to you.

Wednesday: Strength Is in God

Blessed are those whose strength is in you, whose hearts are set on pilgrimage. (PSALM 84:5)

WHAT ARE YOUR STRONG POINTS? What areas are you respectable at your labor?

We all have talent and gifts. We all have particular areas which fit best with our makeup. Some of you seem to be natural in one duty, when other responsibilities are always difficult for you to do.

At times we might focus only in those areas, forgetting what the psalmist prays in Psalm 84:5. Listen again to this confession:

"Blessed are those whose strength is in You, whose hearts are set on pilgrimage."

If our strength comes from God, what can really stand in our way? Nothing! Nothing can stop us, defeat us, overthrow us, or end us. With God as our strength we are always moving forward, always stepping higher, always diving deeper, always seeing victory.

Set your heart on God today. Remember your pilgrimage in this life is not a painful escapade to finish in human ability. You have the Creator giving you strength. You have the Savior giving you life. You have the Counselor giving you peace. You have the Lord giving you authority. You have the Healer giving you health.

You are blessed today, because your strength comes from the Lord.

Thursday: From Strength to Strength

As they pass through the Valley of Baka, they make it a place of springs; the autumn rains also cover it with pools. They go from strength to strength, till each appears before God in Zion. (PSALM 84:6–7)

GOD'S PEOPLE WERE TRAVELING in a journey of endurance. They were finding a healthy place wherever they went because of God's guidance. Fortitude doesn't need to be resting on the muscle of man. Stamina doesn't depend only on the endurance of man.

God can pass His people through valleys and bring them toward a spring. God can chaperone His children as the rains of autumn fill them with nourishment.

That can happen for God's people today also. Traveling in different places in different times, God still gives sustenance to His offspring. Until we all appear before God, He wants to assure us that this is where He is taking us:

· From strength to strength.

If you feel weak today, do not fret. God isn't finished with you. He is guiding you from strength to strength.

If you feel like giving up today, refuse to quit. God is still at work in you. He is raining down His love upon you to calm you; He is shining His light upon you to warm you.

This day is your *strength to strength* day. Refuse to let it be anything else. Pass on through whatever you face today, getting closer to seeing God face to face, knowing He is your strength.

Friday: Receiving God's Favor

Hear my prayer, Lord God Almighty; listen to me, God of Jacob.
Look on our shield, O God; look with favor on your anointed one.
(Psalm 84:8–9)

IT IS WONDERFUL TO RECEIVE the favor of God.

He has that for you today. He has His love and blessings for you today.

Hear the prayers from Psalm 84:

- Hear my prayer
- Lord God Almighty;
- Listen to me
- God of Jacob.
- Look on our shield,
- O God;
- Look with favor
- On Your anointed one.

I believe it would benefit you to pray that prayer throughout the day today. Don't just read it. Don't just study it. Don't just sing it. Pray it. Join with the countless people through the years who have prayed this psalm.

He covers you with His protection. He promises you His provision.

Pray for God to hear your cry. Believe He is looking your way and bringing you favor. Receive God's favor. Choosing to believe and receive is striking a winning blow.

Saturday: No Good Thing Does He Withhold

Better is one day in your courts than a thousand elsewhere; I would rather be a doorkeeper in the house of my God than dwell in the tents of the wicked. For the Lord God is a sun and shield; the Lord bestows favor and honor; no good thing does he withhold from those whose walk is blameless. Lord Almighty, blessed is the one who trusts in you. (PSALM 84:10–12)

WHAT IS YOUR FAVORITE DAY of the week? What is your favorite month of the year? What is your favorite holiday? What is your favorite meal?

Oh, we all have favorites.

Psalm 84—the poetic hymn from the Sons of Korah—made their cravings clear. They had a favorite place to be and favorite things to do.

They knew God would withhold no good thing from them. They knew to trust God when everything seemed to be falling apart. They knew how to look up toward their Leader.

If we could hear them singing this hymn, we would be able to overhear the joy as they chanted:

- Better is one day in your courts than a thousand elsewhere;
- I would rather be a doorkeeper in the house of my God than dwell in the tents of the wicked.
- For the Lord God is a sun and shield;
- the Lord bestows favor and honor;
- no good thing does He withhold from those whose walk is blameless.
- Lord Almighty, blessed is the one who trusts in You.

My dear friends, sing that song today. Pray that prayer today. Better is one day in His courts than a thousand anywhere else. It is better to be a doorkeeper in His house than to dwell anywhere else. He is your sun and your shield. He gives you favor and honor. He is holding nothing back as you walk blameless before Him. As you trust in Him, His blessings are not withheld.

Service Is Gathering Up the Results

Sunday: Never Stop Praying

For this reason, since the day we heard about you, we have not stopped praying for you. (COLOSSIANS 1:9A)

PEOPLE LIKE TO SEE RESULTS. I know I do.

As Christians, we must learn that all results aren't immediate, and all aren't noticeable. They might be slow. They might be distant. But we must keep working and pursuing the right results.

True service for God is gathering up results for His Kingdom, not always for ourselves. I think about times when God has revealed His will. Those do not always come in ways that are easy and simple to accomplish. I look back, though, and give thanks that we knew one key part of pursuing God's will: never stop praying.

Praying helps us know what God's will is. We pray, asking for wisdom. We pray while waiting on an answer. We pray alone with God. We pray together with prayer partners. We pray through acts of worship, Scripture, discernment, intercession, petition, and silence. We might even weep before God. We just might cry out to God as we plead for His supervision.

In each form and method of prayer, we do what we must: never stop praying. That is where the service begins. That is where gathering up the results begins. That is truly placing our trust in God. That is what it really means to look up.

We look up as we kneel down. We look up as we bow. We look up as we lay down at the altar. We look up with eyes closed and hearts opened.

What are you waiting on today? What do you need direction or provision for today?

Whatever it is, never stop praying. Start at this very moment and do not stop.

Monday: Praying for Results

... We continually ask God to fill you with the knowledge of his will through all the wisdom and understanding that the Spirit gives. (COLOSSIANS 1:9B)

RESULTS ARE THE ARTIFACTS OF EVIDENCE that our eyes want to see in order to validate the effectiveness of our prayers. When we see our prayers answered, then we know God has heard us and we don't worry about a thing! The test comes when we pray and nothing happens, at least not in the way we think it should. It can stretch and challenge our faith when we pray and God does not seem to answer.

We all want what we want, but prayer teaches us to want what God wants and to set our wants aside. Jesus said, "You may ask me for anything in my name, and I will do it" (John 14:14). It's easy to fall into the trap of thinking that this means that if we want something, then we pray for it, and when we say, "In Jesus' name," that we should expect the result that we want; but as we grow and come to understand God's Word more deeply, we learn that when we ask for something in Jesus' name, we are submitting our request to the sovereignty of God.

This is what it means to be filled "with the knowledge of his will...." Our requests are subject to God's will.

Isn't that what matters most? May we see God's will be done and His Kingdom come.

Tuesday: A Life of Service

So that you may live a life worthy of the Lord and please him in every way: bearing fruit in every good work, growing in the knowledge of God. (COLOSSIANS 1:10)

WHEN WE THINK ABOUT THE WORD "service," we often associate it with the gathering of believers for a Sunday morning worship experience. This is easy to do when our concept of church is centered around coming together once a week. A life of service goes beyond attending or participating in a gathering and it reaches into the day-in and day-out routines of our lives.

Several times in the story of the Great Exodus, God told Moses to tell Pharaoh to "let my people go so that they may serve me in the wilderness" (Exodus 8:1). That word for service is also translated to mean "worship." The same principle applies in Romans 12:1 where the words "service" and "worship" can be interchangeably translated. This tells us that there is a symbiotic relationship between service and worship. The two concepts go hand in hand. To serve is to worship and to worship is to serve.

When we think of service in this way, then it helps to put our lives into perspective. Everything we do during the waking hours of our lives is to be done with the intention to serve and worship the Lord. In doing this, we find that the real worship service does not begin when we get to the church building; the real worship service begins when we *leave* the church building.

What matters? Living a life of service.

Wednesday: Serving with Endurance and Patience

Being strengthened with all power according to his glorious might so that you may have great endurance and patience. (COLOSSIANS 1:11)

YOU CANNOT LIVE FOR GOD in your own strength.

A life of service is a life of submission, sacrifice, and surrender. Serving Jesus is the most rewarding purpose for anyone to fulfill in their lives. Along with this comes the reality that there are times when serving Jesus can be incredibly challenging and can test the limits of our humanity. It is in these times that we realize how incredibly dependent we are upon the strength of the Holy Spirit in order to please the Lord with our lives.

Life is a marathon, not a sprint.

A sprint requires skill and speed, precision and preparedness, but a marathon requires an altogether different approach. In a marathon, speed is not as important as steadiness and stability. Fast runners can win a sprint, but faithful runners win a marathon.

We must be faithful runners if we want to win the marathon of life. Not distracted by everything we see as we go, not discouraged by temporary pain or discomfort, not disheartened by how far we have left to go; we must remain faithful to finish the task, steady and consistent, and endure to the end.

Thursday: Serving with Joyful Thanksgiving

And giving joyful thanks to the Father, who has qualified you to share in the inheritance of his holy people in the kingdom of light.
(COLOSSIANS 1:12)

THE CONCEPT OF BEING A SERVANT can carry with it a sense that someone has been coerced into doing something that they may not want to do. A servant may be perceived as someone who endures difficult and discouraging circumstances just to muddle through life. What we find when we serve the Lord is that, while there will undoubtedly be difficult and discouraging moments in life, there is a deeply rooted joy that underscores the attitudes and actions of every servant of God.

Colossians 1:12 gives us another glimpse at what else Paul prayed:

- And giving joyful thanks
- to the Father,
- who has qualified you to share in the inheritance of his holy people
- in the kingdom of light.

These components put everything in place. While praying, Paul gave thanks. Let's pray that way today. And, let's remember, our thanks go to the Father who is listening to our prayers and answering those prayers better than we can even expect Him to.

Paul reminded his readers that their Father is the one who qualified them to share in the inheritance of His holy people in the kingdom of light.

Give thanks that way today. Be sure it is joyful thanksgiving. Thank your Heavenly Father—He's the One who has made all of this possible.

And put a smile on your face and joy in your heart as you thank Him. He made this day, so rejoice and be glad!

Joyful thanksgiving is a natural effect of serving the Lord. It is not something that we *have* to do; it is something that we *get* to do. Rather than being forced to serve, we find that we are free to serve. This is the call to every believer: to discover that there is joy in serving Jesus! Psalm 100:2 tells us to "serve the Lord with gladness!"

127

Friday: Remembering the Reason to Serve

For he has rescued us from the dominion of darkness and brought us into the kingdom of the Son he loves. (COLOSSIANS 1:13)

EVERY NOW AND THEN, we need to remember the reason we serve so we can recalibrate our spiritual lives. Do you remember what your life was like before you had an encounter with Jesus? What were your decisions based on? What were your true motives?

The most convincing testimony is the one that is told by someone who knows what God has done for them! The psalmist said it like this:

"He lifted me out of the slimy pit, out of the mud and the mire; he set my feet on a rock and gave me a firm place to stand. He put a new song in my mouth, a hymn of praise to our God. Many will see and fear the LORD and put their trust in him" (Psalm 40:2–3).

When we remember what Jesus has done for us, then we can easily remember why it matters that we serve Him. When we reflect on who we once were before we encountered the Lord and we recall what a difference He has made in our lives, then we can serve Him with a purpose. Even when the world is falling apart, we can do our part in service.

Remember the reasons. Do the service. Make a difference.

Saturday: The Final Results

In whom we have redemption, the forgiveness of sins.
(COLOSSIANS 1:14)

EVERYBODY LIKES TO KNOW the final results. Whether it's from the doctor or the teacher, we want the test results quickly. We watch for outcomes. What is the endgame of serving the Lord?

Paul reminds us that the final goal of our service to the Lord is wrapped up in God's great plan of redemption. When we serve the Lord, we do so as a result of what He has done for us. We remember where He brought us from, what He brought us out of, and our lives become an expression of joy and gratitude. We give our lives to serving God by serving others.

We must keep the final results at the center of our attention as we move through life. Our immediate futures may be somewhat uncertain, but we know the final results are in God's hands. We don't have to wonder about the future; we get to celebrate it in advance!

From Genesis to Revelation, we see the overarching story of Scripture and we are privileged to know the end from the beginning. The story ends with a new creation where heaven and earth are restored, and God's people live with Him forever in the relationship made possible by Christ's work on the cross and victory over sin and death. God's great plan of redemption is summarized as eternity bears out the final results.

Be Kind—Every Person You Meet Is Fighting a Difficult Battle

Sunday: Shining the Lord's Face of Kindness

The Lord said to Moses, "Tell Aaron and his sons, 'This is how you are to bless the Israelites. Say to them: "The Lord bless you and keep you; the Lord make his face shine on you and be gracious to you; the Lord turn his face toward you and give you peace."'"
(NUMBERS 6:22–26)

KINDNESS IS A GIFT that costs nothing to give but is priceless to receive. Every day, everywhere, people are struggling, suffering, fighting, and forging their way through life. When we reflect on the things in our own lives that cause us concern, then we can begin to empathize with others and imagine how the issues they are facing may cause them to be in a position that needs kindness from others. It is in those moments that we are given opportunities to show the kindness of our God and Savior. That kindness can begin with something as simple as a smile. Yes, a facial expression can become the gesture of kindness that lifts another's spirits and helps them make it through another day.

When Moses met God on the mountain, he returned to the people with a radiance on his face so strong that it had to be covered. There was evidence that he had been with God. The same is true for us. When we have been with God, it shows on our faces and we can then represent the face of God to others. When we turn our faces to others, we can be a blessing to them in a way that God, Himself, has blessed us with the light of His face.

Monday: Living with a Kind and Gracious God

The Lord said to Moses, "Tell Aaron and his sons, 'This is how you are to bless the Israelites. Say to them: "The Lord bless you and keep you; the Lord make his face shine on you and be gracious to you; the Lord turn his face toward you and give you peace."'"
(Numbers 6:22–26)

One of the ways we give our attention to others is to look at them. We show our interest in them and we can have our most meaningful communication by engaging in face-to-face conversation. When we try to communicate with someone and they don't look at us, we interpret it as a sign of disinterest and even disrespect. It helps us to understand the significance of Aaron's blessing when we think about what it means to "turn our faces" toward someone.

When Aaron spoke this blessing, no one could ever see the face of God. Although God had come down in a cloud to represent His physical presence, He had never actually shown His face. In fact, it was commonly believed that anyone who saw the face of God would surely die.

The great miracle of the Gospel is that God came to us and showed us His face through the person of Jesus Christ! Now we understand that when someone sees the face of God, they do not die, they truly live!

Tuesday: Living in God's Peace and Passing It Along to Others

> The Lord said to Moses, "Tell Aaron and his sons, 'This is how you are to bless the Israelites. Say to them: "The Lord bless you and keep you; the Lord make his face shine on you and be gracious to you; the Lord turn his face toward you and give you peace."'"
> (NUMBERS 6:22–26)

ONE OF THE SIGNS OF A LIFE spent with God is a life filled with peace. To have the peace of God is to be well and whole on the inside—in your body, in your mind, in your soul.

When God gives this prayer to Moses for Aaron to bless the people, it is so that they will know what it means to be complete and fulfilled in God alone. The peace of God is not only for individuals, but it is also meant to be shared with others. As God brings us into the peaceful place, He uses us to bring in others, as well.

Notice that Aaron's blessing was not only for an individual but for "the Israelites." We can enjoy peace, wholeness, completeness, and fulfillment in God with our family and friends and through us, God brings all of that to our communities.

When the people of God have the peace of God and come together, they share in that peace and enjoy the community. When they go out into the world, God causes that peace to overflow and bring more than enough peace to bring wellness and wholeness to them, too.

Wednesday: Finding Favor with God

If you are pleased with me, teach me your ways so I may know you and continue to find favor with you. Remember that this nation is your people. (EXODUS 33:13)

MOSES WAS CHOSEN BY GOD to lead the children of Israel out of Egypt and across the sea. The people rejoiced but the task was not complete. Between the people and the Promised Land was a vast wilderness that would present a series of setbacks and test Moses' tenacity. There were ups and downs, highs and lows, successes and failures; times when Moses acted with wisdom and times when he acted in anger.

In the midst of these challenges, Moses offers this prayer out of desperation and determination. Moses understands that the favor of God has been on his life and has brought him to this point. His prayer is for God to "continue" to keep His hand on Moses as Moses continues to carry out this difficult and complex task. Moses cannot complete his task without the favor of God.

Each of us has been called by God to complete a certain task and fulfill a certain divine purpose. The reality is that we cannot do this apart from the favor of God on our lives.

From time to time, we are challenged in ways that test us to our limits. We realize that we cannot complete the task alone. Like Moses, we can turn to God. Only His favor can give us the means to follow through and fulfill our calling.

Thursday: Enlarging the Territory

Jabez cried out to the God of Israel, "Oh, that you would bless me and enlarge my territory! Let your hand be with me, and keep me from harm so that I will be free from pain." And God granted his request. (1 CHRONICLES 4:10)

THIS VERSE IS FAMOUSLY CALLED, "The Prayer of Jabez," and is debatably one of the most famous prayers in the Bible. One small, unsuspecting verse in the middle of a long list of genealogies has inspired many to believe God for bigger, better, and greater things.

Jabez gives us a sense of hope that God will answer our prayers—even if that would seem too good to be true. But we can think of this verse in the broader scope how what God does for us can lead us to be kind to others. When God blesses us, we can bless others. It's one thing for God to enlarge our territory, but what if He does it in order for us to enlarge the territory of others? God never does anything just for us. He always intends for us to bless others with the blessings we have received.

God granted the request of Jabez and gave him the things he had asked for.

What are you asking God for and how could you show kindness to others if God answered your prayer?

Friday: Kept from Harm by the Hand of God

Jabez cried out to the God of Israel, "Oh, that you would bless me and enlarge my territory! Let your hand be with me, and keep me from harm so that I will be free from pain." And God granted his request. (1 CHRONICLES 4:10)

WE CANNOT KNOW WHAT MAY HAVE CAUSED Jabez to pray this kind of prayer, but we know that God granted his request. For any prayer to make it into the Bible, it must be significant, so Jabez's prayer must carry some level of meaning that makes it worth investigating.

Half of this short prayer involves a petition for God's supernatural protection from harm. All throughout the Bible, God reminds His people that He is a protector, a refuge, a shelter, a strong tower. God keeps and cares for those who put their trust in Him.

Jabez appeals to this characteristic of God when He makes his petition known and he reminds us that we can call on God. All of us have things in our lives that can cause us to fear.

Rather than attempting to control our own circumstances and be the masters of our own fate, the prayer of Jabez interrupts the genealogy to remind us that, through the years and regardless of what we may face, God keeps and preserves all those who call on and put their trust in Him.

Saturday: Free from Pain

Jabez cried out to the God of Israel, "Oh, that you would bless me and enlarge my territory! Let your hand be with me, and keep me from harm so that I will be free from pain." And God granted his request. (1 Chronicles 4:10)

To be free from pain: what a prayer!

This is a bold and audacious prayer from a man that we know so little about. We don't know what kind of pain he faced; we don't know what his family situation was like; we don't know what his health situation was like.

If it had been the story of Noah or Abraham, Joseph or Job, we would have had at least three chapters or as many as forty-two to tell us their stories, but Jabez is only mentioned in these two isolated verses. We only have one piece of biographical information to put this prayer into context. In verse 9, the Bible says, "His mother had named him Jabez, saying, 'I gave birth to him in pain.'" Jabez had been identified and associated with pain from his birth. He had lived his entire life with pain. His very name communicated the presence of pain. Yet when he prayed to be free from pain, "God granted his request."

God specializes in bringing healing to the hurting and mending the broken. The issues that we were born with or born into do not have to remain the identifying marks of our existence. Jabez's story reminds us that we aren't defined by the circumstances of our past. God comes to us in our pain and responds when we call out to Him.

A Kind Deed Is Never Lost Even Though You May Not See the Results

Sunday: What Good is It?

What good is it, my brothers and sisters, if someone claims to have faith but has no deeds? Can such faith save them? (JAMES 2:14)

ONE OF MY FAVORITE messages in life is this from last week: Be kind—every person you meet is fighting a difficult battle. I also love this week's reminder: A kind deed is never lost even through you may not see the results.

Look back at last week. Think about the people you spoke to and the people you saw walking by. Think about the people you noticed at work and the people you passed on the street. A few of them might have talked to you, telling you their stories. Others might have said nothing at all, but they had facial expressions indicating it wasn't a good day for them.

Now, think about this week. Plan ahead. Plot to shine the Lord's face of kindness to everyone you see. Be kind to them. With a few words or no words at all. With a willingness to listen to their words if you ask them, "How are you doing today?"

Our presence in their lives might be a way for their hopes to come true. We might be the blessing they need. We might be the way God chooses to bless them and keep them. His love might be shining through our faces.

What good is it if we talk about faith but do not live it? It is of no good. We must be people who do deeds of kindness.

Monday: Doing Nothing

Suppose a brother or a sister is without clothes and daily food. If one of you says to them, "Go in peace; keep warm and well fed," but does nothing about their physical needs, what good is it?
(JAMES 2:15–16)

A KIND DEED IS NEVER LOST even though you may not be able to see the results.

Jabez prayed his prayer so that he would be free from pain.

We have encouraged you to pray the prayer for yourself. We now want to encourage you to pray that same prayer for other people. Ask God to let them be free from pain. Mention their names. Describe their pain—though God already knows it, our confessions are a part of the conversation of intercession on their behalf. Stand up for them. Kneel down for them. Lift them to God in prayer.

What might happen? God granted the request of Jabez. Let's believe today He will grant your requests.

And as He does, begin to rejoice. In fact, begin rejoicing even before the final results arrive. Sometimes the rejoicing helps free us from the pain of dwelling on our difficulties or the problems of others.

Once you pray the prayer of Jabez, remember the importance of how we are often part of the answer to our own prayers for others. We can treat folks in ways that might bring healing to their wounds. Be kind—every person you meet is fighting a difficult battle.

Doing nothing isn't the answer. Kind deeds are. Let's do them!

Tuesday: Dead Faith or Deeds of Kindness

In the same way, faith by itself, if it is not accompanied by action, is dead. But someone will say, "You have faith; I have deeds." Show me your faith without deeds, and I will show you my faith by my deeds. (JAMES 2:17–18)

EVERYONE LIKES A BLESSING FROM GOD. To know we have the Lord's favor and that His hand is upon us can bring deep peace.

God had instructed Moses to tell his brother Aaron and his sons how to bless the Israelites. God then voiced a statement, instructing the priests to announce those words to the nation.

The benediction we read last week has been used since then. Churches might close a service with that blessing announced by a bishop. Parents might pray the prayer over their children.

The confession helps us remember what God did—and promised to do—to His chosen people. They were not to allow circumstances to control them. They were not to see with limited vision.

I am convinced we need to hear the Lord's words in our times. Although our situation is different, God is still God. Even if we are not living in the time of Numbers and are not part of the original Israelite audience which received this blessing, we believe in the New Testament promises of God notifying us that we are now the chosen ones of a kind and gracious God. And He has called us to live out our faith with deeds of kindness.

Let our lives be benedictions of blessings to others.

Wednesday: When Believing Isn't Enough

You believe that there is one God. Good! Even the demons believe that—and shudder. (JAMES 2: 19)

REMEMBER THE BLESSING we read and prayed last week:

- The Lord bless you and
- keep you;
- the Lord make his face shine on you
- and be gracious to you;
- the Lord turn his face toward you
- and give you peace.

Read those words again. Read them aloud. Believe God is blessing you today. Choose to believe He is, right now, blessing you.

Accept the blessings of the Lord. Realize the Lord will keep you and never let you go. Appreciate that He is making His face shine on you and is being gracious unto you. Notice He isn't looking away to avoid you but is turning His face toward you. Rest in knowing the Lord is giving you peace.

But realize like we studied yesterday that there is more for us to do.

We are not to be just those who receive God's blessings. We are not just those who believe in God. Faith stated is not enough. Faith is to be shown through kind deeds to others. The Lord might be shining on others through our faces and His blessings might just come to them through us.

Let's not just say we believe in Jesus. Let's live like Jesus.

Thursday: No Announcement

Be careful not to practice your righteousness in front of others to be seen by them. If you do, you will have no reward from your Father in heaven. So when you give to the needy, do not announce it with trumpets, as the hypocrites do in the synagogues and on the streets, to be honored by others. Truly I tell you, they have received their reward in full. (MATTHEW 6:1–2)

LAST WEEK WE READ from 1 Chronicles 4:10 what is called the prayer of Jabez. It is an important prayer. It is a powerful prayer. Though often misunderstood and incorrectly interpreted, those mistakes should not keep us from reading the prayer and praying it.

Today we are listening in on the words of Jesus. He reminded His listeners to not announce their prayers or their good deeds.

Jabez "cried out" to the God of Israel. The prayer of Jabez was an appeal:

- Oh, that You would bless me
- and enlarge my territory!

But today we are to grasp something in addition to a prayer prayed. Today we are to grasp the life we are called to live.

God might answer someone else's prayer of Jabez through you.

Yes, God invited you to ask Him to meet your needs. He also instructed you to care for the needs of others without making what you've done known by others.

Serving in silence, living without applause, our kind deeds will be noticed by God. Others will be helped. What else really matters?

Friday: Keeping a Secret

But when you give to the needy, do not let your left hand know what your right hand is doing. (MATTHEW 6:3)

AS WE READ YESTERDAY, we do not need to make an announcement about our service to others. We just need to live it, expecting no applause for our actions.

Remember again how Jabez pleaded his requests in the Old Testament:

· Let Your hand be with me,
· and keep me from harm
· so that I will be free from pain.

He hoped the hand of the Lord would be with him.

That is what Jesus has called each of us to do. He instructs us each day, whatever is occurring and wherever we are, to let the Lord to be with us and to love through us.

Ask God now for His hand to be with you. Believe by faith His hand is there—right where you need it to be.

Jabez requested that the God of Israel would keep him from harm. Though there is pain in this life, God instructs us to ask Him for health, to ask Him to keep us safe, to ask Him for protection.

Pray today that you will be the person God uses to keep others free from pain. Keep it a secret. Serve in silence. But the people you serve with God's love will never be the same.

Ask God that you will be kept from harm by His hand, and that His hands will work through your hands to help others.

Saturday: An Eternal Reward

So that your giving may be in secret. Then your Father, who sees what is done in secret, will reward you. (MATTHEW 6:4)

A KIND DEED IS NEVER LOST even though you may not be able to see the results.

Don't you want the favor of God? Don't you want God to be pleased with you?

It is okay to tell Him that. It is fine to ask God for His favor. Just love like Jesus did, and expect no rewards here. Only God's eternal reward.

Pray a prayer like this today:

Dear God,

I seek to please you. I want You to be delighted with me. I do not want to fail You, so please teach me Your ways. I know the commandments and I study the Bible. But I need You to help me truly learn from You. There are so many other customs and plans around me, I desperately need for You to teach me Your ways. And here is why I am asking this: that I might know You. I want to fully know You and find favor with You. I do not want to disappoint You. I want us to be your people and for you to be our God. So, reveal to me everything I need to know and do not let me miss anything. I crave Your favor—not that of man. Bless me and keep me today and forever. For You, Father. With the power of the Holy Spirt. In the name of Jesus, I pray, Amen.

God Washes the Eyes with Tears until Tears Shall Come No More

Sunday: Crying Out to Our Help

I will exalt you, Lord, for you lifted me out of the depths and did not let my enemies gloat over me. Lord my God, I called to you for help, and you healed me. (PSALM 30:1–2)

PSALM 30 IS AN ANCIENT SONG about the dedication of the house of David. It begins as it should: crying out to God and asking for His help.

David chose to exalt God, then he revealed reasons—voicing in prayerful celebration and declaration what God had done:

- You lifted me out of the depths.
- You did not let my enemies gloat over me.
- You healed me.

David cried out to God for help by beginning his plea with worship. What a way to begin! What a way to remember! What a way to celebrate!

God had lifted David from the deep, low, throbbing places of pain. Hasn't God lifted you from there? Thank Him for what He has done.

God did not let David's enemies gloat over him. Do you believe God can help you in that same way? Thank Him for what He has done. Thank Him in advance for what you believe God will one day do.

God healed David, who had called out to his Healer for help. "Lord, my God," David titled God. "I called to You for help, and You healed me," David said.

As you cry out to God today and plead for His help, believe He has lifted you, protected you, and healed you. He is your help today.

144

Monday: Brought Up from the Pit

You, Lord, brought me up from the realm of the dead; you spared me from going down to the pit. (PSALM 30:3)

GOD BROUGHT DAVID up from the realm of death. God spared David from going down into the pit.

How does this fit in your life? Do you know about times when everything felt like it was dying? When you felt like life had abandoned you? When your dwelling place mentally, spiritually, emotionally, mentally, physically, financially, and relationally seemed like you were falling deep into a pit?

A pit would be a dark, cold, dangerous, frightening place. Not where we want to go. Not where we want to be. Not where we want to stay. A pit could be a trap we might never escape from.

When you were in your pit, maybe you saw no way out. When you were in your pit, maybe there were times you were ready to give up.

But instead of giving up, you called out to God and He brought you up. You might feel again like not only is the world falling apart but you are in its darkest, deepest pit. But this is not the day to give up. This is the day to let God bring you up.

Believe that can happen again today. Pray that can happen again today. Pray the very words David prayed. Refuse to give up. Let God bring you up from the unfathomable pit of pain.

Tuesday: Joy Comes in the Morning

Sing the praises of the Lord, you his faithful people; praise his holy name. For his anger lasts only a moment, but his favor lasts a lifetime; weeping may stay for the night, but rejoicing comes in the morning. (Psalm 30:4–5)

GOD WASHES THE EYES WITH TEARS until they can behold the invisible land where tears shall come no more. "Weeping may endure for a night," David sang. And, I love the line which follows that one. David confessed, "But joy comes in the morning."

Can this be that morning for you? Can this be a morning of joy for you?

I believe it can. I am convinced it can.

Here is what I want you to affirm as you prepare to receive the joy of the Lord:

- Sing the praises of the Lord,
- you His faithful people;
- praise His holy name.
- For His anger lasts only a moment,
- but His favor lasts a lifetime;
- weeping may stay for the night,
- but rejoicing comes in the morning.

Can you sing that song with David and his people? Can you sing that song during a time of questions and confusion? I invite you to. Sing the praise of the Lord; you are among His faithful people. Praise His holy name! Remember these traits: His anger lasts only a moment, but His favor lasts forever! Remember these truths: your weeping may stay for the night, but joy comes in the morning!

Right now is that morning. Rejoice in the Lord at this moment.

Wednesday: I Will Never Be Shaken

When I felt secure, I said, "I will never be shaken." (PSALM 30:6)

THOSE SITUATIONS COME OUR WAY which cause us to feel shaken. We don't know what will happen next. We heard the bad news and more seems to be on the way. We feel pain physically and emotionally. We wonder where the money will come from. We dwell on sadness that just won't leave us alone.

Times like that cause us to feel very insecure. We are uncertain. We have lost confidence. Our emotions are dull and dry. Our faith has turned into doubt.

What should we do?

We should go back to just where we started this week. Rejoice in the Lord. Remember what He has done. Release our worries to the One who is strong enough to carry them.

Join in with David and make this confession, even when you feel totally insecure—especially when you feel totally insecure: "I will never be shaken."

The ground you are standing on might feel unstable. The enthusiasm you once felt has seemed to depart from you. You wait and wait and wait. You plead and cry and mourn. But now you must make the choice to rejoice. It is a decision, not a feeling. It is a conclusion reached, not a condition reported. Choose to not be shaken. No matter what is happening around you, choose today to rejoice for you will not be shaken. God's strength is enough.

Thursday: The Favor of God

Lord, when you favored me, you made my royal mountain stand firm; but when you hid your face, I was dismayed. (Psalm 30:7)

MAYBE YOU READ YESTERDAY'S THOUGHTS and tried to take those steps toward victory. Maybe a part of you felt like David felt: "God seemed to hide His face from me and I felt dismayed."

Those thoughts and feelings hit us sometimes. That is being human. That is life in a fallen world. That is when the tears keep on falling. That is when we don't know any way out of our situation.

But those very moments of failing to see God's face, those very moments of feeling dismayed, those very moments when the world is falling apart are the very moments when God is about to show His favor. That is His plan for you today.

Gaze toward your God and believe He is rescuing you. Stare in His direction and receive His protection. Put your trust in your Lord and your God. He has promised to be with you and not to abandon you. He has assured you of His empathy. He is hearing the cries of your heart today. And He is responding with deep assurance and concern.

Hear His guarantee today. Believe He will make the mountain of your life stand firm. No wind can blow it down. Not storm can knock it over.

Live today in the favor of God. His face is turned toward you today and His eyes show you love.

Friday: A Cry for Mercy

To you, Lord, I called; to the Lord I cried for mercy: "What is gained if I am silenced, if I go down to the pit? Will the dust praise you? Will it proclaim your faithfulness? Hear, Lord, and be merciful to me; Lord, be my help." (PSALM 30:8–10)

DAVID AND HIS PEOPLE PRAYED together aloud. David and his people sang together aloud. They marched into cities, through villages, down valleys, up hills, atop mountains, confessing the truth they believed. They cried out to God for mercy.

Let us join them today. Though these are much different times in much different settings, two things remain the same: (1) We need God, and (2) He is here for us. Join with the nation of Israel and plead for the mercy of God by affirming aloud Psalm 30:8–10.

- To you, Lord, I called;
- to the Lord I cried for mercy:
- "What is gained if I am silenced,
- if I go down to the pit?
- Will the dust praise you?
- Will it proclaim your faithfulness?
- Hear, Lord,
- and be merciful to me;
- Lord, be my help."

God heard His people in those times.

God hears His people in our times.

Cry for mercy and let Him hear your appeal today. There is nothing to gain if you stay silent, down in the pit of despair. The dust will not praise God or proclaim of His faithfulness. We are the ones to do that. We are the ones to ask God to hear us and be merciful to us. We are the ones to ask the Lord to be our help.

Give to God your cry for mercy today. Believe by faith He will be merciful and bring you help.

Saturday: Mourning into Dancing

You turned my wailing into dancing; you removed my sackcloth and clothed me with joy, that my heart may sing your praises and not be silent. Lord my God, I will praise you forever. (PSALM 30:11–12)

WHEN WE CRY OUT TO GOD as we have this week, great things happen. We release our hurt and sadness. We see God turning our mourning into dancing. We see God remove our feelings of defeat and declare us victorious in Him.

So, receive His victory today. End the time of defeat. Begin the celebration of victory.

Here are a few ways to rejoice:

- Sing songs of celebration to God.
- Tell your story as a testimony of the goodness of God.
- Keep a list of the great things the Lord has done.
- Place a reminder beside your upcoming prayer requests that "the Lord will win again."
- Read Psalm 30:11–12 over and over throughout the day today.
- Write your own prayerful song of praise to the Lord.

There are many other ways for you to rejoice. Just remember this: To rejoice is a choice. It is the right choice, the best choice.

You cannot be silent today. You can praise the Lord today, and forever and ever. Your heart will sing to the Lord. Your body will dance before the Lord. Your mind will remember what the Lord has done.

God washed your eyes with tears but today they have come no more. Today is the day to rejoice!

We Need to Put Matters in the Right Place— God and the Holy Bible

Sunday: How to Know What Really Matters

For this reason I kneel before the Father. (EPHESIANS 3:14)

IN THE SPIRITUAL REALM, we stand taller on our knees than we do on our feet. Paul knew it 2,000 years ago. We can know it right now. Prayer has always been the key to proper perspective.

Think about the things weighing on your heart today.

- Family. Finances. Fears.
- Hopes. Dreams. Questions.
- Burdens. Blessings. Busyness.
- This, that, and
- Everything in between.

For those reasons and for every other reason, we have no better approach than prayer! No better strategy. No better posture. Kneeling before the Father puts the issues of life in proper perspective by tapping our heart into the conduit of heaven's power. Prayer plugs us in to the electricity of God.

Do you want to discern what really matters right now? Do you want to hear the voice of the loving, almighty Father cut through the noise of your busyness and your burdens? Do you want to sense the rod and staff of the Good Shepherd guiding you? Or catch a glimpse into the Holy Spirit's agenda?

Then approach the throne of grace, where Christ sits at the right hand of the Father. Prepare your heart to have an audience with the King. The Author and Perfecter of your faith.

And kneel.

Kneel boldly, gladly, expectantly. Talk honestly and listen urgently. Ask God. Then, be still. Rest on the assurance that as you kneel before the Father, He listens and speaks with you. He gives the riches of wisdom freely.

Trust prayer's process. The Father is giving you His full attention.

Monday: Calling on the Heavenly Father

For this reason I kneel before the Father, from whom every family in heaven and on earth derives its name. (EPHESIANS 3:14–15)

WE DON'T HAVE A DEAF GOD.

We don't have a Father who doesn't care for His family.

Because of this, Paul knelt before the Father. And we should too. As he knelt, Paul knew his Father would not turn away. His Father would not be too busy. Or distant or unloving or too tired to talk.

Instead, Paul knew his heavenly Father would remember that Paul bore His own image and name. Paul knew that being part of God's family meant unlimited access to a limitless Father.

We can know that too.

The Father loves you so much He gave you His own name. This is no small thing. A father's name is his bond of love and his commitment to provide. As imperfect as you are, He delights to speak with you and provide for you. He loves to love you.

This is why calling on your heavenly Father is a joy, as much as it is a command.

Not sure how to pray right now?

Let the Holy Bible help. Try borrowing Paul's prayer from this passage (Ephesians 3:16–21) and make it your own.

"Father, I boldly and gladly ask that out of your glorious riches You would strengthen me with power through Your Spirit in my inner being, so that Christ may dwell in my heart through faith ...."

Start there, and keep going.

Tuesday: God's Glorious Riches

I pray that out of His glorious riches He may strengthen you with power through His Spirit in your inner being. (EPHESIANS 3:16)

SOMETIMES WE FORGET how rich we really are.

Not materially. Material riches have little to do with spiritual ones. They misdirect our priorities if we give them too much attention and affection.

But, spiritually? Yes. Spiritually, we—the family of God—are always and exceedingly rich.

How?

God's glory makes us wealthy. And God's Spirit channels the riches of His own glory to our innermost being, like wind carrying oxygen to our lungs, strengthening and reminding us of what matters most.

Paul spoke excitedly about God's glory. He wanted his faith family to know how blessed and rich their inheritance in Christ was (Ephesians 1:3–4). He wanted them to feel in their bones how powerful a position they were in, just by belonging to the Father (Ephesians 1:5–8; 11–14). He wanted them to live aflame with praise.

Today, child of God, you are in the same supremely, gloriously blessed position.

Today, child of God, you cannot be robbed, cheated, duped, or swindled out of your inheritance. Moths can't devour it. Flames can't burn it. Rust can't corrupt it. Come hell or high water, the glorious riches of God are yours in Christ Jesus.

That's worth praising over. Let us be about our praise today. Let us recall that power and proper perspective comes with praise.

Wednesday: God and His Word in Our Hearts

So that Christ may dwell in your hearts through faith.
(EPHESIANS 3:17A)

IF YOU COULD LOOK INSIDE YOUR HEART today, who would you find dwelling there?

God built our hearts to be lived-in spaces: spiritual homes, over which we preside as spiritual landlords. As landlords, we decide who occupies our heart and sits on its throne. Today, and every day, that is our most crucial choice. Who we become depends directly on who we allow to dwell in our heart.

This is why the Bible teaches us to …

- **Guard our heart above all else**. Everything we do flows from it (Proverbs 4:23).
- **Hide God's Word in our heart**. It's a treasure that surpasses all others, bringing us power and life, lighting our path, and setting our hearts free to run unhindered and unshackled in the life Christ longs to give us (Psalm 119:11, 32, 105).

Today, ask yourself:

- Will I reserve my heart's throne for Christ?
- Will I evict the idols and impostors trying to steal my allegiance and affection?
- Will I make Christ rent temporarily?
- Or will I let him own my heart completely, and live there permanently?

Then, invite the Holy Spirit to help you.

As you do, the Spirit activates the power of the *written* Word of God (the Bible) and prepares the way for the *living* Word of God (Jesus Christ) to draw near and dwell in your heart.

Thursday: A Prayer

So that Christ may dwell in your hearts through faith. And I pray that you, being rooted and established in love.... (EPHESIANS 3:17)

HAVE YOU PRAYED TODAY?

No? Let's pray now. The Father's door and heart are open.

Yes? Let's pray again. The Father's door and heart are still open.

All those things in your life right now. Those burdens. Those blessings that, if you're honest, are still sometimes a burden. Those pitfalls and concerns. Those places where you feel tired or empty or loveless.

All those things in your life right now that are trying to uproot you ...

Pray.

Prayer brings proper perspective. It pulls our eyes back to what matters most. It insulates our ears from the voices that do not matter, and opens them to the whisper that does matter. Prayer heals and stabilizes and inspires.

Prayer roots our hearts in the fertile soil of Christ's own heart. It anchors our weary souls in the only Love that will not let us go.

As you pray, let the Word of God accompany you:

"Lord Jesus, I give you all my burdens and my blessings. Help me make room in my heart, through faith, so you can dwell there with no competition. Root me and establish me in your love."

Times change. Trends come and go. But prayer and Scripture remain the two most powerful ways to commune with God.

They turn the without-God life into the with-God life.

Friday: The Love of Christ

And may you have power, together with all the Lord's holy people, to grasp how wide and long and high and deep is the love of Christ. (EPHESIANS 3:18)

WHAT MANNER OF LOVE IS THIS?

Love so massive, so astonishingly immense, the Apostle Paul knew we needed *power* to grasp it.

Paul could never get over it. Read his letters, and you'll often find him at a loss for words sufficient to describe what He found most glorious in all of life: the arresting, breathtaking love of Christ.

Remember his story? A former murderer, Paul called himself "the worst of sinners" (1 Timothy 1:15).

What about your story?

At times, don't we feel like Paul? Like our wretchedness and shame places us in the "worst" category? Beyond the reach of Christ's love?

But, too often, our opinion of Christ's love is too small. Look around the world—you'll find millions who also think too little of Christ's love, or that Christ's love is too little for them. We're a world of people focusing on the wrong things. How can we govern ourselves when we make what matters most, matter least?

May our heart's priorities shift!

Christ's love *must* become to us the endless treasure it became to Paul. May we, the children of God, drop our shame and grasp for this love with all our might. May it become the matchless treasure—with unending depths, heights, widths and lengths—that we daily seek.

Saturday: The Fullness of God

And to know this love that surpasses knowledge—that you may be filled to the measure of all the fullness of God. (Ephesians 3:19)

How can we know love that "surpasses knowledge?"

How can we—finite, flawed people—possibly be filled with God's own fullness?

Take joy, brothers and sisters. This is a blissful mystery! With God, *mystery is normal.* His Word regularly speaks of wonders. Paradoxes. Logic-defying, heavenly realities. Miracles.

God does not share our limits. When we follow Jesus, our heavenly Father happily inverts our concept of what is possible. He freely reaches into every impossible, off-limits space we never could.

Today,

- What are your limits? List them. Then, next to each one, write: **"*Limitless.*"**
- What are your life's impossibilities? List them. Then, write: **"*Possible.*"**
- In what areas do you feel lack or emptiness? List them. Then, write: **"*Fullness.*"**

As you do, praise God in advance that He is bringing His love and fullness to bear on each burden.

Brothers and sisters, if our heart's priority doesn't rest upon knowing "this love that surpasses knowledge" and being filled to the brim with "the fullness of God," then we will forever run on a half-tank of our own pitiful power—which is as good as running on empty.

Let us instead fix our hearts on God and His Word, and fill ourselves to the brim with His fullness.

This Person Does Not Argue about God's Plan and God's Wisdom

Sunday: Praying Instead of Arguing

Pray for us. We are sure that we have a clear conscience and desire to live honorably in every way. I particularly urge you to pray so that I may be restored to you soon. (HEBREWS 13:18–19)

WHAT ARE YOUR FISTS CLENCHED around today?

What is it? That thing about which your conscience is reminding you: "The more you fight for control, the more you lose it."

Friend: have you prayed?

To argue is our nature. From Adam and Eve, to Jacob, to wayward Israel, to Peter and James and John—we belong to a spiritual lineage of people who instinctively wrestle God.

Sometimes it's our eyes—we can't see what God sees. Sometimes it's our minds—we don't know what God knows. Other times, it's our hearts—we don't want what God wants.

And God is compassionate. Gracious. Slow to anger. Abounding in love and faithfulness. He obliges our wrestling—for a time. But when the necessary moment comes, He impacts our strength, halting our aggression. He reminds us of His goodness and authority and our deep need to trust Him, and let go.

Then, He turns our feverish arguing into fervent praying.

Friend: how much better off are we when we lay down our demands? How much better, to pray instead of argue?

Isn't the cross we carry stained with the crimson love of a *good* Shepherd?

Pray. And trust.

Monday: The God of Peace

Now may the God of peace, who through the blood of the eternal covenant brought back from the dead our Lord Jesus, that great Shepherd of the sheep. (HEBREWS 13:20)

PARTIAL DEVOTION yields partial peace.

God gives us space to grow and wrestle and refine our discipline. He helps us. But when it comes down to it, half-committed followers only experience half-realized results. By carrying their cross only sometimes, they learn all too well the conflict of the cross—how painful and rugged it is. But only scarcely do they realize its victory—how it transforms and gives life through death.

They die partially, and never fully live. They remain in limbo between death and resurrection.

Jesus' commitment to us was not partial. In giving His body to be broken and His soul to be severed, He gave no half-measure. Though He agonized and questioned in Gethsemane, He did not ultimately argue with His Father's wisdom and plan. Facing immense distress, Jesus submitted.

"Not my will," He said.

"But Yours be done."

And in that, He gave us a pattern for finding peace:

Submitting to the God of peace, as the Prince of Peace Himself did.

At times, we agonize and question. We all have our Gethsemanes. And the Father doesn't reject us. But the devoted, committed person who takes the cross and wholeheartedly follows the Lord does not ultimately argue about God's plan and God's wisdom.

Like Christ, our path to peace lies in surrender.

Tuesday: That Which Is Pleasing to God

Equip you with everything good for doing his will, and may he work in us what is pleasing to him, through Jesus Christ, to whom be glory for ever and ever. Amen. (HEBREWS 13:21)

FOLLOWING CHRIST MEANS wholeheartedly pursuing that which pleases God. And pursuing that which pleases God naturally upsets every instinct in us.

Read this verse again slowly. Meditate on each phrase. Notice the motivations (the *why's* and the *what-for's*) found in each:

- The God of peace "equips us with everything good" for what purpose? ... *doing His will.*
- He works in us, through Jesus Christ, what kinds of things? ... *those that are pleasing to Him.*
- To whom goes the glory for ever and ever? ... *Jesus Christ.*

Note the bitter-yet-beautiful pattern hidden in this verse: none of these motivations center on us.

Not our will. *His* will.

Not our pleasure. *His* pleasure.

Not our glory...

Christ's glory.

Carrying our cross is about us learning that things are not really *about us.* This is a lifelong lesson that requires daily commitment and re-commitment. We fall often. But the righteous person always stands back up (Proverbs 24:16).

As we learn to offer ourselves, our Father fills us with more and more of His own peace, pleasures, and purposes. *He* becomes our delight. Christ's Kingdom, our treasure. His gospel, our glory.

God gives us His own heart. And we find, over time, that which pleases Him becomes sublimely pleasing to us as well.

Wednesday: Bear with These Words

Brothers and sisters, I urge you to bear with my word of exhortation, for in fact I have written to you quite briefly. (HEBREWS 13:22)

HOW DOES GOD speak to us?

Through Scripture. Prayer and fasting. Through the beauty of Creation, the changing of circumstance, the wordless whisper of conscience. Through tears, and laughter. Yes, through all these things and more, the Father talks with us.

Are we listening?

He also speaks through relationships.

Herein lies the true excitement and necessity of Christian fellowship—the Church family is yet another way God's voice can reach us. We ourselves can be God's telephones, through which He calls out to people.

This is why Scripture teaches us to treat one another with godly sensitivity. We bear with one another. We bear each other's burdens. We listen to each other's words, and discern. We make love our most common practice.

Love keeps us on our toes. It reminds us that when one of our brothers or sisters opens their mouth, God Himself may just be saying something through them.

Pray today:

- Father, *help me listen* for your voice in the words of others.
- Jesus, *help me stay near you,* so you can speak through me without interference.
- Holy Spirit, *help me discern* ... When I should speak. When I should listen. When it's You I'm hearing. And when it's not.

Thursday: Arriving Soon

I want you to know that our brother Timothy has been released. If he arrives soon, I will come with him to see you. (HEBREWS 13:23)

HARMONY.

Excitement.

Longing.

These words ought to describe the fellowship we share with one another.

- Together, we rejoice and together we weep. Others' concerns and victories are also our own. We live in harmony with one another (Romans 12:15).
- Together, we listen excitedly for news in each other's lives. With interest and energy, we know and learn one another's stories, as well as we know and learn our own.
- Together, we gather. We visit and host each other. We do the simple things, like spending time. We long for one another with a family's love.

Brothers and sisters, don't miss this: Church is personal, because God is personal.

Regardless of the physical distance and time between us, we're called to live with the intimate soul of *"nearby"* neighbors. Our hearts thrive in proximity. Single threads never become alone the tapestry they could when woven together.

Who are the "Timothy's" in your life today? Who has been "released" from prison, figuratively or literally? Whose stories can you show interest in right now? Who is arriving soon? Or departing? Who can you visit, or host?

Live in harmony with the ones God has given you. They, and you, are gifts.

Friday: Greeting One Another

Greet all your leaders and all the Lord's people. Those from Italy send you their greetings. (HEBREWS 13:24)

RELATIONSHIPS ARE communication.

A dance of sending and receiving, choreographed by God to keep our love warm and on the move. Without them, we grow stiff and wooden.

But, we have a choice. We can step back, keep our distance, and deny the dance. We can choose to stay all-business, hurrying along on the surfaces of others' lives. Doing what needs doing, saying what needs saying, and rushing for the exit door.

Or, we can greet one another with the heart of God. We can melt the frost and dive into intimacy, pausing the business to embrace—even though we sometimes get hurt in the process.

God knows that, for His people, all things are best exchanged in relationship. That's why He designed us to long for more from one another than merely goods and services. That's also why it's important we don't skip over tiny verses like this one when we read the Bible. A greeting in Scripture can teach as much as a discourse, if we let it.

Today, let this old greeting, sent and received long ago, teach us about the care we should take with one another. Let it remind us that ...

... If we've only done what needed doing,
and only said what needed saying,
Then we've left undone what needed doing,
and unsaid what needed saying.

We are, after all, more than just each other's business.

Saturday: God's Grace for Us All

Grace be with you all. (HEBREWS 13:25)

DON'T OVERLOOK THE POWER of these simple words.

"Grace be with you all."

To wish the grace of God upon your sisters and brothers is not to *wish* at all. It is to *give* the highest possible blessing with total certainty. Where His grace is sought, God never fails to deliver.

Grace is beautiful in many dimensions:

- It's God's **benevolence**, with which He showers kindness and favor upon us, like a father doting on his beloved children.
- It's His **salvation**, with which He rescues and redeems, like a king defending and fighting for his people.
- It's also His **empowerment**, with which He sanctifies, matures and equips, like a vine dresser pruning, fertilizing, and harvesting fruit from his choicest vine.

In short, God's grace is His supremely good *everything*.

It's the fullest portion of the very best of Himself, given at no cost to us, which all at once arrests our fears, shackles our sins, fans the flame of our giftings, and sends us soaring on wings like eagles. This is why when Jesus told Paul, "My grace is sufficient for you," He was making something of an understatement (2 Corinthians 12:9). More than merely sufficient, Christ's grace is all we'll ever need and the chief treasure for which our soul yearns.

Today,

Ask.

Seek.

Knock for this treasure: amazing grace—the sweet *everything* of God.

The Secret of Patience Is to Do Something Else in the Meantime

Sunday: When Things Seem Meaningless

Again I saw something meaningless under the sun: There was a man all alone; he had neither son nor brother. There was no end to his toil, yet his eyes were not content with his wealth. "For whom am I toiling," he asked, "and why am I depriving myself of enjoyment?" This too is meaningless—a miserable business! (ECCLESIASTES 4:7–8)

ALL HUMAN BEINGS HAVE AN INNATE desire to do something meaningful with their lives. It's part of the way we have been created. There are some people who spend their entire lives searching for that special sense of purpose that underscores their pursuits and plans, while there are others who seem to discover it very early in life.

One of the challenges that we often face is the conflict between tasks that we find menial and tasks that we find meaningful. The menial tasks are those that seem too insignificant to occupy our time, energy, or resources. They are the mundane and redundant tasks that someone *has* to do but no one *wants* to do.

The writer of Ecclesiastes poses a pointed question for all of us to consider: "for whom am I toiling?" How we answer this question can determine whether a task is menial or meaningful. When you do what you do, who are you doing it for? Ecclesiastes reminds us that it is only the work we do for the cause of Christ's Kingdom that brings meaning to the work we do.

C. T. Studd writes in one of his famous poems, "Only one life, 'twill soon be past. Only what's done for Christ will last." Everything we do for ourselves—building up our bank accounts, earning degrees, trying to impress others—is meaningless apart from fulfilling the purpose of God in our lives.

When we find that "sweet spot," then the work that might otherwise seem meaningless takes on a meaning far greater than ourselves.

Monday: No End in Sight

Again I saw something meaningless under the sun: There was a man all alone; he had neither son nor brother. There was no end to his toil, yet his eyes were not content with his wealth. "For whom am I toiling," he asked, "and why am I depriving myself of enjoyment?" This too is meaningless—a miserable business. (ECCLESIASTES 4:7–8)

"IT IS WINTER IN NARNIA," said Mr. Tumnus, "and has been for ever so long.... always winter, but never Christmas." C. S. Lewis wrote these words almost a century ago, but they ring ever the truer. There are ways in which the things that we long for never seem to come to us, no matter how hard we pursue them.

We can work and work, try and try, and still seem to come up short of what we think would fulfill us. It's like a mouse on a wheel or a rocking chair, running and rocking all day but never going anywhere.

It can be difficult to be patient in the moments when what we are striving for still seems unattainable. What we often need to do is to reevaluate whether what we are doing is for the right reasons. It can be depressing to work all day and still have accomplished nothing. "Always winter, but never Christmas." Always striving but never achieving. Always laboring but never resting. Always looking but never seeing. Always hearing but never listening.

God has an expected end for us. When His purpose guides our labor, then He will make sure the task is complete.

Tuesday: Two Are Better Than One

Two are better than one, because they have a good return for their labor. (ECCLESIASTES 4:9)

PARENTS TEACH THEIR CHILDREN to use both hands when they learn to hold their own cup of milk. One old saint used to say of his card-game strategy, "You can't play without a partner." Ecclesiastes emphasizes this eternal truth. If we want to win in life, even if it's just learning to hold a cup or playing cards, then we must learn that we cannot do it alone.

In the garden, God gave Adam a partner to bring him companionship and to work alongside him in tending God's creation. Working alongside another person is part of how God has designed us to grow as a believer. Like two rocks in a stream, they will smooth out one another. Like multiplication rather than addition, the labor of two people is compounded so that the work isn't only twice as great but multiple times.

When we involve another person in our lives, they become a part of making our decisions, shaping our character, and developing our personalities. God uses others to help us become more like Christ. Don't be afraid to involve someone else in what you are doing and don't be afraid to find someone who can see who you really are beneath the surface that others see.

Another set of eyes and ears will help you on your journey with Jesus.

Wednesday: A Return for Our Labor

Two are better than one, because they have a good return for their labor. (ECCLESIASTES 4:9)

IN TODAY'S CULTURE, we do not often celebrate healthy dependence upon another person.

Instead, we celebrate our independence and we are raised to believe that we must be self-sufficient, self-reliant, and self-contained.

This mentality not only means that we end up laboring alone, but it also means that we get to keep everything we earn rather than splitting the wages with another person. While it may seem appealing to keep everything you earn from the work you've done, we also have to remember that two can do more than twice the work that one can do alone. They not only complete the physical labor from a technical perspective, but they motivate one another spiritually, emotionally, and psychologically to accomplish more than what one could do alone.

Who are you investing in today? Who are you seeking wisdom from today? How is God using you to assist the labor of someone else's efforts? How are you fulfilling God's call for you as a part of the body of Christ?

Refuse to live life alone. Pursue other people to be part of your spiritual journey of trusting God even when the world is falling apart.

We always get a greater return for our labor when we are willing to share the experience with others.

Thursday: Helping One Another

If either of them falls down, one can help the other up. But pity anyone who falls and has no one to help them up. (ECCLESIASTES 4:10)

YOU CANNOT SPELL THE WORDS "alone" or "lonely" without the word "one."

God never intended for our Christian lives to be a party of "one." We simply cannot do life alone.

One of the greatest gifts that comes from companionship is the help that one can offer when the other is down. So many people are hurting and in need of help, yet they don't even know it until they need it. The only way we can help someone who has fallen is to be close enough to them when it matters. We cannot help when we are not there. We cannot wait until the crisis hits to get close enough to help. We must be there in the moment of crisis in order for our help to arrive in time.

This means that we must always be striving for healthy relationship with the companions God has placed in our lives. Jesus is a faithful companion to us as we journey through this life. He is constantly near to us and He is available every time we call on His name. We are called to model this for the people God has placed in our lives.

In the same way that He is close to us, walks with us, and helps us in our times of need, we can do the same for others.

Friday: Staying Healthy While Waiting

Also, if two lie down together, they will keep warm. But how can one keep warm alone? (ECCLESIASTES 4:11)

A COLD NIGHT IS A LONELY TIME. It can bring fear and unfamiliarity. It seems endless and uncertain, long and unpredictable.

Many times in our lives, we face circumstances that are just like those nights can be. They make us feel alone, frightened, and unsure of the future. Satan often makes us feel like we have to face these dark cold nights alone, but God would not have us to be alone. It helps us to have a companion when we're waiting through the night for the morning to come.

We may be afraid to ask for help and other times it may be because we don't think we have anyone to ask for help. In any case, the fact is that our own spiritual health depends on having someone else with us to keep us warm through the cold nights. This helps us to stay healthy while we wait.

Make a decision today. While waiting, refuse to wait alone. Find the right voices to help you, encourage you, pray with you. What can you do in the meantime while your patience is developing during this time of waiting: stay healthy by inviting over a friend.

You might not only need them, but you could be the very one to help them today also. Stay healthy together.

Saturday: A Cord of Three Strands

Though one may be overpowered, two can defend themselves. A cord of three strands is not quickly broken. (ECCLESIASTES 4:12)

YOU MAY HAVE HEARD that old saying, "There is power in numbers." This is one of the lessons that we often learn as children. Whether for good or not so good, the more people you get together on the same team, the more power they will have.

The writer of Ecclesiastes reminds us here that the same is true on our spiritual journey. When we walk together with another, the two can strengthen and support one another in ways that one individual cannot do alone. What is more is that when the two come together, Jesus joins them!

The New Testament models this approach with the 72 disciples sent out by Jesus. Whatever ministry the disciples provided as they traveled together, it was all done in the name of Jesus. Read those stories in the gospels and through the Acts of the Apostles. Miracles together. Stories together. Sadness together. Empowered by the Spirit together. Acts 2 reminds us that the followers of Christ—though facing rejection and ridicule, and soon to face severe persecution—devoted themselves to the apostles' teaching, broke bread in the homes, prayed together, enjoyed fellowship, and had all things in common. They ate together with glad and sincere hearts (Acts 2:42–47).

Even with our best intentions, we can only experience the fullness of joy in companionship and meaningful ministry when Jesus is the central cord that keeps us connected. So, let there be no question about it: Jesus is the strand who keeps the cords together!

Don't Be Afraid to Go Out on a Limb —That Is Where the Fruit Is

Sunday: Do You Believe?

Jesus heard that they had thrown him out, and when he found him, he said, "Do you believe in the Son of Man?" "Who is he, sir?" the man asked. "Tell me so that I may believe in him." (JOHN 9:35–36)

THE QUESTION THAT JESUS ASKS the blind man here is an invitation to go out on the limb. To believe in Jesus is to go out on the limb and find the fruit. This same question is the one that you and I must also answer: "Do we believe in Jesus?" When Jesus does something miraculous in our lives, it is not simply so we can enjoy the miracle but to experience the reality of who He is. So after the miracle had already been done and the man had already shared his experience with others, the work that Jesus wanted to do in this man's life was still unfinished. It was not enough that the blind man could now see; Jesus confronted the question of spiritual consequence in the man's life: "Do you believe in the Son of Man?" This is the way to find the fruit.

Nothing else matters as much as being able to answer this question. Notice that every time Jesus responds to a physical need, He also confronts a spiritual reality. The man who had been born blind was not only physically blind, but he was also spiritually blind. Just like this blind man, we have all been born into spiritual darkness, but also like the blind man, we can respond to the question, "Do we believe?" by declaring, "Tell me so that I may believe...." Step out onto the limb and join the adventure with Jesus!

Monday: You Have Seen Him

*Jesus said, "You have now seen him; in fact, he is the one speaking with you." (*John 9:37*)*

SOMETIMES WHEN YOU ARE LOOKING for something specific, it can be so easy to miss it when it is right in front of you. A lost set of keys, a certain pair of shoes, a book in the library, these can all be easily overlooked, even when we are focused on finding them. So it isn't hard to imagine why people would have missed Jesus when He came. For some, they weren't looking for Him, but for others who had given their lives to seeking God's truth, they seemed to miss Him when He was standing in front of them.

Have you seen Jesus? The highest priority you can have is to see Jesus. The miracle of God coming to Earth in the form of a human is that He became visible as God in the flesh. Before Jesus, God often seemed distant and far, only showing up as a cloud or in fire. No one could see God and live. He was so high and holy that He could not be reached by mere mortals. That's why Jesus changed everything. When He came, He showed us what God looks like. When you have seen Jesus, you have seen God.

Tuesday: Choosing to Believe

Then the man said, "Lord, I believe," and he worshiped him.
(JOHN 9:38)

LIFE IS FILLED WITH CHOICES to make and paths to take. Many common decisions are small, like where to eat lunch or what to wear to work on a Tuesday. But there are some decisions we make that can have effects for the rest of our lives. Making the choice to believe the words of Jesus is one of those decisions that changes the trajectory of our lives. For the blind man, the choice to believe the Son was a natural effect of receiving his sight. This story gives meaning to the old saying, "Seeing is believing!"

For a man who had been blind since birth, the cure to his blindness became the bridge to his belief. Imagine the power of the moment when his spiritual eyes were opened to the reality of Who was standing in front of him! This was not just any ordinary person but the man who had given him sight—the Son of Man, the Son of God.

It isn't hard to see how a man who was once blind would be convinced to believe in the person who has just given him sight. He could have settled for physical sight, but he went out on a limb and found the fruit—spiritual sight: the only kind of vision that has eternal value.

Wednesday: Choosing to Worship

Then the man said, "Lord, I believe," and he worshiped him.
(JOHN 9:38)

WE CAN CHOOSE TO WORSHIP. It isn't something forced on us. It is a choice we make.

How are you doing with choosing to worship? I am not talking about singing just right or sounding just right. I am talking about choosing to believe in Jesus and responding to Him with hearts of worship.

That type of worship can come out with our attitudes and our actions. That type of worship is revealed in how we treat other people. That type of worship is on display in our homes, offices, schools, and restaurants. It is not about the music but about how we honor God through our character. Let us live as people who declare our belief in God through everything we do everywhere we go.

That is a choice. A decision we make to be people of worship. A decision we make to honor God with our attitudes no matter what is happening around us. A decision we make to be like Jesus.

How are you doing with that? Is it difficult?

Ask God to help you worship Him. Reveal to Him your deep desire to live a life of worship no matter what you are going through.

Thursday: The Blind Will See

*Jesus said, "For judgment I have come into this world, so that the blind will see and those who see will become blind." (*JOHN *9:39)*

JESUS IS THE GREAT EQUALIZER and the King of an upside-down kingdom. What would seem common and natural becomes uncommon and counterintuitive. In Christ's Kingdom, the way up is down and the way down is up: the poor become rich while the rich are made poor, the last become first and the first are made last, those at the margins are brought to the middle and those in the middle become marginal, and those at the head of the table are moved to the foot and those at the foot of the table are moved to the head. This is the way Jesus operates—completely counter to human intuition.

Jesus gave physical sight to a man who could see spiritually in order to respond to Jesus with the faith to believe in Him, yet those who already had the physical sight to see Jesus were unable to spiritually see Him and believe in Him.

The paradox is that those who had physical sight to see Jesus physically could not see Him spiritually while the blind man becomes the embodiment of those who lack the physical means to notice who Jesus is, yet they are the first to see Him for who He truly is—the Messiah.

When we are confronted with who Jesus is, we have to make a decision that can only be determined by the kind of sight we have. If we only see with physical eyes, then we will miss the spiritual reality that Christ came to reveal to us.

Those who choose to believe and worship will be the ones with spiritual sight.

Friday: They Were Afraid

Some Pharisees who were with him heard him say this and asked, "What? Are we blind too?" (JOHN 9:40)

EVERY NOW AND THEN, it's best to "check yourself."

We will definitely have to go out on a limb to get to this fruit. It's hard to admit when we are the ones responsible and need to change, but this is what happens when we are confronted with hard spiritual truths: they demand that we examine ourselves and check our alignment.

The Pharisees were too spiritually blind to recognize who Jesus was while he was standing in front of them, yet they understood that their confrontation with spiritual truth was requiring self-examination.

It sounds like the disciples at the Last Supper asking, "Is it I, Lord?" Maybe the answer is in the question. If we have to ask it, then the answer is likely, "yes."

When we come to a place where we have to ask this kind of question, life can become very uncomfortable because the answer requires an action. If we are spiritually blind, then there is only one solution, which is to allow God to open our spiritual eyes. This means choosing a new path forward rather than continuing to live in spiritual darkness which can be very scary.

It can be frightening for any of us when we have to admit to any wrongdoing, but to go further and make the decision to do differently tomorrow than we did today is an additional challenge that can scare many away. The Pharisees were afraid because they lived in spiritual darkness with no apparent desire to have their spiritual eyes opened.

You and I do not have to live in this dark place and we have no reason to be afraid.

Saturday: Refusing to Go Out on a Limb

Jesus said, "If you were blind, you would not be guilty of sin; but now that you claim you can see, your guilt remains." (JOHN 9:41)

IT CAN BE DANGEROUS to go out on a limb. It requires risk, vulnerability, and trust. We have to release control of our circumstances and depend on the limb to be strong enough to hold us as we move. The limb requires humility and a willingness to release control. The limb can reveal areas where we need to grow as we move out toward the fruit. The challenge is to be willing to step out on the limb.

For the Pharisees, the challenge was too great. Their physical sight was preferred over spiritual sight. The predictable, what they already knew, kept them from being willing to see Jesus for who He truly was and to learn from Him.

Refusing to go out on a limb is refusing to take the risk of being wrong; it is the risk of not being in control.

To refuse to go out on a limb is to insist that what we already know is enough.

Jesus offers us the opportunity to step out on the limb, to get out of the boat, to go into the realm of what can be rather than what already is, and to rely on Him.

Feed Your Faith and Starve Your Doubts

Sunday: Nothing Will Be Impossible

Then the disciples came to Jesus in private and asked, "Why couldn't we drive it out?" He replied, "Because you have so little faith. Truly I tell you, if you have faith as small as a mustard seed, you can say to this mountain, 'Move from here to there,' and it will move. Nothing will be impossible for you." (MATTHEW 17:19–20)

CHRIST PROMISED US we could move mountains if we only had faith the size of a mustard seed. What a remarkable contrast in size! Mustard seeds are so small a single one would barely cover a quarter of the fingernail on our pinky finger, while mountains are the largest single objects on land.

When we think about this passage, we usually emphasize victory, focusing on Christ's promise that nothing will be impossible for us. And from there we think about getting something we want. Getting that job, or that man, or that woman, or making that shot, or winning that game.

But the immediate context for this teaching is driving out demons. Christ's own disciples, who lived with Him every day and heard His teachings, failed to conquer demonic activity, and Christ's explanation for them was that they had too little faith.

Why don't we take this passage now and apply it not to the things we want, but to our areas of failure, which are possible demonic strongholds? Are you in despair about your marriage? Christ is asking us to have faith, any faith. Just the smallest imaginable faith that God can heal our relationships. Are you struggling with lust, or with other areas of self-control, like your finances? Believe God for them.

Our areas of failure seem bigger than the biggest mountains to us. But Christ wants us to believe in Him, that He can heal us.

Monday: Possible with God

Jesus looked at them and said, "With man this is impossible, but not with God; all things are possible with God." (MARK 10:27)

THIS PASSAGE IS REMARKABLE in context. A man ran to Christ asking, "What must I do to inherit eternal life?" When Christ reminded him of the commandments, he declared, "Teacher, all these I have kept since I was a boy."

The story takes an unexpected turn at this point: "Christ looked at him and loved him." Christ *loved* him. I think Christ loved this man especially because He knew his lack. This man today would be like people who were raised Christian, who grew up doing everything right, but still know they're lacking.

God has a next step for us, but it's hard. He finds what we most value about ourselves and asks us to sacrifice it. This man valued his wealth above all else, maybe because he valued most *the idea of himself as a wealthy man,* so he walked away sad.

The lesson Christ taught to his disciples was that wealth is dangerous, that it's hard to be saved if you're wealthy. The disciples responded, "Who then can be saved?"

And that's when Christ said, *"With man this is impossible, but not with God; all things are possible with God."*

If God is asking you to make an impossible sacrifice, know these two things:

First, you're the special object of God's love.

Next, it's impossible, at least for you. But everything is possible for God. Remember, you just need faith the size of a mustard seed.

Tuesday: Water Will Flow for Those Who Believe

*On the last and greatest day of the festival, Jesus stood and said in a loud voice, "Let anyone who is thirsty come to me and drink. Whoever believes in me, as Scripture has said, rivers of living water will flow from within them." (*JOHN *7:37–38)*

WHEN WE NEED SOMETHING, we look for it. If we're lonely, we look for a friend or a spouse. If we need money, we look for a job. If we need a car, we look for a deal. If we're hungry or thirsty, we look in the refrigerator or head to a restaurant.

These are natural activities. We were created to live within and be dependent upon an external environment. Seeking for our needs outside ourselves is a natural function of biological life.

But what happens when we need life itself? Christ's words were spoken during the Festival of Tabernacles, which was one of three pilgrimage festivals. Jews would travel to Jerusalem from around the world to seek and to honor God and His works. Christ was surrounded by seekers, confronted with the worldwide scope of human need, hunger, and seeking in a microcosm at this feast.

In response to all this need, Christ shouted out, "Come to me." Come to Him. He's not just another external source. Whether He is physically present to us, as He was to the seekers in Jerusalem 2,000 years ago, or whether He is not, Christ will reveal Himself to us within. Everyone who really finds Him, then or now, finds Him within, where He is speaking.

And when we find Him there, we find an inner source. His living waters. When Christ is within us, we carry the source of our life everywhere.

Wednesday: Believing in the Bread of Life

Then Jesus declared, "I am the bread of life. Whoever comes to me will never go hungry, and whoever believes in me will never be thirsty." (JOHN 6:35)

JESUS HAD JUST PERFORMED AN AMAZING MIRACLE, feeding thousands of people with a few loaves and fishes. The next day, the people Christ fed went looking for Him again, but He was gone. They eventually took boats to Capernaum and found Him there.

When they found Him, He knew their hearts: they only followed Him because He had fed them. He told them to do the work of the God who sent Him, and that work was to believe in the One He had sent. They proved the states of their hearts by asking Christ to feed them again, attempting to manipulate Christ to perform another miracle so "that we might see it and believe you."

Because Christ knew their hearts, He brought to them the truth, which is today's passage: "I am the bread of life. Whoever comes to me will never go hungry, and whoever believes in me will never be thirsty." This passage, this glorious promise, is a stumbling block to those who only want Christ to feed their flesh: "I am your food and drink," He says. "I am your provision, your life, and the fulfillment of all of your needs, if only you would believe in Me."

If your deepest needs, even and most importantly legitimate ones, are going unfulfilled, Christ is calling you to look to Him. He will meet all of your needs, but only if you trust Him with them first.

Thursday: Living by Faith and Not by Sight

For we live by faith, not by sight. (2 CORINTHIANS 5:7)

IN THE COURSE OF NORMAL human life we all have to confront death, but so many more of us than usual have had to confront death in recent years.

Paul here meditates on death and on how a Christian should think and feel about it. Sometimes in prison and sometimes pursued, he knew many times what it was like to nearly die. Even apart from special dangers, our bodies are moving toward death on a daily basis. Someday, we will all face it, whether sooner or later. Paul realized the human spirit, not the human body, is our real self, and our bodies are like clothing worn by our spirits. While we are in these bodies, we are physically absent from Christ. Death is not like changing clothing or being unclothed, but like "being further clothed." These decaying, dying bodies won't go away. They will be swallowed up by eternal life.

In the meantime, however, we live out on a daily basis a single truth: "For we live by faith, not by sight." While our eternal bodies will be specially suited for life in the presence of God, our current bodies are like a veil hiding His presence, so Paul encouraged us to *live* by faith, to use our daily lives as preparation for eternity.

Friday: Having Faith to Move Mountains

Early in the morning, as Jesus was on his way back to the city, he was hungry. Seeing a fig tree by the road, he went up to it but found nothing on it except leaves. Then he said to it, "May you never bear fruit again!" Immediately the tree withered. When the disciples saw this, they were amazed. "How did the fig tree wither so quickly?" they asked. Jesus replied, "Truly I tell you, if you have faith and do not doubt, not only can you do what was done to the fig tree, but also you can say to this mountain, 'Go, throw yourself into the sea,' and it will be done." (MATTHEW 21:18–21)

THE DAY BEFORE JESUS CURSED the fig tree, He triumphantly entered Jerusalem, fulfilling prophecies made hundreds of years before in the Book of Zechariah and in the Psalms. After His triumphant entry, one that publicly announced His role as the Messiah, He went to the temple, driving out the moneychangers and those buying and selling there. Then He went on to heal the blind and the lame, and as He did so, children started shouting in the temple, "Hosanna to the Son of David."

At the end of the day, He left for the nearby city of Bethany to spend the night. On the way back into Jerusalem the next morning, He saw the fig tree. Expecting to find fruit because He was hungry, He found nothing but leaves, so He cursed it.

This story could be taken as a lesson about bearing fruit: Christ Himself modeled the fruit-bearing servant of God by fulfilling His destiny, entering Jerusalem triumphantly, casting out the moneychangers, and healing the blind and the lame, while the moneychangers themselves and the Pharisees who profited from them exemplify failing to bear fruit for God.

But Christ in this context chose to teach a lesson about faith. If you believe and do not doubt, anything can happen. That is the real commentary on the triumphal entry, the healing of the blind and lame, and the casting out of the moneychangers. Faith moves these mountains.

Saturday: Believing and Receiving

If you believe, you will receive whatever you ask for in prayer.
(MATTHEW 21:22)

MY BIBLE PUTS BIG HEADERS within the text of Scripture to set off different segments. Matthew 21 is commonly divided into vs. 1–11 (Jesus Comes to Jerusalem as King), 12–17 (Jesus at the Temple), 18–22 (Jesus Curses a Fig Tree), and 23–27 (the Authority of Jesus Questioned), with the remaining verses divided up between the two parables that close the chapter.

But these headers don't exist within the original text, which was just word after word from beginning to end without even much punctuation. Matthew 21:22 does of course go with the preceding story about Jesus cursing a fig tree, underscoring the efficacy of faith. Whatever we ask for we can have, if we believe.

But another lesson can be learned from this passage. It comes just by removing the header. What happens if we read verse 22 as the introduction to the passage starting with verse 23, where the chief priests and elders asked Christ, "By what authority are you doing these things?" while Christ was teaching in the temple? It takes authority to heal, to cast out corruption, and to speak the truth. The answer to their question had just been revealed to Christ's disciples: "If you believe, you will receive whatever you ask for in prayer." Our faith is our authority, and by that authority we can perform the works of Christ.

We can do anything for God in faith when we are doing God's work.

Restlessness and Discontent Are the Necessities of Progress

Sunday: Calling Out to God

My God, my God, why have you forsaken me? Why are you so far from saving me, so far from my cries of anguish? (PSALM 22:1)

EVERYTHING STARTS with our calling out to God, and nothing starts until we have called out to God. We sometimes think we have to meet conditions before we can call out to God. We might think we have to be good enough or need to use the right words. We might think we need to have enough faith, or be spiritual enough, or sinless.

Scripture everywhere teaches us to have faith, shun sin, and seek the things of the Spirit, but nowhere does it teach that there are any preconditions to seeking God. God wants us to come to Him, even when we're not believing, and even when we're coming to Him out of sheer desperation rather than a place of faith and victory.

We might feel like failures, or maybe just terribly selfish, when we call out to God in desperation. If we ever find ourselves feeling this way, we should remember this is a psalm of David, and David was one of God's most beloved servants in the Old Testament, a man who even through failure loved God with all his heart. And even more importantly, we should remember these very words were quoted by Christ on the cross.

If Christ faced these times of darkness, this dark night of the soul, then we should know that we will too. God wants us to call out to Him in the honesty and desperation of our own real pain.

Monday: Feeling Forsaken

My God, my God, why have you forsaken me? Why are you so far from saving me, so far from my cries of anguish? (PSALM 22:1)

SCRIPTURE ABOUNDS with promises of God's faithfulness. Jesus said that He would never leave us nor forsake us. He said that if we came to Him, streams of living water would flow out from within us. He said that He would send a Helper, the Holy Spirit, who would live within us and always be with us.

But at the same time, both Christ and David prayed this terrible prayer in the hour of their deepest needs: *"My God, my God, why have you forsaken me? Why are you so far from saving me, so far from my cries of anguish?"* Just feeling those feelings can feel like failure to us. They sound like the opposite of faith. If Christ said He would never leave us nor forsake us, that He would send a Helper to be within us, why should we ever feel that way?

The truth is that while Christ promised us He would never leave us, He never promised we would never feel left. Since Christ prayed these words too, while He was on the cross, and since He called us to take up our cross and follow Him, we should expect to feel forsaken by God sometimes. We should not condemn ourselves for feeling this way but should call out to God honestly in all of our hurt and pain. When we do so, we can know He understands, because He felt that Himself.

Tuesday: Progress Through Painful Prayer

My God, my God, why have you forsaken me? Why are you so far from saving me, so far from my cries of anguish? (Psalm 22:1)

CHRISTIANS WHO WORSHIP in older traditions pay close attention to "the stations of the cross." In art and liturgy, the fourteen stations of the cross are (1) Jesus is condemned to death, (2) He is made to bear His cross, (3) He falls the first time, (4) He meets His mother, (5) Simon of Cyrene is made to bear the cross, (6) Veronica wipes Jesus' face, (7) He falls the second time, (8) the women of Jerusalem weep over Jesus, (9) He falls the third time, (10) He is stripped of His garments, (11) He is nailed to the cross, (12) He dies on the cross, (13) He is taken down from the cross, and (14) He is placed in the sepulcher.

The traditional stations of the cross are good ways to remember the hours of Christ's life leading up to His death and burial in both words and pictures. They help us remember the story. But I think we should reinvent them for the Christian's spiritual life as well. Christ called us to take up His cross and follow Him. Probably no one reading this will ever be literally crucified as Christ was, but we all carry a cross that leads to death and burial.

Just as Christ progressed through suffering and death, so will we. It helps to remember that He felt forsaken as well, and that He was sinless. When we experience what He did, we should act as He did, and cry out to God.

Wednesday: Praying during Times of Anguish

My God, my God, why have you forsaken me? Why are you so far from saving me, so far from my cries of anguish? (PSALM 22:1)

PSALM 22 IS NOTABLE for the ways in which it anticipates the suffering of Christ on the cross. While David is describing his own physical distress, he sounds as if he were a direct witness of Christ's suffering. Verses 12–18 are particularly graphic in their description of physical suffering, which included feeling like all his bones were out of joint, his heart had melted to wax, his mouth is so dry that his tongue sticks to the top of his mouth, all of his bones seem visible through his skin, and most remarkably, that they had pierced his hands and feet.

All of these descriptions are fitting to a crucifixion and describe intense and extended physical suffering, but both David's and Christ's suffering wasn't only physical. It was emotional as well. They both felt surrounded by enemies, as though everyone scorned, mocked, and stole from them, even gambling away their clothes. And worst of all, they felt like God Himself wasn't listening, that He had abandoned them and seemed deaf to their cries.

Both David and Christ experienced the worst kinds of human anguish, but they also taught us all how to walk through it. Even though they didn't feel God, they remembered Him: "For He has not despised or scorned the suffering of the afflicted one; He. . . has listened to his cry for help." Know that God hears you even if you don't feel that He does.

Thursday: Asking God to Stay Close

Do not be far from me, for trouble is near and there is no one to help. (Psalm 22:11)

THE MOST INTENSE emotional suffering in Psalm 22 comes from feelings of abandonment. Its opening verses convey the extreme anguish of feeling that God has abandoned you. There are two prongs to these feelings of loneliness, however. First, that *trouble is near*. Feelings of isolation and loneliness, feelings of abandonment, do not always, or perhaps even usually, mean that you're physically alone. You might be married or otherwise surrounded with family and feel completely alone. You might be surrounded by friends and coworkers and feel completely alone, or in the fellowship of a good church and feel alone. In the cases of David and of Christ, they weren't alone: they were surrounded by people who were active enemies, people who sought their physical and emotional harm. Perhaps the worst version of this situation is one in which we're surrounded by people who should love us but who seem to act like enemies. When we feel this way, yes, *trouble is near*.

Psalm 22 doesn't give us easy answers. It gives us instead a way to act: call upon God. Especially if you feel that God Himself has abandoned you, call upon God. Ask God to stay close to you when you're surrounded by enemies, including seemingly innocuous enemies like indifference. When no one else seems to want to be near you, or if you're surrounded by people that you wish would leave you alone, ask God to stay close.

Friday: Feeling No One Is Near

Do not be far from me, for trouble is near and there is no one to help. (PSALM 22:11)

THE OTHER PRONG TO ISOLATION is the feeling that *there is no one to help*. Maybe we feel isolated from those around us, enemies or not, so we feel that no one is near. Maybe we should expect them to help, but we believe they can't. It's certainly true from the context of this passage that David, and later Christ, had people around them. In both cases, most of the people around them were enemies. Christ, however, had His disciples with Him at the cross and His mother as well, but still He cried out, and still He felt alone. There are times when we are indeed alone in our suffering, when we are facing trials that we must face alone. This is no fault of ours, and not the fault of those around us. This sense of loneliness and isolation is a necessary part of the trial itself.

The passages leading up to verse 11 tell the most important truths during these times: "Yet You brought me out of the womb; You made me trust in You, even at my mother's breast. From birth I was cast on You; from my mother's womb You have been my God." God is our Father, our Creator, and the One who loves us most and at all times.

We may not feel like He cares, but He does. He loves us infinitely more than we can ever know.

Saturday: Making Progress

Posterity will serve him; future generations will be told about the Lord. (PSALM 22:30)

PSALM 22 TAKES A SUDDEN, triumphal turn starting at verse 19. David turns from describing his present reality, one in which he is surrounded by enemies and facing extreme physical and emotional torment, to declarations of victory. Verses 19–21 conclude David's prayer to God for deliverance, while verses 22 to the end of the psalm are written in the future tense as David imagines the victory of God over His enemies and the future praises that will be offered.

He remembers that God does not scorn the rejected and afflicted, so he calls all Israel to join with him in rejoicing before God. He realizes that in many cases his own enemies are also the enemies of God. David saw into a future in which the enemies of God faced defeat. As Christians, we look forward to a future in which the enemies of God join us in repentance and reconciliation.

Just as the first half of Psalm 22 models our honest suffering, the latter half models our future victory, but it does so by bringing the future in our present. David begins *praising God in the present for the victory He will bring in the future.* He uses the eyes of his faith to see not only the honest reality of suffering in the present, but the inevitable reality of God's victory in the future, and by doing so he makes progress out of his suffering.

What Appears to Be the End
May Really Be a New Beginning

Sunday: When Jesus Doesn't Seem to Be Around

*Immediately Jesus made the disciples get into the boat and go on
ahead of him to the other side, while he dismissed the crowd.*
(MATTHEW 14:22)

MATTHEW 14:1–21 GIVES US important context for what follows. John the Baptist had been vocally critical of Herod because
he had taken his own brother's wife, Herodias, as his own, which is
against Jewish law. Herod, in response, imprisoned John, but didn't
immediately execute him. The daughter of Herodias danced before
Herod and pleased him so much that he promised her anything she
wanted, and at the request of her mother, she asked for John the
Baptist's head on a platter. Herod felt compelled to fulfill her request
because of his promises, so John was executed while in prison.

Christ withdrew to a solitary place after hearing about John's
execution; He was disturbed by the news. But people followed Him
there, so He fed all 5,000 of them miraculously. And then in an act
of care for His disciples, He *"made the disciples get into the boat and
go on ahead of him to the other side, while he dismissed the crowd."*
In the light of recent events, it is plausible that Jesus didn't want
His disciples to be exposed to danger. The size and presence of the
crowd were obvious pointers to Christ's location, so by sending His
disciples across the lake, He was keeping them safe.

While this passage is very topical in nature, we can learn from
it that Christ sometimes sends us ahead while He remains behind.
When He does so, it's for our own good.

Monday: Buffeted by Waves

After he had dismissed them, he went up on a mountainside by himself to pray. Later that night, he was there alone, and the boat was already a considerable distance from land, buffeted by the waves because the wind was against it. (MATTHEW 14:23–24)

CHRIST HAD JUST LOST JOHN THE BAPTIST, who had begun his ministry before His own and recognized Him from the very womb. This chapter shows us Christ's human side more than others: in the face of His grief and loss, and the tragedy of a great prophet of God such as John the Baptist being executed for a trivial reason, a promise made at a party, Christ wanted nothing more than to be alone with God. But people followed Him, so He fed them, sent His disciples across the lake, and then sought the solitude of the mountain once again.

We should see from this passage that Christ did indeed experience grief in the face of the death of a loved one. We should not deny ourselves those feelings as well. Christ's response to that sense of loss and heaviness, though, was to seek God in solitude. He needed to be alone with God to process His grief. Even more remarkably, despite His grief and need to be alone, when people came to Him, He still ministered to them, and He still put the life and well-being of His disciples ahead of His own needs.

From the time Christ sent His disciples across the lake, dispersed the crowd, and went up the mountain alone, the boat carrying His disciples had moved far and was in trouble from the wind and the waves, setting up Christ's next miraculous act of care.

Tuesday: When Jesus Shows Up

Shortly before dawn Jesus went out to them, walking on the lake. (MATTHEW 14:25)

A PASTOR ONCE related an experience he had while preaching an Easter sermon. When he asked the congregation, "What did Jesus say when He rose from the dead?", they sat in silence until a little four-year-old girl stood up, stretched out her arms above her head, and said, "Ta-daaa!" Like that little girl, sometimes we think about miracles the same way we think about magic tricks. We tend to focus on the fantastic. We are impressed with big shows of power, and sometimes feel that such shows of power validate our faith in God, proving His existence and His strength.

But the Bible's emphasis lay elsewhere. Matthew 14 doesn't start with a show of power, but with a show of vulnerability: a great prophet of God had just been executed by a godless king. If John could die, couldn't His disciples die as well? Christ may well have been asking that question. He knew that He had sent them across a lake, and He knew that they were in danger. Surely He could see the storm from the mountain. Seeing His disciples in danger, He walked on the water to reach His disciples.

While we focus on the miracle of the bread and fish and focus on the miracle of Christ walking on water during a storm, let us not lose sight of the most important truth: both of these miracles were acts of care. Let us be so motivated.

Wednesday: Choosing Courage

When the disciples saw him walking on the lake, they were terrified. "It's a ghost," they said, and cried out in fear. But Jesus immediately said to them: "Take courage! It is I. Don't be afraid."
(MATTHEW 14:26–27)

MIRACLES BY NATURE are unnatural, inherent violations of the laws of nature. There is no scientific explanation for feeding 5,000 people with a few loaves and fishes or for a human being walking on water unassisted. So, when Christ came to the disciples in the middle of a storm-tossed lake, walking on the water to them, it was natural for them to be terrified of the sight. They had no explanation, so defaulted to one obvious to them: *"It's a ghost!"*

Of course, it wasn't a ghost. Christ was coming to them Himself, miraculously walking on the water, to protect them from the winds on the lake, which by themselves were probably frightening enough in a small boat. His miracle was His act of care for them, of course, but it was still inexplicably miraculous.

This passage teaches us that even though we're following Christ, maybe even while we are seeing His acts of power, we might still be trapped in superstitious thinking. Scripture doesn't validate the existence of ghosts. Only one appears in Scripture, and it is the ghost of Samuel, who appears to a very surprised witch of Endor to speak God's judgment upon King Saul (1 Samuel 28:3–25). King Saul's lapse into the occult was a sign of God's disfavor with him. The apostles were just afraid and caught off guard. The only real supernatural power resides in Christ, who seeks to save us in our distress.

Thursday: Walking on Water with Jesus

*"Lord, if it's you," Peter replied, "tell me to come to you on the water."
"Come," he said. Then Peter got down out of the boat, walked on
the water and came toward Jesus.* (MATTHEW 14:28–29)

Despite the fact that the disciples had just seen Jesus feed 5,000 people with a few loaves and fishes, they still doubted Christ when He told them He was the one coming to them. That doubt is why Peter said, "Lord, if it's you, tell me to come to you on the water." Peter didn't presume to come uncalled or uninvited, but remembered Christ's temptation, which we have in Matthew 4:5–7: "Then the devil took Him to the holy city and set Him on the pinnacle of the temple. 'If You are the Son of God,' he said, 'throw yourself down, for it is written.' . . Jesus replied, 'It is also written: "Do not put the Lord your God to the test."'" We commit the sin of tempting God by exposing ourselves to unnecessary risks that serve no redemptive purposes, just to force God's hand.

These risks might be refusing to wear a mask during a pandemic or refusing to follow the laws and safety guidelines of any country.

Peter learned this lesson from Christ's temptations, so he asked before stepping out on the water. For that reason, Christ didn't condemn Peter's doubt. He proved Himself instead, inviting Peter: "Come."

When Christ is there ahead of us, then we know we can take risks. When Christ calls us to come to Him, then we know we are safe. And like Peter, we can walk on the water with Christ.

Friday: Beginning to Sink

But when he saw the wind, he was afraid and, beginning to sink, cried out, "Lord, save me!" Immediately Jesus reached out his hand and caught him. "You of little faith," he said, "why did you doubt?" And when they climbed into the boat, the wind died down. (MATTHEW 14:30–32)

We walk with Christ in a physical world, which means that our attention is easily distracted. Peter exemplifies for us all our successes and failures. He was the only disciple bold enough to walk to Christ on the water, but he also only did so briefly. The first and most obvious lesson from this passage is that the world around us will always remind us of why miracles don't happen, so that we must keep our eyes on Christ if we hope to walk on the water to Him. While Peter was watching Christ, he walked on the water. When he looked at the wind, he became afraid and then began to sink.

We act the same in our circumstances, so we need to pay close attention to what happened next. First, Peter called out for Christ to save him. If your faith fails you when you're attempting the impossible, have enough faith to call out to God. Next, Christ did it. Christ is not a sink or swim swimming instructor. He doesn't throw us into the water. Yes, Christ identified the problem, *"You of little faith," he said, 'why did you doubt?"'*, but He wasn't condemning Peter. He was showing him the way forward.

Even when our faith fails us, even when we can't believe, call out to God.

Do not be so ashamed and self-condemned that you lose faith in Christ's love for you. He will catch you.

Saturday: A New Beginning of Faith

Then those who were in the boat worshiped him, saying, "Truly you are the Son of God." When they had crossed over, they landed at Gennesaret. And when the men of that place recognized Jesus, they sent word to all the surrounding country. People brought all their sick to him and begged him to let the sick just touch the edge of his cloak, and all who touched it were healed. (MATTHEW 14:33–36)

AS SOON AS CHRIST ENTERED the boat, the wind died down. The answer to our storms is always the presence of Christ. We should consider the progression of events in this chapter, though, to understand what leads up to our participation in ministry.

First, a prophet of God was killed, almost on a whim. We may experience intense opposition right before God is ready to move us forward.

Then, Christ withdrew. In the midst of that opposition, we may feel alone and abandoned. Know that feeling is part of the trial.

After Christ withdrew, the disciples themselves experienced danger separate from the presence of Christ. Once we see the world is dangerous, we might see that it can be dangerous for us as well.

Then Christ came to them miraculously, and all the disciples but Peter remained in the boat, while the only one bold enough to step out started to sink almost immediately. We may face our own dangers and failures, sometimes both at the same time.

But God saves us, and we come to know His power: *"Truly you are the Son of God."* Through these trials, dangers, persecution, and feelings of abandonment, God is teaching us that one, most important lesson. Christ truly is the Son of God, and He is with us. Once the disciples learned this lesson, then they witnessed once again the healing power of Christ, joining with Him in His care for others.

Difficulties Are Only Miracles That Have Not Yet Happened

Sunday: Remembering What God Has Done

The earth is the Lord's, and everything in it, the world, and all who live in it; for he founded it on the seas and established it on the waters. (PSALM 24:1–2)

HUMAN SOCIETIES ARE RUN on wealth and power: the ability to purchase and the ability to command. These abilities are closely related, but they aren't identical. Scripture says a great deal about what it means to command wealth, and while there were wealthy believers in Scripture, and sincere believers with great wealth today, most of what Scripture says about possessing wealth isn't good.

Christ said that it was hard for the wealthy to be saved, and that it is easier for a camel to pass through the eye of a needle than a rich man to enter the Kingdom of heaven. James records that the wealthy are the ones abusing their position by dragging poorer believers into court. Paul encouraged Timothy to teach the wealthy not to trust in their wealth, but to be thankful for what they have and to give generously.

But the basis of all of these teachings is found here in the Psalms: God is the Creator of all. He owns the wealth. If we are poor, we can take heart: our riches are in Christ. If we are rich, we can be humbled: we do not possess our wealth, we are not the owners of it, but rather the earth is the Lord's and everything in it. He laid the foundations of the earth and He created everything that dwells in the earth and the sea.

We possess nothing but what we have in Christ.

Monday: Who Can Come to the Lord?

Who may ascend the mountain of the Lord? Who may stand in his holy place? The one who has clean hands and a pure heart, who does not trust in an idol or swear by a false god. (PSALM 24:3–4)

ONCE WE'VE SET ASIDE all human notions of merit, we can begin to see from God's eyes. The world values beauty, but God sees the heart. The world values wealth, but God is the true owner of all that is. The world values power, but all of us are powerless before God. The world values intelligence, but God has promised "the intelligence of the intelligent I will frustrate."

It is not that these things are inherently without value. It is that some of them, such as wealth and power, are unnatural. They are based upon a world system that is corrupt. Others, such as beauty and intelligence, are created by God and are good, but they are limited, and they do not win us special favor before God.

Since none of these will win us over to God, and since God is ruler of all the earth and is accountable to none but Himself, we should seek the things that are pleasing to Him and come to Him on His terms.

Those terms are spelled out here in this passage. We must have *clean hands*, or in other words, must not have wronged others without making it right. And we must have a *pure heart*, or have desires that align with God's will. And finally, we must not worship false gods. We ensure that we are not doing so by seeking God on His terms and not on any other.

Tuesday: It Is Time to Receive God's Blessings

They will receive blessing from the Lord and vindication from God their Savior. (PSALM 24:5)

THERE ARE TWO SOURCES of vindication and blessing: God, and this world system. Those who seek out vindication and blessing from this corrupt world system seek to purchase the praise of men through their wealth and power. And sometimes we earn those accolades through genuine accomplishments, through the use of the natural gifts God has given us. But it is important to keep in mind whose blessings we should really seek.

We might desire to be like Esau, who wanted the things of this world. Because he was strong and a hunter he was loved by his father. Esau is the Biblical model of the man of this world: admired, respected, and set to inherit everything, he trades away his birthright for a bowl of food. Jacob, on the other hand, was more known for his cunningness, kept to the tents, and relied on deceit to get the things that he wanted. At first sight, he hardly seems like an admirable figure, and in the end had to wrestle with God to receive God's blessing.

The important difference between Jacob and Esau, however, was that Jacob valued the things of God, the blessings and the birthright of God, while Esau did not. Jacob *wrestled all night with God to receive His blessings*. That is the way in which we should desire to be like him. If we desire the things of God, we will receive the things of God.

Wednesday: Blessings for a Generation

Such is the generation of those who seek him, who seek your face, God of Jacob. (PSALM 24:6)

THE GOD WORSHIPED HERE is specifically named the "God of Jacob." He is the God of the ones who value most the things that He values, and who will do whatever is needed to receive the blessings of God. The generation or people group described here are specifically characterized by the way in which they seek God's face. But what does it mean to seek God's face? So far, the psalm has already provided numerous answers to this question. We must have clean hands and a pure heart. We mustn't worship idols. We should seek out vindication from God, not from men. We should be like Jacob and seek the things of God, and we shouldn't be like Esau, who cared mostly about feeding his appetite.

Today's passage reminds us, however, that in our seeking the things of God, what we are always most seeking is God Himself. We are seeking His face.

What does it mean to seek the face of a person? When applied to the everyday people around us, it means that we have come to know them so well that we recognize them on sight. As a result, when we look for them, we look for their faces. We know them, their look and their expression.

Everything that we do to receive the blessings of God ultimately gives us the greatest blessing of all, and that is to know and love God.

Thursday: Lift Up Your Heads

Lift up your heads, you gates; be lifted up, you ancient doors, that the King of glory may come in. (PSALM 24:7)

TODAY'S VERSE SHIFTS FOCUS radically. It moves from a focus on the God of Jacob and the nature of those who follow Him to a focus on the city in which they live. This passage doesn't speak to the doorkeepers or to the people at the gates, however, but to the gates themselves.

The image here is of the Levites bearing the Ark of the Covenant while it is coming into the city: the ark bearers are calling out for the King of glory to be allowed in. It is also reminiscent of King David in 2 Samuel 6, bearing the ark back to Jerusalem after being victorious in battle, and reminiscent of the Book of Revelation, where the ark is waiting in heaven.

For the Israelites, the ark represented the physical presence of God among them. Wherever it rested, God's blessings came down, and when it goes before the armies of the Lord, Israel experiences victory. In Numbers 10, it went before Moses and the people of God as they sought for a place of rest.

The ark today, the physical presence of God in the world, is embodied in the church. We are the ark, we are the people of God, and we are the city in which the people of God dwell. We call out to let God in, and we are the ones who open the door so that He does. And where He comes, there is victory and blessing.

Friday: The Lord Is Strong and Mighty

Who is this King of glory? The Lord strong and mighty, the Lord mighty in battle. (PSALM 24:8)

THE REMAINING VERSES in Psalm 24 are liturgical in nature, following a question and answer pattern. The question and answer pattern of these closing verses are yet another form of recognition. They indicate our recognition of God and who He is, and they represent our recognition of the people of God, our fellow travelers who also know God. We call out our knowledge of God to one another so that we can all come together and know Him as one.

The Lord in this passage, the King of glory, is given new characteristics, at least new for this psalm so far. The opening verses of Psalm 24 described God as the Creator of all. He made everything, and everything belongs to Him. But here God is *the Lord strong and mighty, the Lord mighty in battle.* This emphasis on warfare further points to the ark of the covenant going out before the people of God, carrying God's presence and winning their battles for them.

But this passage also reminds us that even though the Lord is Creator, and even though everything is His and belongs to Him, He still has to fight for it. God has enemies, and so will we. Though we are sons and daughters of the King of all the earth, we still have to face opposition. Psalm 24 reminds us *that God does fight for us.* He is our warrior and from Him comes the victory.

Saturday: Rejoicing the Lord Who Wins Our Battles

Lift up your heads, you gates; lift them up, you ancient doors, that the King of glory may come in. Who is he, this King of glory? The Lord Almighty—he is the King of glory. (PSALM 24:9–10)

THE CLOSING VERSES of Psalm 24 repeat the liturgical pattern of question and answer. They are written, again, from the point of view of people carrying the ark of the covenant into the city after a victorious battle. We might imagine the ark bearers calling out, *"Lift up your heads, you gates; lift them up, you ancient doors, that the King of glory may come in."* And then we might imagine those standing at the gates responding, *"Who is he, this King of glory?"*, to which the ark bearers would reply, *"The Lord Almighty—he is the King of glory."* In the fellowship of the people of God, we constantly remind ourselves of who God is.

But in the context of Psalm 24, that reminder is playful, joyful, and triumphant. Both the questioner and the respondent already know the answer because they have seen God's victory, and the cycle of question and answer, or of call and response, is an act of celebration.

The Psalms guide us through the deepest pits sometimes, the worst trials of faith. But Psalm 24 teaches us how to be victorious. We gain the victory with clean hands, a pure heart, rejection of idols, and an earnest desire of the blessings of God above all else. We learn to seek His face because we have come to know Him, and in knowing Him, we value what He values as one of the people of God.

Stewardship Is Not a Matter of Funds; It Is a Matter of Faith

Sunday: Faith Is Following Every Command

Be careful to follow every command I am giving you today, so that you may live and increase and may enter and possess the land the Lord promised on oath to your ancestors. (DEUTERONOMY 8:1)

THE BOOK OF DEUTERONOMY narrates the events leading up to the nation of Israel finally fulfilling its destiny and entering the promised land. As you remember, under Moses' leadership God led the nation of Israel out of their bondage in Egypt. But despite God's miraculous deliverance, the habits of mind left over from centuries of cruel slavery caused God's people continual problems. First, when Moses was gone for too long meeting God on Mt. Horeb, they fell into idolatry, and many of them died there. Then when they were on the verge of entering the promised land, only two of the twelve spies sent out ahead believed God could give them victory, so God declared that none of that generation would enter the promised land except for the two believing spies, Joshua and Caleb. Even Moses wasn't going to be allowed to enter.

In Deuteronomy 8, the people of God are on the verge of a new beginning. Ready to enter the promised land under Joshua and Caleb's leadership, God is reminding them of what they need to do to succeed. While God promised on oath that the children of Abraham would inherit the land, that promise was conditional on their obedience. There were always two paths set before the Israelites. One was the path of disobedience that led to bondage, while obedience to God is how we unlock the promises of God to see them fulfilled in our lives.

Monday: Knowing What Is in Our Hearts

Remember how the Lord your God led you all the way in the wilderness these forty years, to humble and test you in order to know what was in your heart, whether or not you would keep his commands. (DEUTERONOMY 8:2)

AS HUMAN BEINGS, it's natural for us to focus on the blessings that could come our way. We focus on the things that come to us, and all the more so when they are the fulfillment of God's promises. Sometimes these are very important, even on a life defining scale. They might be the fulfillment of our deepest desires, and maybe even of the promises of God to us. The things we want can sometimes represent God's plans for us, God's ultimate desire for us. That was certainly true of Israel's inheritance of the promised land. God had spent hundreds of years preparing the children of Abraham to receive the promises He made to Abraham, performing dozens of miracles, including the daily miracle of manna from heaven to feed the children of Israel while in the desert. And yet, He still put off the final fulfillment of His promise another 40 years because His people weren't ready to receive it.

While we are focused on the things that come to us, God is focused on the person to whom the things come. Those trials and wandering were all intended to test the hearts of the children of Israel and prepare them to receive the inheritance He had ready for them. The blessings we receive, even from God, can be harmful to us if our hearts aren't ready for them. We prepare our hearts to receive God's blessing through obedience.

Tuesday: God Provides During Times of Trouble

He humbled you, causing you to hunger and then feeding you with manna, which neither you nor your ancestors had known, to teach you that man does not live on bread alone but on every word that comes from the mouth of the Lord. Your clothes did not wear out and your feet did not swell during these forty years.
(DEUTERONOMY 8:3–4)

GOD BARRED A GENERATION of Israelites from entering the promised land because of their unbelief. God's judgment at the time was final: regardless of their future obedience, they would never enter the promised land. However, despite the fact that those promises of God were closed to them, they didn't cease to be God's children, and they didn't cease to be the object of His care. God continued to feed them, keeping them dependent upon Him on a daily basis with manna. In doing so, God continued to teach them as well. God's word was their sustenance through this daily, miraculous provision of bread from heaven. He turned their eyes toward Him daily. God also continued to protect them and provide for them. In forty years, their clothes did not wear out and their feet did not swell.

God's covenant with the Christian is somewhat different than that with the Israelites. We will never be permanently barred from His blessings or His future destiny for us. But we may be left to wander in the wilderness until we learn dependence upon Him, or learn not to look down to our immediate sources of provision on earth, but up to our heavenly source of provision in God. And we should know that even though we may feel that God has put us on the shelf, He hasn't ceased to be a loving Father who cares for us and teaches us.

Wednesday: The Lord Disciplines His Children

Know then in your heart that as a man disciplines his son, so the Lord your God disciplines you. (DEUTERONOMY 8:5)

WITH EVERY PASSAGE IN DEUTERONOMY 8, we should remember that the nation of Israel was being prepared to finally take the promised land after forty years of wandering in the desert. The most important lesson that God wanted Israel to take from that forty years of wandering was the fact of their sonship. The author of the Book of Hebrews reminds us of this lesson in chapter 12: "Endure hardship as discipline; God is treating you as his children. For what children are not disciplined by their father? If you are not disciplined—and everyone undergoes discipline—then you are not legitimate, not true sons and daughters at all. Moreover, we have all had human fathers who disciplined us and we respected them for it. How much more should we submit to the Father of spirits and live!"

Our hardships aren't the punishment of God, but the work of God in our lives. The external difficulties that we face work eternal good for us as we learn obedience to God in difficult circumstances. God disciplines only His children, so that when we face the discipline of God, we should know that we're not experiencing God's rejection of us, but God's commitment to us.

His desires for us are eternal even though we so often focus on the temporal. His work in us is inner transformation. As we are transformed inwardly, we can be trusted with external blessings.

Thursday: Faith Is Walking in Obedience with God

Observe the commands of the Lord your God, walking in obedience to him and revering him. (DEUTERONOMY 8:6)

GOD'S COVENANT WITH ISRAEL was premised on a single, simple principle that was perhaps most clearly spelled out in Deuteronomy 11: "See, I am setting before you today a blessing and a curse—the blessing if you obey the commands of the Lord your God that I am giving you today; the curse if you disobey the commands of the Lord your God and turn from the way that I command you today by following other gods, which you have not known."

We might best picture the moment of choice between obedience and disobedience as standing at a fork in the road. If we take the right path, obedience, at the end of it lies a blessing. But if we take the left path, disobedience, at the end of it lies a curse. These aren't specially meted out blessings or curses but are the natural result of our choices. The greatest gift that God has given us, however, is that choice itself.

We should always remember that our curse, as Christians, has fallen upon Christ, and He has borne our sins and suffered the curse of disobedience for us.

So we shouldn't despair should we fall into sin, but know that God still cares for us. But we should also know that the path to God's blessing still lies in obedience, and that we should care for Him in return as well and stop sinning.

Friday: Where the Lord Is Taking His People

For the Lord your God is bringing you into a good land—a land with brooks, streams, and deep springs gushing out into the valleys and hills. (DEUTERONOMY 8:7)

THE LAST SETS OF VERSES making up this week's readings focus on the blessings God has in store for His children, especially when they walk in obedience. We should remember that the original covenant with Israel was twofold: first for land, and then for the promise that the Messiah, the Savior of the world, would come through them. When God called the children of Israel into a new land, He chose for them the best of all lands. The land was so good, in fact, that it posed not a physical danger, but a spiritual one.

The danger of material blessing is the danger of forgetting God, as Moses reminded the children of Israel just a little later in the same chapter: "Otherwise, when you eat and are satisfied, when you build fine houses and settle down, and when your herds and flocks grow large and your silver and gold increase and all you have is multiplied, then your heart will become proud and you will forget the Lord your God, who brought you out of Egypt, out of the land of slavery."

Just as hardship drives us to seek God, so do blessings sometimes motivate us to forget God. That is why God is so intent on testing us, on disciplining us and purifying our hearts. He wants to give us these blessings, but He doesn't want His blessings to destroy us.

Saturday: The Land God Has Promised

A land with wheat and barley, vines and fig trees, pomegranates, olive oil and honey; a land where bread will not be scarce and you will lack nothing; a land where the rocks are iron and you can dig copper out of the hills. (DEUTERONOMY 8:8–9)

THE DESCRIPTION OF THE PROMISED LAND provided across verses 7–9 in this chapter is all encompassing. Verse 7 describes the water in the land, while verse 8 describes the food, and verse 9 the iron and copper available. God's ultimate blessings for us are always holistic: He provides everything we need, and in abundance. And He doesn't just provide for our basic needs but gives us great pleasure in our abundance. The promised land wasn't just a land of bread and water, but also of wheat and barley, vines and fig trees, pomegranates, olive oil and honey. In the place that God has for us we will certainly lack nothing, but God's promise goes far beyond basics. The items listed here extend to food items that generate wealth for trade (olive oil) as well as good pleasure in moderation (vines, figs, pomegranates, and honey).

God does not just provide us an abundant life, but an enjoyable one as well.

That is why the preparation described earlier in this chapter is so important. Once we are in the place God really wants for us, the best of all possible places, it will be easy to forget God. That is why we must intently prepare ourselves for God's blessing; our lives must be lived in obedience and our hearts must be right to be able to receive these blessings safely. God is ever present, ever caring, and always teaching us. For that reason we should be always willing to learn.

People Will Take Your Example More Seriously Than Your Advice

Sunday: Leading by Example

Teach me, Lord, the way of your decrees, that I may follow it to the end. (PSALM 119:33)

PEOPLE WILL TAKE YOUR EXAMPLE more seriously than your advice. That is why leaders must lead by actions, not just motivational speeches. We must lead by displaying quality character, not just large stat sheets. Lectures might go on a while, but they can't go long unless the person doing the talking is the same as the person doing the walking.

The psalmist prayed for the Lord to teach His decrees. The reason? So he could follow the Lord's instructions to the end.

That is leading by example. Knowing what is best and doing what is best. Doing what is best the right way for the right reasons with the right attitude.

We have enough poor leaders these days. Bad examples are all around us. Childish, immature attitudes being displayed by famous people? That should upset us. It should also provoke us to be Christlike leaders.

Pray Psalm 119:33 today, asking for God to lead you.

Choose also to live that way, leading like Jesus led. Setting an example other people will want to follow. No, don't just voice your advice. Live as you should. Let that be what those around you see and hear. Let that be what they learn and how they live.

Monday: Receiving God's Understanding

Give me understanding, so that I may keep your law and obey it with all my heart. (PSALM 119:34)

IN TODAY'S VERSE, the prayer asks to receive God's understanding. This is the request:

· Give me understanding.

Invest time now to pray that very prayer. What areas do you need better understanding? Related to what situation do you need God's wisdom? In what encounter do you wait for God's management?

Ask God for His understanding. He has such a better view. He has so much more wisdom. He knows what is best. He loves us and desires to guide us in those righteous paths. Ask Him. Ask Him for His understanding, insight, perception, intuition, and revelation.

The verse shows what the psalmist planned to do with that understanding:

· So that I may keep your law
· And obey it with all my heart.

Knowing isn't the end of the story. We need to know God's wise will, but we need to be willing to obey that plan. Pray to keep God's law. Pray to obey God's instructions with all your heart.

Knowing what is best isn't enough. We must live it. What areas have you struggled to do what you know is right? Lift those to God as you pray.

Ask Him—in faith—to give you understanding so that you can obey Him. Ask for His strength to empower you and enable you. Believe that today is the day you will obey.

Tuesday: Walking Toward God Rather Than for Selfish Gain

Direct me in the path of your commands, for there I find delight. Turn my heart toward your statutes and not toward selfish gain.
(Psalm 119:35–36)

WALKING TOWARD GOD rather than toward selfish gain should be our goal. Ask for direction in the path of God's commands and find delight there. Ask God to turn your heart toward His statutes and not toward any selfish gain.

That can be a wonderful way that we partner with others in the body of Christ. None of this is to be lived alone. We trust God and His people. That helps keep us from selfish motives. It moves us toward cooperation.

> There must be cooperation on the part of the members of the individual church. They can do their best work only as they work together. Paul painted a beautiful picture of cooperation among the members of a church in his epistle to the Philippians: "If there be therefore any consolation in Christ, if any comfort of love, if any fellowship of the Spirit, if any bowels and mercies, Fulfil ye my joy, that ye be likeminded, having the same love, being of one accord, of one mind. Let nothing be done through strife or vainglory; but in lowliness of mind let each esteem other better than themselves. Look not every man on his own things, but every man also on the things of others" (Philippians 2:1–4). He rebuked the church at Corinth for the divisions and strife that existed among them, reminding them that they were "God's fellow-workers" (1 Corinthians 3:9, ASV). **(Blueprint)**

Wednesday: More Than Advice

Turn my eyes away from worthless things; preserve my life according to your word. (Psalm 119:37)

We need more than advice to turn our eyes away from worthless things. To preserve our lives according to God's Word, we need to team with others who also choose to set good examples.

Who do you have in your life right now? Who is there you can trust? Who is there you can learn from?

As we learned yesterday, cooperation is vital. Our eyes will stay toward evil unless we have healthy accountability and partnerships. Oh, the Body of Christ is how it must work. All saved by Jesus, all washed in that same blood, all empowered by the Holy Spirit. All reading the same Word, all seeking the same goals, all building the same Kingdom.

> There must be cooperation among the churches. No single church, working alone, can adequately carry out the program of Jesus for the world. The churches must join together in a cooperative effort.
>
> There was cooperation among the churches in the New Testament era. While there was no definite organization, such as our conventions, Paul and his associates acted as a central committee through which the churches could pool their offerings for a common cause: "But now I go unto Jerusalem to minister to the saints. For it hath pleased them of Macedonia and Achaia to make a certain contribution for the poor saints which are at Jerusalem" (Romans 15:25–26). (Blueprint)

Thursday: God Will Fulfill His Promises

Fulfill your promise to your servant, so that you may be feared.
(PSALM 119:38)

"And we have sent with him the brother, whose praise is in the gospel throughout all the churches; And not that only, but who was also chosen of the churches to travel with us with this grace, which is administered by us to the glory of the same Lord, and declaration of your ready mind: avoiding this, that no man should blame us in this abundance which is administered by us: providing for honest things, not only in the sight of the Lord, but also in the sight of men" (2 CORINTHIANS 8:18–21).

Paul looked on these common funds as a sacred trust that must be administered in a way that would leave no grounds for criticism. They were given for a definite purpose, and Paul and his associates had no authority to divert them to other causes, even if they wished to do so.

This, then, is God's plan for His work: His churches, free and independent, voluntarily entering into a cooperative effort for the promotion of their common causes. (BLUEPRINT)

Those words from Paul remind us again about God's plan the psalmist emphasized. The people in a healthy church have much in common. The people who choose to live healthy lives believe God will fulfill His promises. And they choose to believe together, rather than in isolation.

Friday: God's Laws Are Good Laws

Take away the disgrace I dread, for your laws are good.
(PSALM 119:39)

GOD'S LAWS ARE GOOD LAWS. They are not crafted to cause harm to us, but to keep us from harm. His precepts keep us in safe places.

Disgrace is not the life God has for us. His laws are trustworthy, just, and reliable. Inclinations aren't always right. Replies aren't always right. Moods aren't always right. Perceptions aren't always right. But God's ways are always the right ways.

Those common causes and common goals. Those singular hopes for the Kingdom fulfilled by many people working together as one body. Those central committees after a definite purpose. That is the stuff keeping us in with God's laws. God's ways are offered to supply us with finding hope in Him during grim times.

Today is a Friday, a day nearing the end of another week. How have you done this week in obeying God's laws? Have you chosen to see His decrees as good and right and just? Who has helped you in your journey this week?

Ponder those questions.

Answer them.

And pray for your life to be one of obedience to God and His ways.

Saturday: The Life to Live

How I long for your precepts! In your righteousness preserve my life.
(Psalm 119:40)

"How I long for your precepts," the psalmist confessed. I believe he prayed that with vigor, with declaration, with enthusiasm.

That is the life we are to live—a journey of longing for God's words, His guidance, His direction, His protection, His promises, His assurance.

It is in God and His righteousness that our lives are preserved through Him. That is why we must align ourselves with God. Connecting to the Connector. Trusting in the Truth. Relying on the Redeemer. Crying to the Listener. Pleading to the Comforter.

End this week's study of Psalm 119 by doing exactly what Psalm 119 invites you to do. Join in the prayer. Be a part of the conversation with many believers through the years as you confess the truth about God—and confess it to God. We are to receive God's understanding and walk toward God rather than away from Him, or in the ways of this world.

We cannot endure another day or week in our own strength. People will take our examples more seriously than our advice. We are to walk toward God. Not selfish gain. Not the ways of man. God's promises. God's good laws. God's life to live. With God and with God's people.

Those truths must guide us this week. Refuse to walk alone. Walk with God. Walk with God's people. In God's righteousness, another week will end. In God's righteousness, another week will begin. In God's righteousness, another week of living as examples other people will take seriously.

Lord, Be with Me
in All the Changes in My Life

Sunday: Needing the Lord to Be with Us

May your unfailing love come to me, Lord, your salvation, according to your promise. (PSALM 119:41)

WHAT ARE YOUR BIGGEST NEEDS? If you could place them on a list in the order of importance, what would you write?

It helps us view and endure life better—especially if everything seems to be falling apart—when our largest life goal is to be sure the Lord is with us.

Remember that need today. The need for the Lord to be with us. And notice what the Lord brings when He is with us: unfailing love and salvation, just as He promised.

God does not have an interest in us that goes away when we sadden Him. His love endures every situation. It never fails. It never goes away. It lingers forever and ever.

And it brings salvation—God's rescue through eternity. There are not days of disaster in heaven for those who are with the Lord. It is a life of peace forever.

The Lord has promised that. He will keep His promises. He will never leave us or abandon us (Deuteronomy 31:6, Hebrews 13:5).

That is our biggest need, isn't it? To be sure of the Lord's presence with us. Even with countless changes going on in our lives, the Lord will be with us, His people.

Monday: What to Trust in These Uncertain Times

Then I can answer anyone who taunts me, for I trust in your word. (PSALM 119:42)

WHEN THE WORLD SEEMS TO BE FALLING APART, we often wonder if there is anybody we can trust.

People offer their views with slants from personal opinions rather than clear information. We begin to doubt whatever we are told.

But, for us as followers of Christ, we have found where our trust can stand. We can place our trust in Scripture. Our confidence and conviction can remain stable in the security of God's Word. The Bible provides what is missing in this world of confusion.

Please remember that. Understand God has not provided His wisdom to us so we can use it as a lucky charm or a complicated habit. It is nourishment for our souls. It is healing for our hearts. It is wisdom for our minds. It is true and just. It brings insight and guidance. It offers hope and endurance. It is stable and secure. It does not waver. It lasts forever. It fits today. It fits tomorrow. It fits next week.

Step away from unhealthy sources of information. Invade God's truth. Read it. Study it. Trust it.

You can do that no matter what the world around you brings. No matter the weather or your schedule, no matter your mood or what awaits you tomorrow, trust God and His Word during these uncertain times.

Tuesday: Where to Place Our Hope

Never take your word of truth from my mouth, for I have put my hope in your laws. (PSALM 119:43)

WHEN WE GET READY FOR A TRIP, we need to be sure to pack all that we want to take with us. When we prepare to purchase something, we need to have cash or a card set to seal the deal. When a couple pledges to marry one another, they publicly voice their vows before people and God.

We don't just do something halfway. We do what is best by giving our best. Take all we need on the trip, have a card ready to make a purchase, publicly pledge a promise. We are serious. We are dedicated. We are committed.

The reason is because if we hope for a healthy outcome, we see the benefit of placing investments into the experience. We want to do it right.

How does that help us today? By reminding us that we are to place our hope in God. His truth gives us hope. All might be changing around us, but we can stay stable when we carry a deep assurance in God's truth. His wisdom does not waver. His hope is in place.

Let that hope be your hope today. His stable and sure hope can give you assurance that He will be with you no matter what else is going on around you.

Wednesday: Always

I will always obey your law, for ever and ever. (PSALM 119:44)

THINK ABOUT CERTAIN THINGS in your life that will not change. Your weight might change but your height will stay the same after you reached your full altitude. You might have a favorite sports team—cheering for them whether they win or lose. Your date of birth, your heritage, your ancestors.

Other things change. We age. We lose hair. Voices change, friends might change, lives on earth end. Weather changes with seasons and geographical locations.

Our lives are filled with seasons of many changes. Unexpected alterations. Unpleasant adjustments.

How were you affected by those changes? Did you become better or bitter? Did you adjust and learn, or did you give up and feel defeated? A mixture of both sides?

Well, whatever has happened to us and whatever will happen to us, we can rely on this. God is still God. He is an "always God." And because of who He is and what He has promised to us, we can continuously obey Him forever and ever.

Believe now that, as the world continues changing, God will keep you stable and obedient in Him. Believe now that, whatever happened last month or last week or yesterday, that God is always God. Believe now that, however you feel and whatever you fear, your "always God" is giving you strength to always obey.

Thursday: Walking in Freedom

I will walk about in freedom, for I have sought out your precepts. (PSALM 119:45)

SOME PEOPLE SEEM TO THINK that focusing on God's Word and His ways limits us. Some people act like God's precepts prohibit us from experiencing the best in life.

Oh, how wrong those perspectives are. The psalmist said, "I walk about in freedom." That is how we all want, and need, to walk. Living a life in freedom is much better than a life of bondage. Living a life in freedom is much more pleasant than a life of legalism.

After that phrase, the writer gave a reason—the same phrase used throughout this lengthy prayer. "For I have sought Your precepts," he wrote.

Can we make that confession today? We are free, living in liberty rather than bondage. We are about our Father's business and find freedom in such a lifestyle. Set free—those two words should describe our lives. They should explain who we are and what we do. We are walking in freedom.

Walk in freedom today. Liberty to obey. Assurance to stay with God. Focusing on God's Word—not seeing limitations and condemnation but seeing an adventure of abundance and grace.

It is the life where the Lord is with you, no matter what else is changing around you. Today you are free. Walk in that.

Friday: Speaking to Leaders

I will speak of your statutes before kings and will not be put to shame, for I delight in your commands because I love them.
(Psalm 119:46–47)

THE THEMES FOR EACH WEEK in this book came from my heart. I deeply believe these phrases are worth stating and repeating. I firmly believe these statements are worth hearing and receiving. I certainly believe these comments are worth believing and applying.

That is why my life has been spent proclaiming what I believe is the truth. I could not risk someone missing the gospel. I had to speak. With boldness and confidence, I had to speak. To friends and foes, I had to speak.

Like the writer of Psalm 119 I had to speak of God's ways. Before kings and servants, before church people and sinners, before every tribe and tongue, I had to speak of God's statutes. And like the psalmist, I found delight in God's commands because I love them.

Will you speak up? Will you raise your voice the right way and the right time?

If you know God and believe in what He has done, speak up. Find delight in God's commands because you love Him, and you love them. Speak before leaders—you might be the one voice God plans to speak through and bring change to the world.

Speak in the Spirit of God. Not fleshly talk where you say just what you want to say the way you want to say it. No, speak on behalf of God. What an honor. What a calling. Don't miss it. Tell it. Speak up in this season of change. Speak as the one helping bring the right change.

Saturday: How the Lord Will Change My Life

I reach out for your commands, which I love, that I may meditate on your decrees. (PSALM 119:48)

ANOTHER WEEK is about to end. So, what will you do to finish this week well?

Can I suggest this? Reflect on what you have read this week. Go through the thoughts again and choose to believe again.

My friend, change is coming. I want it to be the right change. And I want you to be a part of bringing that change.

But how does it start? It begins by letting God bring change to your personal life. Don't shout it to the street before it comes into your own life in the prayer closet. Don't expect the world to hear you until you have chosen to hear God.

Reach out for God's commands. Love His words. Believe them, study them, repeat them, obey them. Those words in God's Word are there to change us. As they change us, we change the world. See how it works?

I firmly believe you are a key voice to bring change. Refuse to doubt. Refuse to quit. Refuse to waver.

This is your time. The Lord will change the world through your life. He will be with you.

Let Us Feed Our Faith and See Our Fears Starve to Death

Sunday: Seeing What the Lord Has Given You

When you have eaten and are satisfied, praise the Lord your God for the good land he has given you. (DEUTERONOMY 8:10)

GOD SPOKE TO HIS PEOPLE. The nation of Israel had battled war after war, expedition after expedition, adventure after adventure. They had obeyed God and disobeyed God. But God did this: He spoke to His people.

His promises are astounding. The Israelites had waited and longed for this season. And it was upon them.

His promises to us are also astounding. The Bible is covered with His promises.

My invitation to you today is to look and see what the Lord has done. Glancing at God's goodness can feed your faith for more good to come. Starve your fears to death and give life to your faith. We must believe that God can do all He promised to do.

The Israelites battled that over and over. We have too, haven't we? One moment we believe and the next moment we doubt. One morning we wake with faith, but we've lost it all before that day ends.

But not this day. Not this week. We begin and end in faith. We open our eyes and see with faith today. When those feelings of doubt come, we will choose to starve them.

Let us open our eyes and see what the Lord has given us.

Monday: Refusing to Forget What God Has Done

Be careful that you do not forget the Lord your God, failing to observe his commands, his laws and his decrees that I am giving you this day. (DEUTERONOMY 8:11)

HOW DO WE FEED OUR FAITH and let our fears starve to death? God instructed His people to be careful to never forget what He had done, and never fail to obey His commands.

We must remember what the Lord has done. We testify to remind ourselves and inform others of what He has done. We read and write books to keep the works of the Lord alive. What the Lord has done is so good and so great and so real that we must not forget.

What are ways you can do that today? How can you find a practical method of remembering what the Lord has done?

Here are some ways:

- Write a list of God's works done throughout the Bible.
- Write a list of God's works done through church history.
- Write a list of God's works done in the lives of others during your life.
- Write a list of God's works done for you.

Those will be some long lists. Some amazing lists. Those are lists of faith in action. Those are lists allowing us to be careful and refusing to forget what the Lord has done.

Can't that give you faith for today? Can't that give you faith for tomorrow?

Refuse to forget what the Lord has done!

Tuesday: We Must Believe!

Otherwise, when you eat and are satisfied, when you build fine houses and settle down, and when your herds and flocks grow large and your silver and gold increase and all you have is multiplied, then your heart will become proud and you will forget the Lord your God, who brought you out of Egypt, out of the land of slavery. (DEUTERONOMY 8:12–14)

IF WE LOOK BACK at those lists from yesterday, our vision should change. We might just believe a little bigger and trust a little better.

Isn't that what we should do?

God did not want His people to forget what He had done. He brought them out of Egypt. He provided their meals. He met their needs. God was their protector. God was their guide.

Isn't He that for us?

We must believe in God's provision. What do you need? Tell Him. Ask Him to provide the manna for you. Ask Him to bring the feast for you. Pray in faith, believing.

We must believe in God's protection. Do you feel afraid? Confess that to the Lord. Ask for His covering to hover over you. Pray in faith, believing.

We must believe in God's guidance. Are you unsure where to go? Seek God's will. Ask Him to direct every step, and to keep you from taking any wrong steps. Pray in faith, believing.

God has brought you out. God will bring you through. Believe. We must believe and receive.

Wednesday: We Must Remember!

He led you through the vast and dreadful wilderness, that thirsty and waterless land, with its venomous snakes and scorpions. He brought you water out of hard rock. He gave you manna to eat in the wilderness, something your ancestors had never known, to humble and test you so that in the end it might go well with you.
(DEUTERONOMY 8:15–16)

TO FEED OUR FAITH and to see our fears starve to death, we choose to believe. We believe, and we remember what He has done. Deuteronomy 8:15–16 offers reminders of what God did for His chosen ones. Focus on each phrase and think of how it applies to what God has done for you:

- He led you through the vast and dreadful wilderness,
- that thirsty and waterless land,
- with its venomous snakes and scorpions.
- He brought you water out of hard rock.
- He gave you manna to eat in the wilderness,
- something your ancestors had never known,
- to humble and test you
- so that in the end it might go well with you.

Listen in to those statements from so long ago. Hear them again. And remember.

God has led you through vast and dreadful wildernesses. God has guided you through thirsty and waterless land with its venomous snakes and scorpions. God has brought you water and food, not letting you starve in your own wilderness. God has done things for you even your ancestors never experienced.

Be humble today, and remember. We must remember.

Thursday: The Ability to Produce Wealth

You may say to yourself, "My power and the strength of my hands have produced this wealth for me." But remember the Lord your God, for it is he who gives you the ability to produce wealth, and so confirms his covenant, which he swore to your ancestors, as it is today. (DEUTERONOMY 8:17–18)

LOOKING BACK and remembering can inspire us to look forward in faith. But we cannot say the wealth is the result of our own efforts. Not our power and strength. It is from God. It is all from God. He had, and still has, the ability to produce all the wealth we needed, and all that we still need.

These days we see so much promotion about how we can do whatever we want. We hear promises of having faith only in ourselves.

Positive thinking is not enough. We must direct our thoughts correctly. Our faith must be in God and not in ourselves.

God told the Israelites that the miracles did not happen by their own abilities. God did what God does. God is the one who had the ability to provide for their needs. God is also the one who has the ability to produce your wealth.

Admit that to the Lord today. Pray for Him to provide. Wait in faith, putting your trust in Him rather than yourself.

Friday: Being Sure to Remember

If you ever forget the Lord your God and follow other gods and worship and bow down to them, I testify against you today that you will surely be destroyed. (DEUTERONOMY 8:19)

DESTRUCTION.

That is not a pleasing word. That is a frightening word.

Deuteronomy 8:19 makes it clear, though. Destruction awaited the people of God if they turned away from Him. If they forget the Lord and worship other gods, they would surely be destroyed.

Destruction awaits those who turn from God. In Deuteronomy we can read it. Throughout history we can study it.

But in our times and in these days, we must not allow it to happen. We must be sure to remember who God is and what God has done.

These devotions this week have reminded us over and over. We have invited you to remember, to believe, to trust.

Today is not the day of destruction. It is a day of restoration. It is a day of promise. It is a day of hope. It is a day to feed our faith. It is a day to defeat our doubt. It is a day to see our fears starve to death. It is a day to believe God can do what God promised to do.

Be sure to remember and not be destroyed. Remember and be victorious. We are triumphant in the promises of God.

Saturday: Never Let This Happen

Like the nations the Lord destroyed before you, so you will be destroyed for not obeying the Lord your God. (DEUTERONOMY 8:20)

OH, THOSE FEARS WILL NOT WIN. We have thought about faith and fear again this week. We have remembered God's Word to His chosen people. We have studied about how those words apply to us.

And we have decided to be people of faith. We refused to let destruction happen because of lack of faith. We choose to believe.

Don't you? Don't you choose today to believe?

Faith is risky. Faith is challenging. Faith is daring. But faith is the way. It is the only way.

Without faith we cannot please God (Hebrews 11:6). Trusting God. Believing what He has said. Obeying His instructions. Basing our beliefs and our actions on our relationship with God, not on temporary pleasure. We are in for the long haul. We are in to win. That happens by faith and obedience.

Let us feed our faith and see our fears starve to death. We must believe that God can do it.

Other nations will be destroyed. Other people will be destroyed. But those who have faith in God will triumph. Victory is waiting for those who place their hope and trust in God.

If we choose to live that way and love that way, the results will be fascinating. The world is going to change as people of faith starve their fears, knowing God can and will do what He has promised.

The Person Who Sows Seeds of Kindness Can Expect a Perpetual Harvest

Sunday: Planting Seeds of Kindness

Love is patient, love is kind. It does not envy, it does not boast, it is not proud. (1 CORINTHIANS 13:4)

THROUGHOUT 1 CORINTHIANS 12, Paul describes in detail how the church is the body of Christ, and each individual Christian is one of its parts. The different functions of the body are carried out by the different gifts of the Spirit (wisdom, tongues, healing, etc.) and offices within the church (apostles, prophets, pastors and teachers, etc.) distributed throughout the church. The goal of the gifts and offices is always "the common good" (1 Corinthians 12:7). The Holy Spirit in us unites the church, distributes the gifts, and all of the gifts and offices, however diverse they are, are united by the working of the Spirit. Because we all serve different offices and function in different gifts, we all need one another.

But we can function in the gifts of the Spirit with a worldly mind and fall into the trap of comparing ourselves with others (1 Corinthians 12:14–26). That thinking destroys the unity that the Spirit seeks to preserve. That is why Paul ends 1 Corinthians 12 by saying there is a more excellent way to serve the edification of the church than even the greatest gifts, and that is love.

Without love, the gifts are useless in the service of Christ and His goals. Even miracles and deep understanding, without love, count for nothing to God. Love is so important that Paul spends 1 Corinthians 13 describing what love is and how it acts: patient, kind, and not proud.

Monday: Love Is the Seed to Plant

It does not dishonor others, it is not self-seeking, it is not easily angered, it keeps no record of wrongs. (1 CORINTHIANS 13:5)

THE GOAL OF ALL GIFTS is the common good, and love is the greatest way of serving that good. Love is both a frame of mind and a way of acting. That frame of mind and way of acting should be seen as two sides of the same coin: we can't have one without the other. If one is present, the other will be as well.

But we need to fully grasp what this means. Many times, Christians are told their emotions don't matter. We should focus on what we should be doing and not what we are feeling.

1 Corinthians 13 teaches us this is only part of the truth. When we are told to be patient and kind, and to reject pride, boasting, and envy, it is telling us to choose one emotional tone over another. When it tells us not to dishonor others, not to be self-seeking, not to be easily angered or keep a record of wrongs, it is telling us to forbid ourselves from acting in these ways, but we always do so because they are emotionally gratifying.

Our emotions don't have an on-off switch. Their presence means we need to grow, and this chapter teaches us how to begin that growth. Sometimes it is just a process of denial. We want to keep a list of what someone else has done wrong. When we feel that desire, Paul teaches us not to feed it.

Tuesday: What Love Does Not Do

Love does not delight in evil but rejoices with the truth.
(1 CORINTHIANS 13:6)

PAUL CONTINUES HIS DESCRIPTION of love in the Christian's life with emotional language: delight and rejoicing. When we love, we do not delight in evil. When we love, we rejoice in the truth. The word "evil" is used in English translations of Scripture to cover both bad or hurtful events or actual moral evil that stands in opposition to God's will. Both senses of the word "evil" could be brought into this context.

We don't delight when bad things happen to other people, and we don't delight in things that are evil in themselves. When we love, we take no pleasure in that which is inherently opposed to God or harmful to others.

Significantly, Paul juxtaposes "delighting in evil" with "rejoicing in the truth." We tend to think that goodness or holiness stand in direct opposition to evil, but to Paul, truth does. Jesus taught His disciples, "I am the way and the truth and the life. No one comes to the Father except through me" (John 14:6), while he said of the Pharisees, "You belong to your father, the devil, and you want to carry out your father's desires. He was a murderer from the beginning, not holding to the truth, for there is no truth in him. When he lies, he speaks his native language, for he is a liar and the father of lies" (John 8:44).

Love rejoices in the truth, because Christ is Himself the truth.

Wednesday: What Love Does

It always protects, always trusts, always hopes, always perseveres. (1 Corinthians 13:7)

Paul continues his description of love with four of love's continual acts: protects, trusts, hopes, and perseveres.

Love always *protects*. Love seeks to shelter the object of its love. Rather than seeking the harm of others, love seeks their safety. This safety could be socially defined, seeking not to defame another person, the way Joseph sought to put away Mary quietly when he learned she was pregnant, before the angel appeared to him (Matthew 1:19). But it can also be seeking the physical safety of others, such as wearing masks or driving carefully.

Furthermore, love always *trusts*. Love always trusts God, certainly, but does love always trust people? That seems harder, especially when we've been wronged so many times. But love wants to believe the best of others, so it trusts.

Love always *hopes*. It is quite possible that *love always hopes* is the most difficult of these, especially the longer we live. It is so easy to despair in the face of continual failure and disappointment, both in our own lives, the courses they have taken and the growth we have experienced, and in the lives of others, especially when we have felt let down so often. But love *always hopes*. In other words, love doesn't give up.

The final act of love, always *perseveres*, is the capstone of them all. Because the love of God in us always perseveres, love always hopes, always trusts, and always protects.

Thursday: Success

Love never fails. (1 Corinthians 13:8a)

VERSE 8 IS THE CAPSTONE of what Paul has to say about love itself: *love never fails*. Paul moves from the four "always" that define love in the present time, here on earth—protects, hopes, trusts, and perseveres—to the eternal nature of love. Love never fails. We need to understand why Paul can say that love never fails, however.

Love never fails because love is the fruit of the Holy Spirit in the church (Galatians 5:22). What seems impossible to us is made possible through the Holy Spirit within us. When our emotions are everywhere but on God, feeling the worst about ourselves and others, we need to remember that we are not the source of this love. The Holy Spirit within us is. When patience and trust seem impossible, it is not impossible for the Spirit within us.

But love never fails for a second, even more profound reason: love is the defining characteristic of God Himself: "God is love" (1 John 4:8). John did not say that "love is God," but that God is love. We don't worship an abstract idea or principle, but the God of all creation is love Himself. We need to fully consider the implications of this truth. Because God is love, and God created all, love is the foundational principle of all creation. More specifically, it is the foundational principle of our very being.

We were created by, in, and for love.

Friday: Seeds of Love Remain

Love never fails. But where there are prophecies, they will cease; where there are tongues, they will be stilled; where there is knowledge, it will pass away. (1 CORINTHIANS 13:8)

1 CORINTHIANS 13 is the middle chapter of Paul's discussion of spiritual gifts. Paul begins his discussion in chapter 12 with an explanation of how we should view the gifts and offices within the church. The gifts and offices of the church function like different parts of the body. They serve exclusive functions, so that each member of the body is dependent upon every other member of the body for the body to function.

Chapter 14 continues Paul's teaching about the gifts and offices within the church with practical instruction about what concrete purposes they serve and how they are to be used when the congregation is gathered together.

1 Corinthians 13:8–13 is a transition between Paul's discussion of love and Paul's return to instruction about the gifts and offices. Love is at the literal center of this instruction, so before Paul returns to a discussion of the gifts, he wants to remind us of where they really stand.

Love never fails, but all of the gifts of the Spirit will one day pass away. God's eternal nature is characterized primarily by love, but only by love.

So, while love never fails, the temporal expressions of God's love in the church will indeed cease one day. That is why we shouldn't fall into comparisons of ourselves with others about the gifts, not looking down on others for their gifts or looking down on ourselves for ours.

Only love is eternal.

Saturday: The Greatest Harvest

And now these three remain: faith, hope and love. But the greatest of these is love. (1 CORINTHIANS 13:13)

PAUL EXPLAINS in verses 8–12 how and why the gifts of the Spirit will all pass away. They serve an immature and incomplete church, while we "know in part" and are still like children in the Kingdom.

Paul's language of incompleteness should be understood in terms of growth and maturity. We are immature children in the Kingdom of God at present, so the gifts operate among us to help us grow. When we grow into maturity, they won't be necessary any longer. That growth into maturity is related by Paul to how well we know Christ.

Even with the Holy Spirit within us, our knowledge of Christ is partial. But at the end of days, He will appear before us without anything hindering our seeing Him and knowing Him, and then we will grow into the people He intends us to be. Until then, the gifts operate.

But what will remain in that day, when the gifts cease to operate? Faith, hope, and love.

The element of our faith that stands in juxtaposition to sight will end, because then we will have sight, and we will know God by sight. But faith itself as trust in God will remain. Our hope will transform as well, because we will be receiving so much of what we have hoped for all along. But love is the greatest of these, because the love that God has placed in us will never change for eternity.

Maturity Is Knowing When to Speak Your Mind and Mind Your Speech

Sunday: The Importance of Words

Remember your word to your servant, for you have given me hope. (Psalm 119:49)

JAMES WROTE about the importance of words:

We all stumble in many ways. Anyone who is never at fault in what they say is perfect, able to keep their whole body in check.

When we put bits into the mouths of horses to make them obey us, we can turn the whole animal. Or take ships as an example. Although they are so large and are driven by strong winds, they are steered by a very small rudder wherever the pilot wants to go. Likewise, the tongue is a small part of the body, but it makes great boasts. Consider what a great forest is set on fire by a small spark. The tongue also is a fire, a world of evil among the parts of the body. It corrupts the whole body, sets the whole course of one's life on fire, and is itself set on fire by hell.

All kinds of animals, birds, reptiles and sea creatures are being tamed and have been tamed by mankind, but no human being can tame the tongue. It is a restless evil, full of deadly poison.

With the tongue we praise our Lord and Father, and with it we curse human beings, who have been made in God's likeness. Out of the same mouth come praise and cursing. My brothers and sisters, this should not be. Can both fresh water and salt water flow from the same spring? My brothers and sisters, can a fig tree bear olives, or a grapevine bear figs? Neither can a salt spring produce fresh water (James 3:2–12).

Let us speak with maturity today.

Monday: Words to Preserve Life

My comfort in my suffering is this: Your promise preserves my life.
(PSALM 119:50)

OUR WORDS are very important. Every statement we voice has an impact. Please do not forget that.

God speaks to give us hope rather than harm. Going through these devotions has allowed us to dwell on good words rather than harmful words.

We do not want to be the people who talk about being mature but then talk in ways which prove immaturity. True maturity is knowing when to speak your mind and how to say what needs to be said. Minding one's speech is proof of maturity.

God's Word can preserve life. It can move us from defeated to victorious. It can shift us from darkness into light.

God's declarations to us bring comfort when we are suffering. Read His comments of peace today. Receive His truth into your mind and your heart. Let your conversations be flavored and filtered by God's statements. Let your decisions be crafted and constructed by God's assertions.

Ask yourself: What statements does God want me to say today? What comments does God want to declare through me today? Do I allow my emotions to speak with more volume that I allow God's Word to speak through me?

His way brings endurance. His Word offers life in abundance.

Tuesday: Those Who Speak Their Mind

The arrogant mock me unmercifully, but I do not turn from your law.
(PSALM 119:51)

THERE ARE TIMES we offer this as a compliment to someone: "Well, he's just speaking his mind." If the words from a mind through a mouth are not pleasing in the sight of God, what good are they? Is it really okay to say whatever we want however we want to say it to whomever we want to say it? Speaking our mind can be okay if it is biblical and led by the Spirit. But it should not be allowed when arrogant words mock others unmercifully.

Where are your words coming from today? What is your reason for stating those words?

Read again words from the book of James:

My dear brothers and sisters, take note of this: Everyone should be quick to listen, slow to speak and slow to become angry, because human anger does not produce the righteousness that God desires ... Those who consider themselves religious and yet do not keep a tight rein on their tongues deceive themselves, and their religion is worthless (James 1:19–20; 26).

Keep a tight rein on the tongue today. Be quick to hear, slow to speak, and slow to become angry. The world might be falling apart with words, but we don't need to fall with it. Our words can bring life as we rise up and grow toward maturity.

Wednesday: What to Never Forget

I remember, Lord, your ancient laws, and I find comfort in them. Indignation grips me because of the wicked, who have forsaken your law. (PSALM 119:52–53)

HERE WE ARE IN THE MIDDLE of week thirty–five. What do you remember most of the words you have read in this book? What has inspired you to trust God? What are some ways you feel like you have applied what you've learned?

Take a few moments to think about and answer those questions.

And, friends, I do not want you to ever forget what I have stated to you. Please never forget how you can trust a true, wise, secure, and loving God even when so many things are going wrong. Please let Him be your security. Please let Him be your joy. Please let Him be the One meeting all of your needs. Please let Him be the One converting your dreams into realities.

Never forget it. Remind yourself day and night. Tell others. Believe in faith that the Lord brings His comfort to you even in the middle of a week and the middle of a year and the middle of a day and the middle of a night.

Thursday: A Theme Song

Your decrees are the theme of my song wherever I lodge.
(PSALM 119:54)

DOES YOUR LIFE have a theme song? If so, what is it? If not, why don't you select one today?

The psalmist chose to let his theme song be the decrees of the Lord. The verdicts and declarations of God offer a whole new sound than the songs we often hear in this world.

- We hear songs of defeat. God sings victory to us.
- We watch news reports of divisions. God unites us together.
- We read stories of a downfall. God declares to us that He will lift us up.
- We feel emotions of exhaustion. God breathes life into our spirits and our lungs.
- We physically can't seem to stand up. God holds us and carries us with His strong arms.

Be held by the arms of your Father today. Be assured of your future by the Word of the Lord today. Hear the song of the Lord today, and let it be your theme.

Friday: How to End Each Day

In the night, Lord, I remember your name, that I may keep your law.
(PSALM 119:55)

PEOPLE END THEIR DAYS differently. Some fall asleep quickly. Others take forever to rest. Some eat a lot before bedtime and refuse to worry about those calories. Others resist any food after dinner. Some watch television. Others read or write.

What about you?

We might end our days differently, but I invite us all to remember the Lord's powerful name before we let our day reach its conclusion. We hear heaps of words throughout each day. We read a lot, write a lot, speak a lot, and forget a whole lot. But there are some words we must choose to never forget or ignore. Those are the words we must keep in our minds and in our hearts. The name of the Lord is the most important.

He is God the Creator. He is Jesus the Lord and Savior. He is Father. He is Counselor. He is Judge and Jury. He is King. He is Shepherd. He is Ruler of All. He is the Great Physician.

As you near the end of this week, end this day like we should end every day: dwell on the name of the Lord.

Saturday: Living a Mature Life

This has been my practice: I obey your precepts. (PSALM 119:56)

SOME FOLKS SEEM TO NEVER GROW UP. I have mentioned that in other ways throughout my talks and my books. I have to say it again here, though, because we often just let it happen.

We must grow up.

End your week reading these verses, as you pray for God to help you live a mature life:

For this reason, since the day we heard about you, we have not stopped praying for you. We continually ask God to fill you with the knowledge of his will through all the wisdom and understanding that the Spirit gives, so that you may live a life worthy of the Lord and please him in every way: bearing fruit in every good work, growing in the knowledge of God, being strengthened with all power according to his glorious might so that you may have great endurance and patience, and giving joyful thanks to the Father, who has qualified you to share in the inheritance of his holy people in the kingdom of light (COLOSSIANS 1:9–12).

We ought always to thank God for you, brothers and sisters, and rightly so, because your faith is growing more and more, and the love all of you have for one another is increasing (2 THESSALONIANS 1:3).

But grow in the grace and knowledge of our Lord and Savior Jesus Christ. To him be glory both now and forever! Amen (2 PETER 3:18).

If You Find a Path with No Obstacles, It Probably Does Not Lead Anywhere

Sunday: Led by the Shepherd

The Lord is my shepherd, I lack nothing. (PSALM 23:1)

ONE OF THE MOST POPULAR prayers of all times and in all languages is Psalm 23. Most people call it The Twenty-Third Psalm.

David, the man who was close to God and lived with a heart like God's heart, wrote most of the Psalms. As a shepherd, he inscribed this prayer from his personal experience. The illustrations reveal his heart for God and his experience with sheep. He knew about life—as a child caring for sheep and eventually as a king caring about a nation. He had learned much—spending time with sheep, understanding nature, encountering danger, facing darkness, trusting the light. He knew about obstacles, and he found a path from God through those obstacles which turned him into a true leader.

But what this psalm and his many other poetic prayers remind us is that David knew God, and he knew how to talk to God.

I hear so many people saying that they just don't know how to pray. They confess that they would pray more if they just knew how.

Well, my friends, Psalm 23 is a delightful case we can follow.

Look at the first line. That sentence confesses two declarations:

· The Lord is my shepherd.
· I lack nothing.

Don't know how to pray? Yes, you can just begin there. Start with that sentence highlighting two truths. Open your prayer with a statement about who God is and what that means to you. You can be led by a Supreme Shepherd, the One who will never leave you in need.

Monday: A Path Providing Rest

He makes me lie down in green pastures, he leads me beside quiet waters. (Psalm 23:2)

As your Shepherd, what does God do? He doesn't sit off at the distance giving instructions and grading you on how well you follow His orders. He is your Shepherd. He leads like a shepherd.

The paths He takes you down provide the rest you desperately need:

- He makes me lie down in green pastures.
- He leads me beside quiet waters.

In your busy, hurried pace, let your Shepherd lead you in a path providing respite today.

He invites you to lie down. Rest. Step aside from your busy stride. Take a nap. Remember the importance of the Sabbath. Be still and know that the One leading you is God.

David knew that while watching over the sheep he needed to rest when he could. The rest prepared him for battles, for caring for the sheep, for travel. It gave the energy he needed.

God wants you to lie down and rest. Where? A beautiful place of green, plentiful, abundant, rich pastures.

The Shepherd also leads you beside calm, peaceful, still, quiet waters. Away from the noise. Away from the show. Away from the performance. Resting in the stillness. Rewinding in the place of peace.

God created times for rest. Our cultures often ignore their importance though our minds and bodies cry out for such peaceful waters.

Travel that path today. Stop and be still. Rest a while.

Tuesday: Refreshing the Soul

He refreshes my soul. He guides me along the right paths for his name's sake. (PSALM 23:3)

TODAY'S PRAYER is just what you need today, I believe. Whatever your year has been like, however your week started, whatever it is you are facing, however you usually respond to stress, this is the day for your soul to be refreshed.

David confessed that his Shepherd refreshed his soul. Does your soul need refreshing today? Does it need restoration today? Does it need invigorating today? Does it need renewal today?

We often work while needing rest. We also tend to hurry right past our cries for refreshing.

The world finds other ways for temporary refreshing. Those momentary experiences can cause permanent regrets.

Not the Shepherd's way. His way brings peace through a calming we crave. Look at these three confessions together, and pray they are what you receive today from the Lord:

- He makes me lie down in green pastures.
- He leads me beside quiet waters.
- He refreshes my soul.

That rest and rejuvenation allows you to be ready for what God does next: the Shepherd will guide you along the right paths. He knows where to take you. He knows how to take you there. And it is all for His name's sake. Not for ourselves or for anyone else. All for Him.

That is the journey awaiting you. Let your soul be refreshed so you'll be ready to go there.

Wednesday: Obstacles Are Waiting

Even though I walk through the darkest valley, I will fear no evil, for you are with me; your rod and your staff, they comfort me.
(PSALM 23:4)

THE POETIC PRAYER of David helped us confess God's provision. It helped us rest for our own renewal. It then allowed us to follow the path of God's direction.

And sometimes in life, obstacles await us. If you find a path with no obstacles, it probably doesn't lead anywhere. It probably isn't somewhere of importance. It probably isn't a place where a giant is waiting for you to defeat as you rescue a nation. It probably isn't a place where conflict needs someone to trust God to bring peace.

But, I know. You have found the path of obstacles. We all have. So many times I thought I had gone the wrong way because everything went wrong. But those wrong things proved I was on just the right path. There was no better path because there was no better place for God to do His best thing.

David referred to this as the darkest valley. We might not enjoy those times at first. But because God is our Shepherd we don't need to fear any evil at all. Don't let fear stop you. Don't let fear control you.

David turned directly toward communicating with God, his Shepherd:

- I will fear no evil.
- For You are with me.
- Your rod and staff comfort me.

David knew about a rod and a staff. He knew how to direct and protect and correct his sheep. David also knew that God knew how to direct and protect and correct him.

Even with obstacles waiting, David refused to be afraid. So, your two words for today: Fear not!

Thursday: Blessings When Facing the Enemies

You prepare a table before me in the presence of my enemies. You anoint my head with oil; my cup overflows. (PSALM 23:5)

WHAT MIGHT GOD DO for us even when it feels like our enemies are nearby?

Oh, He still wants you to just trust Him. He has blessings for you right when you are facing enemies. He has blessings for you when the world is falling apart. He calls you to look up when everything else seems to be looking down.

David confessed:

- You prepare a table before me in the presence of my enemies.
- You anoint my head with oil; my cup overflows.

An enemy might want to fight. But God is bringing you a feast. The enemy might want to distract you and make you feel defeated. But God is reminding you He has already won the war. No need to keep fighting if the war is over. Oh yes, we fight the enemy. But we fight by realizing the war is already won. We receive God's blessings when the enemy wants to curse us.

God is anointing our heads with His purity and His power. We have more than enough. The adversaries might come, but just go to the table. The haters might shout, but just receive the anointing. The accusers might rant, but just let your cup overflow.

God brings His blessings to you no matter what the enemy wanted to do.

Friday: God's Goodness and Love

Surely your goodness and love will follow me all the days of my life, and I will dwell in the house of the Lord forever. (PSALM 23:6)

WHAT DO YOU WANT to keep with you wherever you go? Your driver's license, your bank card, your credit card, your insurance card, your contact information, your passport?

We like to keep important things close by. We want to be sure to know where they are always.

Though, like David, we travel down paths that have some obstacles, we believe all is okay. We have faith today that God has already provided everything we need to go where He leads us.

David was convinced of these realities:

- God's goodness and love would follow him all the days of his life.
- He would dwell in the house of the Lord forever.

Goodness.

Love.

Those two blessings from God were following David? What more did he need? Did he really need to carry anything else with him on his journeys?

God's goodness and love would be what David needed in every battle, in every struggle, in every conflict, in every need, in every phase. Battling a giant or a king or a temptation or a nation, David needed the goodness and love of God following him.

Don't we need God's goodness and love following us today?

Saturday: Where God Leads Us

Surely your goodness and love will follow me all the days of my life, and I will dwell in the house of the Lord forever. (PSALM 23:6)

DAVID ALSO KNEW the end of the story. He would dwell in the house of the Lord forever. He had permanent residence in the ideal location. That means that goodness and love from the Lord would never, ever end. That meant the Shepherd would also be caring for His sheep.

When you ponder about heaven, what comes to your mind? I know, we think about missing those we are saying goodbye to. But think about who all we are saying hello to. Our family and friends who have gone before us. The people of faith who helped open the doors for us to walk through. God our Father. Jesus our Lord and Savior.

Consider also what will not be there. All the troubles we face on this planet. All the wars and fights and struggles. Those do not belong to the eternal house of the Lord.

But, if you are reading this, you are not there yet. So, let me remind you. Your life can be lived on earth with an awareness of God's house being the place you are already living. He is with you. He will never leave you. He hears your cries. He answers your prayers.

God is your Shepherd. You lack not one thing. Don't wait on heaven for your blessings; God has already brought them to you. Now be still and rest beside those calm waters. Let your soul be restored. Place your trust in your True Shepherd today.

To Get Ahead You Have
to Know Somebody

Sunday: Knowing Myself and My God

You are my portion, Lord; I have promised to obey your words. (PSALM 119:57)

PEOPLE OFTEN INSTRUCT US that we must know the right people if we want to get ahead. They are correct in part of the statement, but might be wrong in their understanding of the statement.

We need to be sure to understand the correct meaning of "getting ahead." Is it just a cultural success story? Is it just about money and fame? Or is it about the Kingdom of God? Is it about being the greatest where it really matters?

I believe we all want to get ahead. And I believe we all need to pursue getting ahead. But we must know that getting ahead with God is different in many ways than getting ahead in this world.

Also, we need to see the two key components of getting ahead: knowing ourselves and knowing our God.

God must be our portion in life. He must be what really matters. And we must see value in God's plan for our lives. Promising to obey His words voices our pledge to His guidance.

Getting ahead is a healthy goal. As long as we know what it truly means—knowing God and knowing ourselves—we can endure the adventure. These daily readings remind us of the steps to take. Your prayers help keep you on the path God has planned. Stay the course.

Monday: Desiring to Know God Better

I have sought your face with all my heart; be gracious to me according to your promise. (PSALM 119:58)

THE WAY TO BE SURE we are taking the best steps to "get ahead in life" is to desire what matters the most. Our deepest desire should be to know God better.

How well did you know God last year? How have you grown in your knowledge of God this year? What steps would you suggest to help yourself improve in knowing God better in the future?

Seeing His face with your whole heart is the place to start.

You can't know a friend or relative better if you never spend time with them. How can you strengthen a relationship if you are never around one another? Conversations together, meals together, prayers together, events together: a variety of encounters together can enhance relationships.

The same with God. Make sure to take time with Him. And time with God might happen sometimes when we least expected it, but we should be sure to schedule and plan time with Him. It is important—vital for our personal growth and development.

Do that today. Do that now.

Desire to know God better and spend time with Him at this very moment.

Tuesday: Getting Ahead

I have considered my ways and have turned my steps to your statutes. (PSALM 119:59)

I MUST REMIND YOU today that, from a biblical perspective, getting ahead in life is all about knowing God and knowing ourselves. How do you feel like you are doing with that?

As you think about yourself, consider your ways. Into what have you invested your time, money, and energy? What really matters the most to you? What has God called and equipped you to do? Consider, ponder, process, and think about your ways.

Now, consider the ways of God. To truly get ahead we must look ahead. Looking in the mirror isn't enough. Looking in the bank account isn't enough. Looking at a list of accomplishments isn't enough. We must look up, from where our help truly comes (Psalm 121:1–2). All the other places we stare and pay so much attention to can be paths that lure us away from truly getting ahead because they turn our eyes away from God. Getting ahead starts with getting our lives in touch with our God and our Creator.

Pray this prayer today:

"Oh, God, You are my Guide and my Leader. I must not go the ways that are not Your ways. Please reveal myself to me. Please reveal Yourself to me. I want to know You and help others get to know You. Direct my steps toward the successful journey you have for me. In the name of Jesus, Amen."

Wednesday: No Delay

I will hasten and not delay to obey your commands. (PSALM 119:60)

NO DELAY!

Those two words are important. Though we misunderstand them from a biblical perspective, we need to see life correctly with no delay.

Why do we often wait so long to obey God? Why do we seem to put our spiritual lives on hold, while letting all other aspects be priorities?

There are many reasons. But today that must change. Don't you want obedience to God to be your main priority?

Those other aspects of life shouldn't carry the weight we often let them carry. Those other goals shouldn't be as important as we often let them be. Those other statements on our lists shouldn't be ranked as high as we often place them.

Today is the day to obey God. Today is the day to trust God. Today is the day to step out in faith. Today is the day to seek first the Kingdom. Today is the day to let go of all those unneeded things which have held you back. Today is the day when God is true priority.

No more delays. Only steps of faith and obedience. Only decisions directed by the Spirit of God.

You know those people who waited and waited, and never turned toward God? We all have friends who said they would make things right with God, but their lives ended before they stepped forward in faith.

That is not the way.

God's path is the way—the right way. That is the way to travel today.

Thursday: Learning to Know God Better

Though the wicked bind me with ropes, I will not forget your law.
At midnight I rise to give you thanks for your righteous laws.
(PSALM 119:61–62)

IN OUR WILLINGNESS to obey God instead of the ways of this world, it isn't always simple. There are some rough routes we must take. There are some stormy nights we must travel.

But even in those dark nights we can decide. We can choose to learn to know God better.

The ways of the wicked take turns which distance them from God. The ways of the righteous choose to learn more about God and how to serve Him. Each turn can teach a lesson. Each hill can motivate trust. Each marathon can inspire endurance. Each path offers opportunities for people to truly love the God they claim to love.

And that is what this is all about. It is loving God. It is receiving God's love in our personal lives.

As we love Him we can learn to know God better. Every day, every moment. Better aware of God's voice. Better sure of His will. Better connected to the Spirit.

God is the Somebody we must know as we seek to take the right steps in life and get ahead. He will lead us correctly.

Friday: Knowing God and His People

I am a friend to all who fear you, to all who follow your precepts. (PSALM 119:63)

WHILE WE EMPHASIZE the importance of knowing ourselves and knowing God, that is another portion we cannot leave out. We are to be a friend to all who fear the Lord and follow His precepts.

What does that mean? We must be true parts of the body of Christ. We must live as key components of the church. We must not live life alone. We must be among the people of God.

How are you doing with that? Have you let past hurts in relationships keep you at a distance?

Today, please choose to change that. No longer bitter. Better. No longer hateful. Loving. No longer alone. Part of the body. No longer in isolation. Within the community of faith.

Let that be your decision today. Don't just wait for another person or a church to invite you. God already has invited you. Say yes. Say yes to His invitation.

Knowing God's people will help you know God better. That is getting ahead the right way!

Pray together with those friends. Spend time with God and His people. Living alone is not New Testament church.

Yes, we take time away from people to be in private prayer with God. But, in the big picture, we are not alone in our walk with Jesus. Our fellow travelers need to be in our lives. Welcome them.

Saturday: God's Creation Is Teaching Us about His Love

The earth is filled with your love, Lord; teach me your decrees.
(PSALM 119:64)

WE HAVE TALKED throughout these devotions about spending time with God and His people. We have repeated over and over about God's love. We have encouraged you to notice God's love all around you.

Today is another day to sit outside a while and see what God has created. I don't know your favorite pastime, but I know this: God is inviting you to step away from your ordinary routine and notice the goodness of God.

His love fills the earth. The clouds in the sky, the grass on the land, the leaves on the trees, the stars in the evening. So much beauty all around us. But you know how we are. We often stare straight ahead and miss what is right there for us to see.

Not today. This day we must choose to let God's creation teach us about His love. Slow down a little and give a few moments to stare at God's creation. Small town or big city, mountains or plains, north or south, east or west. God has crafted a lovely planet in this vast universe.

Nothing is too big. Nothing is too small. God is God. Believe in Him again today as you see what He has done.

Life Is Tragic for the Person Who Has Plenty to Live on, but Nothing to Live For

Sunday: Why Do We Live?

Do good to your servant according to your word, Lord. Teach me knowledge and good judgment, for I trust your commands.
(Psalm 119:65–66)

SOME PEOPLE HAVE a lot to live on but have very little to live for. They live on bank accounts and jobs and investments and material possessions. But what do they live for? They wake up each day and go to work with no true, lasting, valuable, eternal purchase in life.

God has a much better plan than that. He wants His people to receive His knowledge and to trust in His commands.

I do not want your life to be another tragic experience of missing God's true purpose in life. That happens to too many people. But, my friend, it must not happen to you.

On this day choose to grasp the large calling of God on your life. He created you and rescued you. He won't leave you now. He knows why you're here on earth. He placed you here for a reason for this season.

Ask yourself, "What is the reason God has placed me here during this season? Why am I here? What eternal difference does God want to make through me?"

Ponder those questions. God will do good through you, His servant. The world will be a better place because you are one of those better people making a bigger difference.

Monday: God's Word as Our Guide for Life

Before I was afflicted I went astray, but now I obey your word.
(PSALM 119:67)

GOD'S WORD CAN GUIDE OUR LIVES, informing us of our true-life purpose. There is no need to live with no good reason. I can give you many reasons. Those would not be just my reasons, but the reasons God has placed you on this earth during this season.

Look back at the questions you asked yourself yesterday. Did the Holy Spirit help reveal God's answers? Are you getting a new glimpse at your calling?

Even while you wait for the right time or the right move or the right provision, there is one thing already waiting to give you help. That is God's Word. It is available to you right now.

That is why I preached God's truth for so many years to so many people. That is why I could not quit. That is why I could not give up. God gave me a purpose. He planned for me to develop the gifts He gave me and—as He empowered me with His presence—to use those gifts for the building of His Kingdom. I want His words heard. I want His words studied. I want His words obeyed.

Don't look around to some other source for guidance. God gave it to you already. Open the Bible and receive it. Open the Bible and obey it. God will be true to His promises and He will speak them to you—and through you to this world.

Tuesday: Learning from Our Good God

You are good, and what you do is good; teach me your decrees.
(PSALM 119:68)

WE ARE TALKING ABOUT learning from God and His Word as giving us true reasons to live. It is so sad to see so many people with no purpose in life.

We can have a different way to live. We can see a larger perspective. We can be learning from our God, and realizing our God is a good God.

God is always good. Everything God does is good.

Don't forget that. Don't let someone else take that off your mind. You must believe that today. You must rejoice in that today.

Why don't you take a few minutes—push aside whatever else is on your schedule for this instant—and just tell God all the good you see in Him. Thank Him for His creation, for His kindness, for His Scripture, for His holiness, for His justice, for His compassion, for His forgiveness, for His promises, for His provision.

Here is something else you should do. Not only thank God for what He has done and for who He is, write a list of lessons you have learned from God's character traits. Glance at the list in the previous paragraph from today's devotion: God's creation, kindness, and other traits and actions. Beside each one, write a statement about what you learned. Maybe something like this: *Through God's creation I have learned to trust His ability to do what is best in my life.* Or something like this: *Through God's holiness I have learned that He is stable in character and will never waver in what He says to do.*

God is good. Let's learn from our good God.

Wednesday: Life Does Not Need to Be Tragic

Though the arrogant have smeared me with lies, I keep your precepts with all my heart. (Psalm 119:69)

Disasters happen. Catastrophes occur. Conflict continues. Devastations transpire. Maybe last year was a difficult year. Maybe you have faced trying times this year. Maybe this week has already disheartened you.

I am not suggesting we deny those sad moments. I believe we should face those scenes, address them carefully and faithfully, call out to God and His people, and wisely pursue a victory.

It also helps us to do this crucial act: Remember that life does not always need to be tragic. Situations might seem troublesome, but they can end peacefully. With the precepts of God in our hearts and the Holy Spirit guiding our responses to circumstances, peace can prevail. Panic is not our calling. Fright is not the force to control us. Dread isn't to be our mood to start an experience, a conversation, a relationship, a job, or a day.

Say goodbye today to an unneeded and unhelpful mindset. Refuse today to let your view be controlled by hurts. Deny the lie that everything in life is tragic.

God brings good to His people. His decrees declare it. His promises assure it. Believe it today. No matter what has already come your way this week, believe it today.

Thursday: Finding Our Way

Their hearts are callous and unfeeling, but I delight in your law.
(PSALM 119:70)

YOU WANT TO MAKE A WISE DECISION, don't you? As you consider various options, you need inner assurance that your choice is the right choice, don't you?

We have already emphasized—and will continue to accentuate—how God desires to guide us along the correct paths. These pages are covered with words underscoring God's Word about provision and direction. He hands us what we need. Then those hands of God carry us to where we need to go.

So, how do we find our way? We must find God. He can then take us along the best way possible. Don't spend all your time looking for the way to go. Spend your energy and effort pursuing God, then trust Him as your chaperone.

He will remind you today that you have much to live for.

He will remind you today how to be in the right place to fulfill what He wants you to live for.

God will prompt you in the right way at the right time. Remember, though, it will be His way and His time that are right. Remember, also, that He will give you the heart He has to care for the people around you.

Want to find your way? Find God. Trust His way. Rely on Him along the way.

You want to make a wise decision, don't you? That, my friend, is how you make it.

Friday: When Hurt Helps Us Learn

It was good for me to be afflicted so that I might learn your decrees.
(PSALM 119:71)

HOW HAVE YOU LEARNED your most important lessons? Teachers teach us. Preachers inspire us. Motivational speakers motivate us. Mentors train us. But sometimes we learn outside the classroom and in the training room, outside the sanctuary and in the battle, outside the celebration and in the skirmish.

Go back through your life. Haven't you seen that? Haven't you learned deep lessons from God right in the middle of your storms of life? Those winds are blowing and those waves are crashing around, and God stops you right where you are to teach you a lifechanging lesson. Your body is in pain and your mind can hardly think anymore, and God speaks clearly to you about paths He knows you must take.

See what I mean? Lessons can be learned when it feels like the world is falling apart.

Don't miss them. Don't focus on a quick solution and fail to learn a crucial life lesson.

Whatever you are facing today, place your trust in your Teacher. He has all knowledge. He possesses all wisdom. He seeks to direct your paths correctly. Though He might direct you past some valleys and shadows of death, do not miss the opportunity to become better as you pass through.

It might hurt.

It also might help you.

Agree to endure. Agree to learn. Agree to trust your Teacher.

Saturday: What We Must Really Rely On

The law from your mouth is more precious to me than thousands of pieces of silver and gold. (PSALM 119:72)

ANOTHER WEEK is now ending. Tomorrow another day will begin.

What have you learned this week about trusting God? What are hopes you have about applying that trust better next week than you ever have before?

It might help you to write your own list here.

Before writing your list, look again at today's verse. God's law is more precious than thousands of pieces of silver and gold. His Word is what we must rely on. Reflect on His Word we have studied and thought about. As you think of the will of God and the Word of God, as you realize He is the one to really rely on, now put together your list of ways you will rely on God:

"I choose to rely on God for ..."

-
-
-
-
-
-
-
-
-

Look through your list several times. Pray and think slowly. Listen to what God is saying to you.

End by asking yourself a few questions. How can you rely on God in those areas? What does that mean to your attitude and your actions? How can this week end well, and a new week begin better because you have chosen to rely on God?

Generosity Is Giving a Little from a Lot; Sacrifice Is Giving a Lot from a Little

Sunday: Learning God's Way

Your hands made me and formed me; give me understanding to learn your commands. (PSALM 119:73)

IN THESE DEVOTIONS we have included many thoughts on Psalm 119. Not only is the prayer the longest chapter in the Bible in the number of words and verses, it is classic Hebrew poetry written as an acrostic poem. The entire psalm focuses on God's Word. This week we want to fill each day with more Scripture, so we fit the mood of the psalm spiritually and poetically.

And the verses we will use this week emphasize how God is calling us all to be sacrificial givers. Though generosity is giving a little from a lot, sacrifice is giving a lot from a little. This week, let's study God's wisdom and obey His instructions to give. And let us give gladly.

In the New Testament, this verse describes the early church: they sold property and possessions to give to anyone who had need (Acts 2:45).

In the Old Testament, these words were said to Moses, "The people are bringing more than enough for doing the work the Lord commanded to be done" (Exodus 36:5).

Look at the results of learning God's way for the early church which had an attitude of giving: "That there were no needy persons among them. For from time to time those who owned land or houses sold them, brought the money from the sales" (Acts 4:34).

Learn and live God's way this week. Choose to sacrifice.

Monday: Putting Hope in God No Matter What Happens

May those who fear you rejoice when they see me, for I have put my hope in your word. (PSALM 119:74)

PUTTING OUR HOPE in God's Word doesn't just mean liking what He says. It means living by His principles and obeying His instructions. Giving is what the Lord has commanded us to do—and He's told us to give with joyful hearts and sincere motives.

Like yesterday, we want to meditate on God's Word today about giving—putting our hope in God no matter what else might be happening around us.

Look at these two examples from the life of Jesus:

• Jesus Anointed at Bethany

While Jesus was in Bethany in the home of Simon the Leper, a woman came to him with an alabaster jar of very expensive perfume, which she poured on his head as he was reclining at the table (MATTHEW 26:6–7).

• The Widow's Offering

As Jesus looked up, he saw the rich putting their gifts into the temple treasury. He also saw a poor widow put in two very small copper coins. "Truly I tell you," he said, "this poor widow has put in more than all the others. All these people gave their gifts out of their wealth; but she out of her poverty put in all she had to live on" (LUKE 21:1–4).

What can we learn from the woman who came to Jesus with an alabaster jar? What can we learn from the poor widow with two very small copper coins? What can we learn from statements of Jesus about what the widow did, compared to what others had done?

Today, let us learn and give, putting our hope in God even when the world is falling apart.

Tuesday: God as Our Example

I know, Lord, that your laws are righteous, and that in faithfulness you have afflicted me. (PSALM 119:75)

THE LORD'S LAWS are right and just. His faithfulness is the example we must follow. That example includes giving much when there doesn't seem to be much available.

Elijah knew about giving and taking risks. He knew about trusting in God to supply even when we give all, and nothing seems to be available. Elijah spoke words which offered assurance for a widow to sacrifice:

Elijah said to her, "Don't be afraid. Go home and do as you have said. But first make a small loaf of bread for me from what you have and bring it to me, and then make something for yourself and your son. For this is what the Lord, the God of Israel, says: 'The jar of flour will not be used up and the jug of oil will not run dry until the day the Lord sends rain on the land.'" She went away and did as Elijah had told her. So there was food every day for Elijah and for the woman and her family (1 KINGS 17:13–15).

Look at the promises. Realize God has given you promises today. Remember also the example God is for us. He gave His son. He gives us His love. What an example God is on this life of giving!

Wednesday: Living as God's Servant

May your unfailing love be my comfort, according to your promise to your servant. (Psalm 119:76)

TO BETTER UNDERSTAND this giving as a way of living, let's remember the unfailing love of God. That is our comfort. We live as servants because that is what God has taught us.

Today we want to continue reading from His Word, allowing Him to continue teaching us to live—and give—as His servants:

For I testify that they gave as much as they were able, and even beyond their ability. Entirely on their own, they urgently pleaded with us for the privilege of sharing in this service to the Lord's people (2 CORINTHIANS 8:3–4).

For if the willingness is there, the gift is acceptable according to what one has, not according to what one does not have. Our desire is not that others might be relieved while you are hard pressed, but that there might be equality. At the present time your plenty will supply what they need, so that in turn their plenty will supply what you need. The goal is equality, as it is written: "The one who gathered much did not have too much, and the one who gathered little did not have too little" (2 CORINTHIANS 8:12–15).

If any of your fellow Israelites become poor and are unable to support themselves among you, help them as you would a foreigner and stranger, so they can continue to live among you. Do not take interest or any profit from them, but fear your God, so that they may continue to live among you. You must not lend them money at interest or sell them food at a profit (LEVITICUS 25:35–37).

Learn from God's Word and live as His servant today.

274

Thursday: Giving with God's Compassion

Let your compassion come to me that I may live, for your law is my delight. (PSALM 119:77)

THE EXAMPLE OF GIVING we must follow is God's compassion. He is our leader. He is the one who has called us to give, and He is actually giving to others through us. That is how it works.

Reflect on God's Word again today—from Deuteronomy 15, Psalm 41, and Luke 6:

If anyone is poor among your fellow Israelites in any of the towns of the land the Lord your God is giving you, do not be hardhearted or tightfisted toward them. Rather, be openhanded and freely lend them whatever they need (DEUTERONOMY 15:7–8).

For the director of music. A psalm of David.

Blessed are those who have regard for the weak;
* the Lord delivers them in times of trouble.*
The Lord protects and preserves them—
* they are counted among the blessed in the land—*
* he does not give them over to the desire of their foes.*
The Lord sustains them on their sickbed
* and restores them from their bed of illness* (PSALM 41:1–3).

"Do not judge, and you will not be judged. Do not condemn, and you will not be condemned. Forgive, and you will be forgiven. Give, and it will be given to you. A good measure, pressed down, shaken together and running over, will be poured into your lap. For with the measure you use, it will be measured to you" (LUKE 6:37–38).

Giving instead of judging. Trusting the Lord's care as we give. Being openhanded and lending freely. That is the way we are called to live and give.

Friday: A Lot or a Little?

May the arrogant be put to shame for wronging me without cause; but I will meditate on your precepts. May those who fear you turn to me, those who understand your statutes. (PSALM 119:78–79)

GOD'S STATUTES INSTRUCT US to give and keep on giving. God's precepts direct us to give a lot, not just a little.

Here are more words from God we must hear today—we begin with the words of Jesus talking about a treasure in heaven, then we include wisdom from Proverbs:

Do not store up for yourselves treasures on earth, where moths and vermin destroy, and where thieves break in and steal. But store up for yourselves treasures in heaven, where moths and vermin do not destroy, and where thieves do not break in and steal. For where your treasure is, there your heart will be also (MATTHEW 6:19–21).

Whoever shuts their ears to the cry of the poor
    will also cry out and not be answered (PROVERBS 21:13).

One person gives freely, yet gains even more;
    another withholds unduly, but comes to poverty.

A generous person will prosper;
    whoever refreshes others will be refreshed (PROVERBS 11:24–25).

Whoever is kind to the poor lends to the Lord,
    and he will reward them for what they have done
    (PROVERBS 19:17).

The generous will themselves be blessed,
    for they share their food with the poor (PROVERBS 22:9).

Choose today to give a lot, not just a little.

Saturday: When God Is Everything

May I wholeheartedly follow your decrees, that I may not be put to shame. (PSALM 119:80)

GIVING REMINDS US THAT GOD is everything. We shouldn't choose anything else or anyone else to take His place. We wholeheartedly obey His decrees on giving and loving, as our way of letting Him truly be our everything.

To end our week of Scripture about giving, here are texts from the Gospel of Matthew and the Acts of the Apostles:

And if anyone gives even a cup of cold water to one of these little ones who is my disciple, truly I tell you, that person will certainly not lose their reward (MATTHEW 10:42).

Now I commit you to God and to the word of his grace, which can build you up and give you an inheritance among all those who are sanctified. I have not coveted anyone's silver or gold or clothing. You yourselves know that these hands of mine have supplied my own needs and the needs of my companions. In everything I did, I showed you that by this kind of hard work we must help the weak, remembering the words the Lord Jesus himself said: "It is more blessed to give than to receive" (ACTS 20:32–35).

When God is our everything we choose to give—and to give wholeheartedly. When God is our everything, we give even when it feels like everything else is falling apart. When God is our everything, we give a lot rather than a little. End this week by giving, and by giving a lot.

In Spite of the Cost of Living
It Is Still Popular

Sunday: Hope to Live

My soul faints with longing for your salvation, but I have put my hope in your word. (PSALM 119:81)

IN SPITE OF THE COST OF LIVING, it is still popular.

But what is our true view of living? What keeps us motivated to "keep on keeping on?" What gives us hope for another month, another week, another day, another moment?

I believe we find hope in God's Word.

Not always in the news or in the latest trends. Not always in how others treat us or what we include on our resume. Not always in just going to church or just thinking a positive thought.

If the hope is dependable and reliable, it must come from God's Word.

Oh, we have all tried so many other things. But what does it come back to? Stories in Scripture remind us about many victories and defeats. Those narratives tell us where to go to get those victories instead of those defeats. God's Word guides us, directs us, assures us. It offers us the news we won't hear on television or online. Better news. News of hope for eternity. News of gladness during times of sadness. News of peace during times of war. News of health in times of sickness. News of care in times of conflict.

Don't let your soul faint today. Don't pay the price of your own demise. Eternal salvation and hope lie on those pages of truth. Open the book. Read God's Word. Meditate on those statements. Receive hope for living.

Monday: Hoping While Waiting

My eyes fail, looking for your promise; I say, "When will you comfort me?" (Psalm 119:82)

WELL, MAYBE YOU WANT TO SAY, "I have tried that."

Maybe you want to say, "I have read and studied God's Word, but I am still waiting for God's promises to come true."

Yes, we have all felt that way. During those seasons of waiting, the delays feel like defeats. The postponements seem like they'll last forever. The rearrangements can't be seen clearly. The reorganizations make us feel like everything is falling apart.

But, oh, from God's eyes, the victories are coming our way.

Today, for you, that long-awaited answer is coming your way.

Your human eyes might fail to see it. But look on through. Rather than watching what is obvious, glance toward the promises of God. See through the now. See all the way to God's plan.

- Rest in His unfailing love.
- Trust in His consistent care.
- Believe in His astonishing capacity.
- Wait for His remarkable redesigning.

Ask God, "When will You comfort me?" Listen as He answers, "I am your Comforter. I am with you now. Let me console you. Let me reinstate you. Let me bring you peace as the miracle is coming."

Receive that. Receive the comfort from God while waiting on the fulfillment of His promise. He is with you in the waiting. Today, He is with you.

Tuesday: Never Forget

Though I am like a wineskin in the smoke, I do not forget your decrees. (PSALM 119:83)

WE OFTEN FOCUS too long on what can harm us. It is better to place our attention on God's decrees. Even when we feel like we are burning into bits, we can shift our focus on what God is doing and who God is.

I am not suggesting we ignore life's perils. I am not instructing us to forget life's hazards. I am not informing us to abandon reality.

What I am saying is that while waiting, we must place our attention on what matters most. Those are God's decrees.

His ways—that is what we must dwell on. Not all those negative thoughts blowing into our minds like storms whirling danger our way. Such harmful views need to go. We are to replace them with God's declarations.

Try to:

- Read God's Word aloud.
- Read God's Word slowly.
- Tell others about what God has done in your life.
- Write your own story about what God has done in your life.
- Place a list of God's decrees to keep near you every day.
- Meditate on that list each day.

Focus on the helpful rather than the harmful. Concentrate on the decrees of God rather than the opinions of people.

Let God be the One—the only One—guiding you today. Refuse to forget His decrees.

Wednesday: So Many Questions

How long must your servant wait? When will you punish my perse-cutors? The arrogant dig pits to trap me, contrary to your law.
(PSALM 119:84–85)

EVEN AS WE TRY TO TRUST God and overcome negative thoughts, we often deluge our minds with questions. Look at these two the psalmist wrote from Psalm 119:

- How long must Your servant wait?
- When will You punish my persecutors?

That *first question* is asking God what is taking Him so long to bring His answer. As we have reflected on before, those thoughts come to our minds. We must choose to respond properly so we do not become consumed or obsessed by such questions. We can pray them out like the psalmist did, as we begin to adjust our views to see God's way.

It helps to see the waiting as a time of preparing. God is getting us ready for the provision. God is getting those around us ready for that revelation. God knows the time and the place and the method to bring His will to life.

What about the *second question*, "When will you punish my persecutors?" Oh, that is a tough one, isn't it? We feel betrayed, ignored, mistreated, neglected, rejected, hated, persecuted, deceived, abandoned. We have stayed true to God during a season of torture. We know now must be time for God to destroy those foes.

But maybe that is not God's plan for them. Though those arrogant ones decided to dig pits to trap you, maybe God's plan is to rescue them from their own hurts which caused them to mistreat you.

So, pray those prayers to God. As we live with so many questions, pray those prayers to God. All while remembering, He is your rescuer and He is their rescuer too. Pray for those who harm you to also be healed.

Thursday: There Is No Reason for This Struggle

All your commands are trustworthy; help me, for I am being perse-cuted without cause. (PSALM 119:86)

THERE MIGHT SEEM to be no reason for the struggle you are enduring. I know we have all faced such seasons.

During our waiting, during those times of struggling with no reason, during those times of being persecuted without a cause, what can you do to apply the principles of trusting God when the world is falling apart?

Here are a few ideas for you today:

- Remember who God is.
- Remember what God has done.
- Remember what God has promised to do.
- Rejoice in who God is.
- Rejoice in what God has done.
- Rejoice in what God has promised to do.
- Receive who God is.
- Receive what God has done.
- Receive what God has promised to do.

Who God is—His character. What God has done—His fulfill-ment. What God will do—His promises. Welcome the assurance those thoughts bring.

When there seems to be no cause for the waiting or the agony, rest in God. Trust Him. He can be your peace during the struggle.

Friday: I Am Still Holding On

They almost wiped me from the earth, but I have not forsaken your precepts. (PSALM 119:87)

SOMETIMES THERE IS A PLACE we just need to go. I'm not talking about the restaurant or the ballgame. I'm not thinking about the family reunion or the business meeting. I'm not suggesting the convention or the long drive.

What am I talking about? The altar.

Sometimes we just need to go to the altar.

These prayers we are studying and reflecting on from Psalm 119 reveal similar confessions over and over, just using diverse words and in different ways. One thing the writer was doing while he wrote and prayed these statements was this: he was still holding on.

Though the weight might have been heavy, he didn't let go.

Though the trials might have been difficult, he didn't let go.

While praying, he was still holding on. While holding on, he was still praying.

He felt wiped out from the earth, but he refused to forsake the precepts of God.

That is the place I want you to go today. Go to the altar. When feeling defeated and abandoned, when feeling rejected and forsaken, go to the altar. Be honest with God—as we've said, He already knows. Let go of those worries and those fears. Surrender them to Him.

Hold on to this truth: God is holding on to you!

Saturday: All Will Be Well

In your unfailing love preserve my life, that I may obey the statutes of your mouth. (PSALM 119:88)

WE LOOK FORWARD to a time when all will be well. And, I know, there are moments when we feel convinced things just keep getting worse and worse. It seems like they'll never get better.

The psalmist wanted to obey all of the Word of God. He did not want to falter. He did not want to fail. He sought to obey all the statutes from God's mouth. Even when waiting seemed to last forever, he prayed, asking God to preserve his life. Even when he saw no glance of God's grace, he had faith, knowing it was somehow there.

To help you choose to endure today, dwell on two words from this ancient prayer. Think about these words: *unfailing love.*

He asked God to preserve his life that way: in God's *unfailing love.*

Oh, it helps us to dwell on God's *unfailing love* instead of only fix on our many failures. Absorbed by our blunders, thoughts push us away from believing all will be well.

Instead of just waiting for better weather or more money or a nice job to make your life better, try this. Concentrate on God's *unfailing love.* It is dependable. It is always there. It is reliable. It will never leave.

We need His steady love in these seasons of uncertainty. That love is available for you today. Welcome His love and believe all will be well.

Two Things I've Had:
Good Advice and Bad Examples

Sunday: God's Advice Is Great Advice

Your word, Lord, is eternal; it stands firm in the heavens. (PSALM 119:89)

LATELY I'VE BEEN THINKING about two things I have had in life: Good advice and bad examples.

You can relate, can't you?

Most folks can tell us what the right things are that we should do. They can instruct us and advise us, inspire us and direct us, rebuke us and correct us. They try to get our attention and try even harder to keep our attention. They give us lists and goals and plans.

Their guidance might be helpful. Their intelligence might be advantageous.

But how does it make you feel if you see them not following their own advice? We don't like that, do we? Their hypocrisy causes reluctance. Setting a bad example can be louder than the advice they offer.

The psalmist knew that God doesn't work that way. He gives wisdom in word and in action. God's advice is great advice. God reveals the advantages of His direction through His character and His Scripture. His Word is eternal. It stands firm in the heavens.

Receive God's guidance today. Trust His wisdom. His good advice and His great example offer you a chance to be a good example to yourself. Refuse to let anything stop you from living each day by following God's directions.

Monday: God Is True to His Word

Your faithfulness continues through all generations; you established the earth, and it endures. (PSALM 119:90)

IF WE LIVE EACH DAY fulfilling God's directions, we live with faithfulness. That is a character trait we should desire.

Look at what Psalm 119:90 reveals about our lives displaying God's truth in His Word:

- God's faithfulness continues through all generations.
- God established the earth.
- God's faithfulness will endure.

God is true to His Word. God keeps His promises. Such faithfulness can change the world—beginning with us.

Glance outside and notice the wonder of the planet earth. It is stable and secure. Storms come and bring changes, but the earth remains. Weather shifts through the seasons, but the earth remains. This planet is in her place, spinning around in her regular routine.

The verse says God is He who established the earth. Its stability and security come from Him.

That is why we can stand on the solid foundation of God's Word. It is stable. It is secure. In a world of many opinions and perspectives and moods, God brings stability. In a world of hate and hurt and division, God brings security.

God not only established the earth, but God has a faithfulness that will endure. He is here for the long run. He stays on track for the marathon.

True to His Word—that describes this faithful, stable, secure, strong, powerful God. And that truth can motivate us to be faithful and endure our journey.

Tuesday: Finding Delight in God's Way

Your laws endure to this day, for all things serve you. If your law had not been my delight, I would have perished in my affliction.
(PSALM 119:91–92)

LIFE CAN CARRY MANY IFs. If the weather stays nice, we might go on a trip. If the money comes in, we might purchase that gift someone has requested. If the church keeps us happy, we might stay at that church. If the doctor's appointment goes well, we just might feel a little better about things. If the right leader takes over, we can see some good changes happen.

If this and if that. So many IFs.

Here is an IF from Psalm 119:92:

"If your law had not been my delight, I would have perished in my affliction."

Oh, what a different experience life could be for us if we chose to realize the larger IF. We need to realize we will perish unless we find delight in God's law. His Word should be our IF. His truth should be our guide. His instructions should be our path.

We do not need to perish in whatever affliction we are facing today. Even when suffering, we can find peace in God through His law. Even when the storms come our way, we can live with calmness because God's Word is true and stable.

Let God's law be your delight today. Desire it. Seek it. Stay committed to it. Find delight in it. And let that be the IF for today and every day.

Wednesday: Perseverance

I will never forget your precepts, for by them you have preserved my life. (PSALM 119:93)

"I WILL NEVER FORGET THAT DAY."

Haven't you said that before? One of those times when everything went right. One of those experiences when all your hopes came true. One of those situations when your prayers were answered.

Take a few moments today to think about times you will never forget. Talk about it with a friend or family member. Look at a few old pictures. What food did you eat? What was the weather like? What time of year was it? Who all was there? What is the real reason that event meant so much to you? If you wrote a story about it, what would you title it?

It is nice to think back about those times. Positive memories can motivate us to persevere. Today's verse helps us know what is worth never forgetting:

"I will never forget Your precepts, for by them You have preserved my life."

God's precepts. His guidelines. His instructions. They can offer stability in these grim days.

We are reading God's Word every day. We are meditating on it and believing it. We are contemplating on it and receiving it. His Word is what we must never forget. It helps us persevere no matter what is happening around us.

Never forget that.

Thursday: Rescue

Save me, for I am yours; I have sought out your precepts.
(PSALM 119:94)

"SAVE ME," David prayed. "For I am Yours," he stated as the reason. "I have sought out your precepts," David said in his conversation with God.

What an honor we have to listen in to their conversation.

This psalm, written in an acrostic pattern in the Hebrew alphabet, was very structured. It contains 22 units with eight verses each. Those units all begin with one of those Hebrew letters. The organized prayer continues emphasizing God's precepts, while asking for God's rescue.

What about you today? However your week is structured, and whatever seems to be the alphabet of this season of your life, you can request God to rescue you from any harm. Worry does not promise safety. Fear cannot assure protection.

God is the One to call.

Call Him. In a time of prayer—simple and honest prayer—call Him. Maybe your prayer won't be as systematized as David's, or as poetic as David's, but it can still be as candid as his prayer.

"Save me," is the prayer you can pray today. "Rescue me," you can pray, because you belong to the God who rescues His people. "I am Your child," you can confess to your Father.

Don't just listen to David's conversation with God. Pray those words yourself. Believe God is answering.

Friday: Bad Examples

The wicked are waiting to destroy me, but I will ponder your statutes.
(PSALM 119:95)

WE BELIEVE THERE IS AN ENEMY who seeks to destroy God's people. We also believe that foe does not win in the end.

David wrote the Psalms while he faced many enemies: Opponents from other nations and rivals in his own tribe. A king who depended on him turned against him. An army might protect him or could help Saul attack him.

David chose to pray. That isn't avoidance or escape. It is wisdom. Prayer allows our hearts to be made clean and our minds precise. Prayer connects us with our true protector, God.

How can we pray more like David? The best way is just to pray. Begin by admitting to God what is going on. You feel like the adversary is out to destroy you today? Talk about that to God. You sense this is a decisive time of crisis you are facing? Talk about that to God.

Put all those needs before God. Beside those concerns, place the promises of God.

See Him as your

- Protector
- Provider
- Rescuer
- Healer
- Savior
- Director

Let God be that for you today. Yes, He is willing and waiting, wanting to offer His help in your time of need.

Those wicked folks and the enemy are bad examples. Their goal is destruction.

God will not let them bring devastation your way. He will not let you be ruined. This is THE DAY God will come your way and rescue you.

Saturday: How to Win

To all perfection I see a limit, but your commands are boundless.
(PSALM 119:96)

THE THINGS WE SCHEDULE have a time set for them to occur. Usually, a time to begin and a time to end. We set our calendars and we plan our agendas. We write our lists and finalize our outlines.

But God's commands have no end. His perfection has no borders. His commands, David wrote, are boundless.

That is what we need to hear when we sometimes feel like we are losing—financially, relationally, spiritually, physically. That is what we need to believe each day as we hope to find ways to win.

We have seen the bad examples about winning in this game of life. We have heard those telling us what to do and how to do it—while they themselves didn't obey. Remember again the two things: good advice and bad examples. God's boundless commands come from the One who is holy and just. God never fails. God never leaves us or forsakes us. God is right all the time and always right on time.

As this week ends, remind yourself that God's commands never end. They were with us last week. They are still with us this week. They will be with us next week. God—and His words—are eternal.

If we want to win, we must stay true to the boundless commands of God.

Live Each Day So That You Will Neither Be Afraid of Tomorrow Nor Ashamed of Yesterday

Sunday: Take the Better Way

Oh, how I love your law! I meditate on it all day long.
(PSALM 119:97)

OUR GOAL FOR THIS WEEK can help us live with a new perspective. Think about giving this a try: Live each day so that you will neither be afraid of tomorrow nor ashamed of yesterday.

Too often we live with fear about the days waiting for us. Too often we live ashamed of those days we have already experienced.

That needs to change. We need to choose to take a better way to live.

You have been reading these thoughts about how to truly place our complete trust in God. You have been thinking and praying about verses from the Bible which have all reinforced the importance of looking up.

Let me ask you now, how are you doing with it? I know, through this year like any year, you have faced struggles. No one said this life would be easy. We studied passages and read stories which have shown the need to endure even in difficult times. But we have also reinforced over and over that this is not a solo journey. The Lord is with us. He is our help and our strength.

Taking the best way to travel this journey is to place our eyes on the finest route to take. That is the Word of God. Begin this week by paying your full attention to what really matters most.

Monday: Living Each Day

Your commands are always with me and make me wiser than my enemies. (PSALM 119:98)

GOD'S COMMANDS do not come just a few days of the week. They are always with us. In the Bible. On our desks. In our minds. On our phones. In our conversations. We sing and pray and teach and study and preach God's commands.

Those instructions from God give us wisdom to be living each day. We can apply His instructions of love and forgiveness as the Holy Spirit gives us strength to do so.

That is what it is like to live each day with God's direction even when bad things keep on happening. We make the right choices when others don't. We are willing to change for the better when others just seem to get bitter.

Look at today's date. You have not been on this day before and you'll never be here again. But you are here now. Refuse to waste it. Choose to embrace it. This is God's day and you are His chosen one. Live today like you want to make a difference. Live today like you want to bring God's love to this world.

I am convinced you can do it. I am certain you can do it. The reason? Because God has called you and equipped you. So, do not miss the chance to live today like what you do really matters.

Tuesday: Living Without Regrets

I have more insight than all my teachers, for I meditate on your statutes. I have more understanding than the elders, for I obey your precepts. (PSALM 119:99–100)

I KNOW WE AREN'T supposed to brag. But we just need to tell the truth. That is what the psalmist did. Look at these two positive statements:

- I have more insight than all my teachers.
- I have more understanding than the elders.

No, I am not suggesting we become cocky. That is not what was happening there. What was being stated was what it is like to live without regrets, to live each day not afraid of tomorrow and not ashamed of yesterday, to truly trust God.

Notice now the other parts of these verses—the statements give reasons the psalmist is living wisely and without regrets:

- For I meditate on Your statutes.
- For I obey Your precepts.

That is talking about taking time to study God's Word and obey it. Guided by God means living without regrets.

Look back on your life. Remember those regrets? Remember those victories? What made the difference? Following God or disobeying God.

How will you live today? With, or without, regrets?

Wednesday: Nothing to Fear

I have kept my feet from every evil path so that I might obey your word. (PSALM 119:101)

TAKING A LONG WALK gives us time to think and reflect. We can walk through a neighborhood or walk in a park. We can walk in the morning, afternoon, or evening. We can walk with family members or friends. We can walk while praying or we can walk while listening to someone tell us his or her story.

Such a walk can move us away from our normal life of hurry. It can allow us time and space to take deep breaths, to see lovely stars, to observe a gorgeous sun rising or setting.

When we walk, though, we need to be sure we are taking steps on the right roads or paths. We need to stay off the street. We can't tread right in front of vehicles. We must not place ourselves or others in dangerous areas.

It is the same in life. We have nothing to fear if we keep our feet from the evil paths. We have nothing to fear if we choose to obey God's Word.

This might be a good day for you to step outside and take a walk. Depending on the weather, of course. And depending on your safety, of course. But, whether or not you can physically let your feet take you on a long walk, you can spiritually live your life with nothing to fear. You can walk God's safe path of obeying His Word and He will keep you safe.

Thursday: A Better Time

I have not departed from your laws, for you yourself have taught me.
(PSALM 119:102)

I MUST REMIND YOU that there is no better time than now. Whatever the circumstances, whatever the news reports, whatever the weather, whatever your age, whatever last week brought you, there is no better time than now.

Why do I say that?

Because now is the time we have.

We can't go back to yesterday and do it over again. We can't jump ahead to tomorrow and do something before that day even comes. We are here now. You are right where you are right now.

What are you going to do about it? What does God want you to do about it?

God has taught you His ways. He has kept you from departing from His laws, and He has not departed from you.

Take another look at today's day. Yes, as I have said, this day only comes once. And it is here now. It won't be here again.

Take another look in the mirror. Yes, as I have said, you are the only you. Nobody else is called to do just what God has assigned for you to do the way He wants you to do it.

There is no better time than now. This is the best time. Make everything else better by doing just what God has taught you to do.

Friday: Optimist or Pessimist?

How sweet are your words to my taste, sweeter than honey to my mouth! (PSALM 119:103)

ARE YOU AN OPTIMIST or a pessimist? Do you see the good or do you dwell on the bad? Do you see a glass half empty or half full? Do you see just the problems or do you notice the potential?

God's Word is sweeter than honey, than our favorite dessert, than our preferred season of the year.

We shouldn't see the Bible through the eyes of a pessimist. Some people choose to complain about Scripture—the Old Testament laws, the wars, the prophecies, the deaths. Those people might have tendencies to find negatives in just about anything. It does them no good. And it sure does them no good to look at the Bible that way.

Make choices today to see God's Word as a lamp unto your feet and a light unto your path. Believe the Bible is directing you and protecting you. Have faith that Jesus loves you because the Bible tells you so. See the future as a powerful victory for the people of God.

I think that is a much better view than just seeing negative after negative. Stop seeing just the bad. Start seeing all the good.

God's Word is just what we need to taste and digest today, receiving the positive effects of its nourishment.

Saturday: Gaining Understanding

I gain understanding from your precepts; therefore I hate every wrong path. (PSALM 119:104)

THE PSALMIST ADMITTED two key things in Psalm 119:104. One is what he has gained. The other is what that first action has allowed him to resist.

· I gain understanding from Your precepts.

Do you realize that each day as you open this book, understanding is coming your way? Each day and each Bible verse are breathing new life to you. Instead of hastening through your day and forgetting spiritual nutrition, you are gaining strength and wisdom and guidance. God's Word is giving you understanding too many people are missing in this world. Gain that today. Read and reflect on what I am saying to you. Read and reflect on what God is saying to you.

Look at the final words in today's verse—they tell us what the writer hated:

· Therefore, I hate every wrong path.

We must not hate people. But we should hate the wrong paths many people take.

Oh, the hurt which comes to them as they take such streets in life. Gaining understanding from God's Word instructs us to avoid those pathways.

What can you do today to gain understanding from God? Will you do it? Yes, I believe you will. I believe you will avoid the wrong paths and choose the right ones. I believe you will gain an understanding that will not allow you to be ashamed of yesterday or afraid of tomorrow.

God Loves Us the Way We Are, but Cares Too Much to Leave Us That Way

Sunday: Our Loving God Will Guide Us

Your word is a lamp for my feet, a light on my path. (PSALM 119:105)

MAYBE YOU HAVE HEARD the statement before: God loves us just the way we are, but He cares too much to leave us that way.

That is our theme for this week. I want you to let that statement penetrate in your mind and your heart. Instead of dwelling on negative thoughts and untrue statements, why not focus on that phrase? Isn't it true? Isn't it just what we need?

I believe strongly that is what we need. My years of ministry have reminded me over and over about those two parts on one declaration:

- God loves us just the way we are!
- God cares too much for us to leave us just the way we are!

But what does God decide to do with those two parts? How does He love us completely while seeking to transform us? How can grace bring God's acceptance to use us just as we are, and also assure us that God is refusing to let us stay just as we are?

His Word. Through His Word we are guided and directed on where to go, what to do, and how to get there. We are informed that the instructions are only possible to obey as the Holy Spirt empowers us.

Begin this week by dwelling on God's Word. It is a lamp for your feet—each step matters. It is a light on your path—the journey is directed by God.

God loves you today. He loves you so much He won't leave you just as you are, or just where you are. Our loving God will guide you.

Monday: What Is Our Part?

I have taken an oath and confirmed it, that I will follow your righteous laws. (PSALM 119:106)

YESTERDAY WE FOCUSED on what God does. He loves us. He plans to change us—not so He can love us more but because of how much He already loves us. He hopes to guide us in this life of change and transformation.

But what role are we to play? What is our part?

We've focused often through these devotions that our part is not to take the place of God. Only God can do what God can do. We must let God do what God can do. We must receive His work into our lives.

He will lead. We are to follow.

When we are too weak to walk another step, we are to let Him hold us and carry us. And that is not just in theory. It is practical and applicable. It is for each of us in seasons like we are facing.

Giving our lives to God means we have taken an oath. We have agreed to surrender all to Him. That is our part. To trust God to do His part is really our part. And that is what we are to do today. Follow the Leader. He knows what is best.

Tuesday: God's Love During Our Suffering

I have suffered much; preserve my life, Lord, according to your word. (PSALM 119:107)

"PRESERVE MY LIFE," the psalmist prayed. "According to Your Word," he voiced the prayer as the method he believed God could answer him. "I have suffered much," the poet confessed.

Take time to reflect on how each portion of this prayer is healthy in our own conversations with God. And remember: God loves us, but He loves us too much to leave us as we are. He loves us and is changing us to become more like Him.

As we suffer, God loves us. As we hurt, God loves us. As we wait, God loves us. As we doubt, God loves us. Look at how all three parts of this confession reinforce such love to us:

- I have suffered much.
- Preserve my life, Lord.
- According to Your Word.

How have you suffered this year? How have you suffered the last few years? What situations would you never want to endure again? Well, I am sad for what you've experienced. I am sorry you have suffered much. Our suffering has been painful. It hasn't been easy. The rocky roads have been lengthy, and the sharp mountains have been lofty.

But, though we have—like the psalmist—suffered much, we know we must call out to God. Pray today along with this verse, "Preserve my life, Lord." It is okay to pray such a prayer. Though desperate, plead to God. Though frantic, state your request to Him.

And, choose to believe that according to His promises, God will save you. He will not leave you alone in the valley. Trust Him even when you are falling apart.

Wednesday: Praising God through Our Words

Accept, Lord, the willing praise of my mouth, and teach me your laws. (PSALM 119:108)

ASK GOD TO TEACH YOU His laws. Ask God to accept the praise of your mouth.

Oh, what a difference it would make if we did those actions more often. If we agreed to praise God through our words, our whole world would feel like a different place. It might take a while. It might not begin changing just how we want it to. But trust me on this. Praise the Lord and watch how so much shifts from darkness to light, from hate to love, from defeat to victory.

Praise God through actions and attitudes, yes. But we are reminded in today's verse to praise God with our mouths.

State words of thanksgiving to God today. This very day. Do not wait. Do not sit back until everything becomes better. Do not wait to bless God until you can see the way He's blessing you. Begin. At this very moment, begin to praise God.

Here are a few ways:

- Make a list of what you are grateful for today.
- Sing songs of praise to God.
- Let your prayer time be a praise time.
- Tell a testimony which gives all the glory to God.

Look up. Praise God through your words. See what those words do as you believe them and state them. When you tell God why you love Him so much, you might be in a better place to let God change you even more.

Thursday: Refusing to Stray Away

Though I constantly take my life in my hands, I will not forget your law. The wicked have set a snare for me, but I have not strayed from your precepts. (PSALM 119:109–110)

TODAY'S TWO VERSES expose candid prayers to God. Notice these points from verse 109:

- Though I constantly take my life in my hands,
- I'll not forget Your law.

Notice these points from verse 110:

- The wicked have set a snare for me,
- But I have not strayed from Your precepts.

Can you perceive the stress in this prayer? Can you see the battle? Even though we face an enemy who seeks to steal, kill, and destroy us (John 10:10), we can refuse to drift away from God. Here is how: we must call out to Him.

These devotions have encouraged you to pray, to pray honestly, to pray often, and to pray believing God will answer your prayers better than you can ask Him to or hope that He will (Ephesians 3:20).

So, though you might have times when you feel like life isn't worth living, and though you have times when the enemy seems to be setting a snare for you, you can choose to remember God's truth and refuse to stray from it. You refuse to take any other way. God's way is truly the only way. His way brings us to Him. His way keeps us in line with Him.

Other paths bring harm and danger—even eternal danger. Refuse to stray. Choose to stay.

Friday: Our Heritage and Our Joy

Your statutes are my heritage forever; they are the joy of my heart.
(PSALM 119:111)

IN PSALM 119:111 THE WRITER PRAYS a wonderful confession. His words state what should be our heritage and our joy. They were his. They should be ours, also.

God's statutes—His laws, instructions, guidance, direction, warnings, commands, promises—are so vital that the psalmist explains them as:

- My heritage forever.
- The joy of my heart.

When we think of a heritage we can think of things we want said about us at our funerals. Or what people might say when they are gossiping about us behind our backs. Or what might be placed in our bios. Or what might be the main points if a story was written about our lives. We crave leaving a lasting heritage where we are remembered in positive ways. We long to pass along to others optimistic assertions of the goodness of God. And we want that heritage, those memories, that biography to last forever. We hope it has eternal, heavenly, godly value.

Now look at the next line. Not just a heritage. We want God's truth to be the joy of our hearts. Oh, how that should change what we do. It should change all we do. Joy coming into our lives through God rather than the things of this world—now that is what we must pursue.

Are you going after those goals today? Are you being sure that your loving God is changing you so that your heritage and your joy are based on His guidance?

Saturday: My Heart Is Set

My heart is set on keeping your decrees to the very end.
(PSALM 119:112)

CHANGE ISN'T ALWAYS FUN or easy. It sometimes comes in hard ways and at hard times.

That is when our hearts are to stay set on God and His ways. Those aren't times to waver; those are times to remain. Those aren't days to wonder; those are days to persist. Those aren't seasons to shift our focus; those are seasons to stay right on course.

Join in this confession today:

- My heart
- is set
- on keeping
- Your decrees
- to the very end.

Let that be a confession you make. Let that be a testimony you live. Let that be a description of your life purpose.

Even when changes come, one thing can persist just as it is. A heart can stay set on keeping God's decrees to the very end. Not changing along with moods or money. Not changing along with news or seasons. A heart can be set—refusing to shift from the path of righteousness.

Pray this prayer from Psalm 119:112. This verse, like all of God's Word, wasn't just for the original audience. This verse is for you. It is for you right now.

Live today adaptable where you need to be but set with a heart toward God.

Smiles and Frowns Cost Nothing, but the Difference in Effects Is Enormous

Sunday: Choosing to Do What Is Right

I have done what is righteous and just; do not leave me to my oppressors. (PSALM 119:121)

MANY OF YOU HAVE SEEN a smile on my face. Yes, I love to smile. Frowns don't look pretty, and they don't make us feel any better.

Smiles bring a difference in effects that are enormous. Smiles yield more smiles. Smiles help another person feel like they are welcomed by you. Make some eye contact and show a genuine smile, the person seeing you might start feeling better—right when they notice you.

Why don't we smile more often?

Why don't we do something like that to help others more often?

No, we aren't promoting a fake grin. No, we aren't encouraging deception. No, we aren't asking you to pretend all is well when it isn't. We've said throughout this book many ways to deal with our many questions and hurts. What we are saying here is this: choosing to do what is right just might be smiling today.

It might not mean stating many words, though sometimes it will.

It might not mean singing a beautiful song, though sometimes it will.

Choosing to do what is right today could be you letting the love of God shine through your smile to help someone else feel a little better. Today, that might be just the right thing to do.

Monday: Looking for God's Promises

Ensure your servant's well-being; do not let the arrogant oppress me. My eyes fail, looking for your salvation, looking for your righteous promise. (PSALM 119:122–123)

"WELL," YOU MIGHT SAY. "I don't have anything to smile about today." Can I offer one suggestion? I encourage you to smile as you look at these promises of God.

For no matter how many promises God has made, they are "Yes" in Christ. And so through him the "Amen" is spoken by us to the glory of God (2 CORINTHIANS 1:20).

Now I am about to go the way of all the earth. You know with all your heart and soul that not one of all the good promises the Lord your God gave you has failed. Every promise has been fulfilled; not one has failed (JOSHUA 23:14).

Now, Lord, the God of Israel, keep for your servant David my father the promises you made to him when you said, "You shall never fail to have a successor to sit before me on the throne of Israel, if only your descendants are careful in all they do to walk before me according to my law, as you have done" (2 CHRONICLES 6:16).

For I tell you that Christ has become a servant of the Jews on behalf of God's truth, so that the promises made to the patriarchs might be confirmed (ROMANS 15:8).

Look again and again at God's promises. Believe them today.

Tuesday: Learning from God's Loving Direction

Deal with your servant according to your love and teach me your decrees. (PSALM 119:124)

Those promises we included yesterday should encourage you. Learning from God's loving direction can bring us smiles. Not only on our faces. But also deep smiles in our hearts.

Continue reading God's Word as He speaks to you today:

For no matter how many promises God has made, they are "Yes" in Christ. And so through him the "Amen" is spoken by us to the glory of God (2 CORINTHIANS 1:20).

Therefore, since we have these promises, dear friends, let us purify ourselves from everything that contaminates body and spirit, perfecting holiness out of reverence for God (2 CORINTHIANS 7:1).

Is the law, therefore, opposed to the promises of God? Absolutely not! For if a law had been given that could impart life, then righteousness would certainly have come by the law (GALATIANS 3:21).

Do you hear what He is saying to you? Will you allow His words to bring direction in your life? His promises are real. They are yes and amen! They are for you to believe and receive.

He loves us to guide us where He knows is best for us to go. His direction is protection. His direction is provision. His direction should inspire us to choose a time of celebration.

Wednesday: Seeking Understanding

I am your servant; give me discernment that I may understand your statutes. (PSALM 119:125)

Maybe you are trying to do all I am suggesting but you find it hard. As you seek and pursue better understanding of God's plan for your life, I ask you again to read, reflect, study, pray, and meditate on verses from the Bible.

These are words from God. These are words for you.

It is because of him that you are in Christ Jesus, who has become for us wisdom from God—that is, our righteousness, holiness and redemption (1 CORINTHIANS 1:30).

Let the message of Christ dwell among you richly as you teach and admonish one another with all wisdom through psalms, hymns, and songs from the Spirit, singing to God with gratitude in your hearts (COLOSSIANS 3:16).

Let us draw near to God with a sincere heart and with the full assurance that faith brings, having our hearts sprinkled to cleanse us from a guilty conscience and having our bodies washed with pure water (HEBREWS 10:22).

Read those three passages of Scripture. Seek understanding through God's Word. His words are strong, powerful, transformational, assuring, daring, confirming, comforting, cleansing, directing, correcting. His words are real, firm, gentle, close. His words are ancient and modern. His words are for us today. Seek understanding through them. State them. Pray them. Believe them. Receive them.

You are in Christ Jesus. He has become for us the wisdom from God. See it—its righteousness, holiness, and redemption. His understanding becomes yours.

Thursday: Time for God to Act

It is time for you to act, Lord; your law is being broken.
(PSALM 119:126)

REFLECT AGAIN on two of the verses from yesterday:

Let the message of Christ dwell among you richly as you teach and admonish one another with all wisdom through psalms, hymns, and songs from the Spirit, singing to God with gratitude in your hearts
(COLOSSIANS 3:16).

Let us draw near to God with a sincere heart and with the full assurance that faith brings, having our hearts sprinkled to cleanse us from a guilty conscience and having our bodies washed with pure water
(HEBREWS 10:22).

Today's main verse says it is time for God to act. Well, God often acts in ways that empower us to let His actions come through us. When that happens, the world around us is changed. God's will is being done.

Paul wrote in that passage from Colossians that followers of Jesus should let the message of Christ dwell in them richly as they teach and admonish others with all wisdom. They were to do that through psalms, hymns, and songs from the Spirit—singing to God with gratitude in their hearts. My friends, if we choose to do that today, God will act! Singing with gratefulness changes the climate around us. Shouting for joy shifts things around us. It prepares us for the powerful presence of God.

In that verse from Hebrews 10 we are instructed to draw near to God with a sincere heart. Full assurance. Hearts sprinkled. Cleansed from guilt. Bodies washed clean in pure water. Wow. See what can happen when we let God act? We are changed. Let His message dwell in us. Let us draw near to Him. Let this be the time for God to act.

Friday: More Than Gold

Because I love your commands more than gold, more than pure gold. (PSALM 119:127)

I WANT YOU TO REFLECT on these four words:

"I loved Your commands."

The psalmist confessed that powerful claim. So, now, let me ask us: "Do we love the commands of God?"

His commands are right and just. They bring the truth we desperately need. Our responses often miss the points God is making. We fail to see the value of His decrees.

We must change that. It begins by noticing again what we have focused on so often through these pages. It all comes back to this one key word: TRUST.

God's Word is:

T—truthful
R—right
U—uplifting
S—stable
T—transformational

Isn't that, as the psalmist wrote, better than gold, than pure gold? I say it is. It is better than material possessions. Loving God's commands allows us to trust Him. His ways. His thoughts. His guidance.

Trust God today. Trust God's Word today. More than your money or your inheritance or your talent or your goals or your gifts or your investments, trust God. His commands can keep us on that path we are created to take. His map points us in proper places. His hands hold us to take us there. Trust Him.

Saturday: What to Consider

And because I consider all your precepts right, I hate every wrong path. (PSALM 119:128)

THE PSALMIST DECIDED to consider all the ways of God correct.

Remembering taking those tests in school? There were times you thought you had the answer right, but the teacher told you it was wrong. You didn't feel too good. You might have argued your case—and lost. That teacher had to show you not just that the answer was wrong but why it was wrong.

Good teachers help students not only know what is right and wrong, but also how to decide what is right in the future.

God is that kind of teacher. He reveals truth, then He also helps us discern truth. He states facts, then provides us gifts of wisdom to detect correctness.

He also empowers us to obey Him. We might be weak, but He makes us strong. We might have failed in the past, but He's giving us a new chance today.

Please take that chance. This is your time to consider the ways of God as the right ways, the best ways, the holy ways.

No other road is right, but His road.

No other god is a true god, but our God from the Bible.

No other leader can guide you like our true God can. He instructs you, then He empowers you. Wrong paths are not yours to take today, my friend. Just the right roads. Led by God, consider His ways and walk therein.

The Christian Is Not Ruined by Living in the World, but by the World Living in Them

Sunday: Choosing God's Statutes Rather Than This World

Your statutes are wonderful; therefore I obey them. (PSALM 119:129)

ON THE NIGHT BEFORE His crucifixion, Jesus prayed for His disciples. That includes you and me.

Jesus did not ask for us to be taken out of the world, but to be protected from the evil one (John 17:15).

Living in an ungodly world, we are in need of protection and direction. As we walk the straight and narrow path marked out by Jesus, voices are calling to us from left and right:

- The voice of greed says, "You have to buy this now; just put it on the card."
- The voice of anger says, "What she said is unforgivable. You can't let her get away with it."
- The voice of lust says, "You can give in just this once, no one will know."
- The voice of envy says, "Why does he get all the breaks? It isn't fair."
- The voice of pride says, "No one appreciates all your work and sacrifice. Why go on?"

How can we keep from being led astray by seductive voices? We can't shut their mouths, and we can't shut our ears.

What we can do, is to tune our ears to the voice of God. The statutes of the Lord are given to protect us, to keep us on course. If we focus on obedience to the Word of God, we won't stumble or step off the path.

Keep your focus today.

Monday: Longing for God's Commands

The unfolding of your words gives light; it gives understanding to the simple. I open my mouth and pant, longing for your commands. (Psalm 119:130–131)

HAVE YOU EVER BEEN RELAXING at home alone in the evening when suddenly the power went out in the neighborhood? No house lights, no street lights. Only darkness.

Suddenly you're not relaxed anymore. What to do? Wait for the power to come back on? As the minutes tick by, anxiety builds. The room that was so familiar is not so comfortable in the dark. You have to find light. A flashlight, maybe some matches. Now where did you put your cell phone?

You can't sit still any longer. You get up and feel your way in search of light. You strain your eyes to make out the furniture, but the shadowy shapes look strange. You can't get your bearings. You're getting desperate. You need light!

This world is cloaked in spiritual and moral darkness. Men and women stumble around in the dark, crashing into one another, tripping over the realities they can't see. They harm each other and themselves, because they can't see where they are or where they're going.

The Word of God offers light for individuals to find their way and for societies to function successfully. Sadly, many think God's commands are optional or outmoded, and have turned their backs on the light source they so desperately need.

Lord, we long for Your light! Let Your light shine in the darkness!

Tuesday: Seeking God's Mercy

Turn to me and have mercy on me, as you always do to those who love your name. (PSALM 119:132)

IF YOU SPEND ANY TIME on social media, you know how a seemingly harmless post can draw hateful comments. Express an opinion of any kind, and people you don't even know will tell you why you're wrong, and ridicule you for even daring to think that way.

You can be attacked for your race, your political affiliation, your diet, your religion, your musical tastes, and even your grammar. Say the wrong thing and you may find yourself "cancelled."

But we can't blame Twitter and Facebook. They only provide a platform for people to express what's in their hearts. The world is a merciless place.

Thankfully, we know where to turn to find mercy. There is an endless supply of mercy flowing from the throne of God and poured upon His people. Do you realize how dependent you are upon the mercy of God?

- Because of God's mercy you woke up this morning.
- Because of God's mercy you haven't perished in your sins.
- Because of God's mercy the devil hasn't destroyed your life.
- Because of God's mercy you have hope for the future, no matter what happened in your past.

Two things to always remember about the mercy of God:

1. His mercy is new every morning (Lamentations 3:23). Why? Because you need His mercy every day.

2. His mercy endures forever (Psalm 107:1). Why? Because there will never come a time when you don't need His mercy.

Thank God for His mercy!

Wednesday: God's Guidance in Our Journey

Direct my footsteps according to your word; let no sin rule over me. (PSALM 119:133)

WHAT IF THE HIGHWAY DEPARTMENT decided to take down all the road signs regulating traffic and indicating directions? What if drivers could set their own speed limits and make up their own rules of the road? The result would be chaos, with people smashing into each other and ending up in places they never wanted to go.

That sounds a lot like society today. People want to make up their own rules for living. It's no longer a matter of right and wrong, but only of deciding what's "right for me." So they barrel down the highway of life with no clear idea of where they are or where they're going.

But all roads don't lead to the same destination. You may be looking for a place of happiness and peace, but you'll never find your way there on your own.

It isn't enough to just follow your heart. How does your heart know the way?

You can't just follow your dreams. The devil can turn your dream into a nightmare.

You'd better not try following the crowd. They're as lost as you are.

In the end, there are only two ways to go: God's way or some other way. In His Word, God has given us signposts, warning lights and guardrails to keep us on track. Pay attention to God's Word, and you won't go wrong.

Remember, the Bible is your GPS—God's Positioning System!

Thursday: Obeying God's Precepts

Redeem me from human oppression, that I may obey your precepts. (PSALM 119:134)

A LOT OF PEOPLE have a negative image of religion as a system of rules and regulations that restrict our freedom, and keep us from enjoying life. If God insists that we live by His precepts, then we'd better obey if we know what's good for us. But we don't have to like it.

That's not the way the ancient Hebrews thought about it. They considered the laws God gave Moses on Mount Sinai to be a precious gift. Obedience to God's laws was a sign that they were God's chosen people, privileged to be in covenant relationship with Jehovah.

The divine precepts revealed in God's Word are not intended to limit our freedom, but to enable us to experience maximum freedom. God created us, and He knows what's best for us. In His Word, He shows us how to live so as to fulfill our purpose and potential. Consider:

- Only the disciplined athlete who follows the training regimen is able to achieve greatness.
- Only the disciplined musician who masters the scales is able to play beautiful music.
- Only the disciplined farmer who sows and waters and cultivates at the right time is able to reap a harvest.

If we ignore the precepts of God's Word, we become less free, not more. We end up in bondage to sin, and lose the ability to do what is right.

God's precepts are a sign of His love for us. In obeying them, we find true freedom.

Friday: God's Shining Face

Make your face shine on your servant and teach me your decrees. (Psalm 119:135)

A BABY LEARNS EARLY on to recognize the faces of his mother and father. A baby's first smile comes in response to his parents' smiles. Nothing stops a baby's cries and sparks more joy than the sight of Mommy's or Daddy's face.

Children never outgrow the need for their parents' approval. The toddler who brings a crude crayon drawing to her mother is happy to see a beaming smile. The Little League boy who hits a home run looks to the stands to see the joyful reaction on his father's face.

What we see in these human relationships is a reflection of the deep-seated desire in our hearts to know that God's shining face is turned our way, and smiling upon us.

When Moses came down from Mount Sinai after receiving the Ten Commandments from God, the people of Israel were surprised and frightened to see that his face was shining with the glory of the Lord (Exodus 34:29–30).

When Jesus went up on the mountain with Peter, James and John, and was transfigured before them, His face shone like the sun in brightness and glory (Matthew 17:2).

We were created not just with a desire to behold God's shining face, but with a capacity to shine ourselves in reflection of His glory (2 Corinthians 3:18).

The more time you spend in God's presence seeking His face, the more His glory will be reflected in your life.

Saturday: A Stream of Tears

Streams of tears flow from my eyes, for your law is not obeyed. (PSALM 119:136)

PEOPLE SHED TEARS for all sorts of reasons.

Babies cry when they're hungry, uncomfortable, or frightened.

Children cry when they're hurt, made fun of, or when they don't get their way.

Adults may cry over a broken heart or a joyous reunion. Some will cry over a sad movie, though few men will admit it.

We could say that tears don't really originate in the eye, but flow from a hidden source deep within the heart. God created us with the capacity to shed tears as an expression and release of emotion.

The psalmist sheds tears because God's laws are broken. And no wonder. Breaking God's laws brings immeasurable pain and suffering into the world:

- Broken families.
- Abandoned children.
- Assaulted and trafficked women.
- Lives destroyed by crime, terrorism, and war.

We were created in God's image. Did He give us the capacity to cry so we would know how He feels about sin and its devastating effects?

Jesus wept at the grave of Lazarus, face to face with the tragedy of death and the grief it causes. Jesus was called "a man of sorrows, and acquainted with grief" (Isaiah 53:3).

Christians are not stoics, hiding their emotions and pretending all is well. It's right and proper to shed tears of sadness in this sin-sick world.

But never forget: there will come a day when God will wipe away every tear from our eyes, and the time for crying will be gone forever (Revelation 21:4).

Hallelujah!

A Friend Is One Who Walks in When the Rest Walk Out

Sunday: The Lord Can Be Trusted

You are righteous, Lord, and your laws are right. The statutes you have laid down are righteous; they are fully trustworthy.
(PSALM 119:137–138)

DURING ELECTION SEASON, presidential candidates are all about making promises to voters. One promises to cut taxes, another promises to increase benefits. One promises to strengthen our defenses, another promises to bring our troops home. All promise to make our lives better than they are now. But reality sets in shortly after Inauguration Day, and most promises go unfulfilled.

Of course, it's not just politicians. In a world where almost everyone is selling a product or pushing an agenda, hucksters and swindlers abound. It's easy to get taken if you put your trust in the wrong place.

But it's one thing to be let down by strangers, and something else altogether to be let down by a spouse or a close friend. The friend who fails to keep his word, the husband or wife who fails to keep their vows—these personal betrayals cut deep and leave lasting scars.

Thankfully, there is One who will never let us down. Our God never changes, and His Word endures forever.

People may lie to your face or stab you in the back, but God speaks only truth and makes good on everything He says.

Even the preacher may let you down, but the God he preaches about never will.

Take your stand on the Word of God. It's a firm foundation.

Put your trust in the Lord today. He will hold you up when everyone else lets you down.

Monday: Some Will Walk Away

My zeal wears me out, for my enemies ignore your words.
(Psalm 119:139)

DEFENDERS OF CHRISTIANITY have developed philosophical arguments for the existence of God, scientific arguments for God's design in creation, and historical arguments for the resurrection of Christ. Yet no matter how powerful and persuasive these arguments are, many people simply reject them.

Zealous Christians have developed evangelistic tracts, songs, skits, books and films to present the gospel. There are witnessing programs that train believers in how to share the gospel in a winsome way, using Scripture along with their testimonies. Yet even with all these opportunities to hear and receive the good news, some just walk away.

It is frustrating to pour our hearts out in prayer for friends and loved ones, and do our utmost to persuade them to repent and believe, but still fail in our quest to bring them to Christ. It is heartbreaking to watch them turn away from God, and we may wonder: Could we have done more?

Consider that Judas spent over three years with Jesus, and had a front-row seat to see His miracles. He heard the truth from the mouth of the Lord. Yet in the end, he chose to go his own way rather than enter the Kingdom.

Let us do all we can to win people to Christ, while remembering that in the end, they must choose for themselves.

As for us, our watchword remains: "Though none go with me, still I will follow Jesus."

Tuesday: The God of Promises

Your promises have been thoroughly tested, and your servant loves them. (PSALM 119:140)

GOD PROMISED TO GIVE ABRAHAM a son through whom his descendants would number more than the sands of the seashore. But years passed, and nothing happened. Abraham tried to produce an heir in his own strength and in his own way, and succeeded only in making trouble for himself and his family. It was a full 25 years after the promise was made that Isaac was born, as God showed His power to fulfill the promise.

God sent Moses to Egypt in His Name to lead His people out of bondage into a land that He promised to give them. Yet Moses battled with Pharaoh over the course of 10 plagues and battled with the stubborn Israelites over a period of 40 years, without making it into the promised land. But God's promise was fulfilled in the next generation, as Joshua led the people into Canaan.

God spoke through the Old Testament prophets again and again over hundreds of years, promising to send a Messiah to save His people and set up an eternal Kingdom. When Christ came, His people did not recognize or receive Him, and crucified their Lord and Savior. Yet in spite of the opposition of Satan and the unbelief of His people, God's promise was fulfilled for them, and for us.

Does it look like God's promises are failing in your life? Don't give in to doubt and despair. The God of promises never fails.

Wednesday: God Holds Us Even When We Feel Down

Though I am lowly and despised, I do not forget your precepts. (PSALM 119:141)

HEROES OF THE FAITH don't always feel like heroes.

Take Elijah. What a man of courage! He faced 450 prophets of Baal in a showdown, and beat them by calling down fire from heaven!

Elijah was a conquering hero, boldest and baddest in the land. Except the very next day, a threatening word from Jezebel sent him running for his life. He ended up hiding in a cave, holding a pity party. He was ready to give up on everything, even life itself.

Elijah went from the top of the world to the pit of despair and wallowed there for 40 days. But God brought him out! Elijah may have given up on himself, but God didn't give up on him. He showed Elijah that He was still in control, and still had plans to use him. He gave Elijah a new assignment, and sent him back into the fray.

James tells us that Elijah was a man with a nature like ours (James 5:17). That means we can expect to have the same kind of ups and downs. We're never as strong as we think we are, and we need God's grace to accomplish anything for Him. And when we're down, things are never as bleak as we think they are.

God meets us where we are and lifts us up again. He is faithful!

Thursday: God Never Walks Out

Your righteousness is everlasting and your law is true.
(PSALM 119:142)

REMEMBER JESUS' PARABLE of the prodigal son (Luke 15:11–32)?

The younger son demanded his inheritance, and left home to see the world. With his pockets full of cash, he soon attracted a crowd of friends to help him spend it. With no thought for the future, they partied every day, until his pockets were empty. And when the cash was gone, so were his "friends."

The young man was left on his own. The only job he could find was feeding pigs, a disgraceful and disgusting task for a Jewish boy. His wages were so low he couldn't buy enough food to fill his belly. When he found his mouth watering for the pig slop, he knew he'd reached rock bottom.

Only one thing to do. Go home and face the music. He had squandered his inheritance and shamed his father. But better to "eat crow" than to stay here and starve. Maybe his father would at least give him a job as a hired hand on the farm.

He swallowed his pride, gathered his courage, and headed home. What would he find? A closed door? No, open arms! He was welcomed, celebrated, and restored to the family.

God is a faithful Father to His children. His love is a gushing fountain that can't be plugged by our foolishness and failures.

God will love us all the way home.

Friday: God's Words Are Our Delight

Trouble and distress have come upon me, but your commands give me delight. (PSALM 119:143)

THE SOUND OF A FAMILIAR VOICE can bring back distinct memories and stir up strong emotions.

For some children, a mother's voice sounds soothing and comforting, while for others it sounds critical and grating. For some children, a father's voice communicates strength and safety, while for others it provokes fear and anger. Some voices are attractive, and others are repellent, depending on our past experiences.

What about the voice of God? How does that sound to you?

When the Lord came down to Mount Sinai to give His laws to Israel, His visit was accompanied by smoke, thunder and lightning. The people trembled with fear and did not dare to approach the mountain. They begged Moses to listen to God and deliver His words to them, but they were terrified of hearing the voice of God for themselves.

Do you imagine God's voice as stern and scolding, condemning your every sin and threatening judgment?

Listen to the voice of Jesus: "Come to me, all who labor and are heavy laden, and I will give you rest ... I am gentle and lowly in heart, and you will find rest for your souls" (Matthew 11:28–29).

Today God has a personal message for you. It isn't a message of rejection, but a message of welcome. Don't run *from* Him, run *to* Him.

Saturday: God Gives Us Understanding

Your statutes are always righteous; give me understanding that I may live. (PSALM 119:144)

WITH SMART PHONES, Google and Wikipedia, the answer to most of our questions seems to be only a few clicks away.

- What is the capital of Liberia? (*Monrovia*)
- Who won the US presidential election of 1856? (*James Buchanan*)
- How far away is Jupiter? (*365 million miles at its closest point to earth*)

But these questions are trivial compared to the really important questions of life:

- Why am I here?
- What makes life worth living?
- What is God like?
- How can I be saved?
- What happens after I die?

Sadly, many people never learn the answers because they don't even ask the questions. Maybe they think there are no answers, or maybe they don't know who to ask. Often it seems they are satisfied with not knowing, as long as they can keep themselves distracted and entertained.

How can we find the answers to the questions that really matter?

Thank God, He has not left us in the dark. The Bible presents a panorama of God's plan for the world, and for our lives. God is producing a Grand Cosmic Drama, with phases of Creation, Fall, Redemption and Consummation. God's Word reveals the plan and helps us to discover our place in it. Jesus is the hero of the story, but each of us has a role to play.

Including you.

People Seldom Appreciate Their Blessings until They Are Afraid of Losing Them

Sunday: Calling on the God Who Answers Us

I call with all my heart; answer me, Lord, and I will obey your decrees. I call out to you; save me and I will keep your statutes. (PSALM 119:145–146)

IN THE SHOWDOWN between the prophet Elijah and the 450 prophets of Baal, the issue was simple: Whose God will answer?

Starting in the morning, the prophets of Baal spent hours crying out to their God, with no response. Elijah began to mock them: "Shout louder! Maybe he's on a trip, or maybe he's asleep, or maybe he took a bathroom break!" The false prophets went wild, screaming and dancing around the altar, and cutting themselves until the blood gushed out. But nothing happened.

It's foolish to believe that a lifeless idol can answer your prayers. But what about the true and living God? Is it also foolish to believe that He would pay attention to us and our needs?

The psalmist asks a legitimate question: "When I look at your heavens, the work of your fingers, the moon and the stars, which you have set in place, what is man that you are mindful of him, and the son of man that you care for him?" (Psalm 8:3–4).

What right do we have to call upon the Lord? What reason do we have to expect the God of the universe to answer our prayers?

Simply because He invites us to call upon Him: "Call upon me in the day of trouble; I will deliver you, and you shall glorify me" (Psalm 50:15).

Call upon the Lord with confidence. He is listening!

Monday: Thankful for Our Hope in God's Word

I rise before dawn and cry for help; I have put my hope in your word. (PSALM 119:147)

AS THE SAYING GOES, "Where there's life, there's hope." But where there's no hope, there's no life.

Hope is essential for human existence. In order to endure and overcome the troubles of today, we need a solid, secure hope for tomorrow. Where can we find such hope?

Many put their hope in wealth, but Jesus warned that this is foolhardy. Even if we guard against moth and rust, we remain vulnerable to inflation, stock market crashes, and economic depression. No amount of money can guarantee immunity from calamity or misfortune.

Some put their hope in politics, but it's clear that no candidate or party is capable of solving the problems of society. Sin is too deeply rooted to be eliminated by a social program. Government can barely deliver the mail; it sure can't deliver us from sin!

Some put their hope in science and technology, but every new discovery or invention can be used for evil purposes as well as good.

Some hope in themselves, but this is a dead end. None of us is wise enough, strong enough, courageous enough, or good enough to cope with the tribulations of life and the temptations of the devil.

There is only one foundation strong and stable enough to sustain our hopes: the unchanging, everlasting, ever-living, Word of God. God cannot lie, and His Word cannot fail. Those who put their hope in God's Word can look forward to the future with unshakeable confidence.

Tuesday: Standing on the Promises of God

My eyes stay open through the watches of the night, that I may meditate on your promises. (PSALM 119:148)

MARRIAGE VOWS are the most solemn promises a man and woman can make. By God's grace, a new union is formed, and the two become one. There is a mutual commitment to love, honor, and cherish, for as long as both shall live.

We rightly celebrate couples when their marriages reach milestones of thirty, forty, fifty years, and even longer. Tragically, we all know couples whose marriages have collapsed, and what God has put together has somehow been torn asunder.

How is this possible? How is it that these sacred promises are broken?

The devil makes it his business to destroy marriages. As a symbol of Christ and the Church, every marriage becomes a target for Satan's attacks. He fires arrows of temptation and discord at husband and wife, and some strike exposed areas of weakness or sin. Promises are broken, and hearts are shattered.

Thankfully, divine promises are not the same as human promises.

There is no accusation Satan can bring against you to weaken God's commitment to you.

"Who shall bring any charge against God's elect? Christ Jesus is the one who died—more than that, who was raised—who is at the right hand of God, who indeed is interceding for us" (ROMANS 8:33–34).

Listen to the words of Jesus: "I will never leave you nor forsake you" (Hebrews 13:5).

When you stand on the promises of God, you will stand firm.

Wednesday: God Will Preserve His People

Hear my voice in accordance with your love; preserve my life, Lord, according to your laws. (PSALM 119:149)

THE WORLD THAT GOD made doesn't keep running on its own. It is God's preserving power that keeps stars in their courses and atomic particles bound together. God keeps the sun shining, the wind blowing, and the waters churning. If God were to let up for an instant, everything would dissolve into chaos.

In the same way, God continually preserves our individual lives. He enables our lungs to breathe the air and process the oxygen, and then causes the blood to carry it throughout our body. He enables us to eat and digest our food, and causes it to nourish and strengthen us. God keeps us alive every day.

Not only our physical lives, but our spiritual lives are also sustained by God. Some people have the idea that we are saved through a miraculous new birth, and then complete the journey to heaven on our own steam. But the truth is that we are just as dependent upon the power of God for living the Christian life as for being born again. It is the preserving power of God that carries us through day by day.

Just as God sustains your body through material bread, He sustains your spirit through the bread of His Word.

Make sure your diet meets the daily requirement for spiritual health.

Thursday: Those Who Miss the Blessings of God

Those who devise wicked schemes are near, but they are far from your law. (PSALM 119:150)

ESAU WAS THE FIRSTBORN SON of Isaac, just ahead of his brother Jacob. The boys were born into a family that God had chosen to carry His blessing for generations to come.

Their grandfather Abraham provided for them an unforgettable example of faith, having left his homeland and stepped into the unknown in obedience to the call of God. While by no means perfect, Abraham lived as the friend of God, and his faith was credited to him as righteousness.

Their father Isaac was born a miracle child, a testimony to the power and promise of God. Their mother Rebekah was selected to marry Isaac through God's specific guidance. Esau should have been eager to carry this precious legacy of faith and blessing into the next generation.

Yet we read that Esau despised his birthright and was willing to sell it to his brother for a bowl of stew. Esau was more concerned about hunting wild game than seeking God's will for his life. He was more concerned about filling his belly than filling his mind with knowledge of God. As a result, he missed the destiny and blessing that could have been his.

America has been blessed with a rich history of religious freedom. The Bible is widely available in all formats of media, is preached from thousands of pulpits, and is broadcast around the clock. Yet many gorge themselves on entertainment, while giving scant time to the Word of God.

Don't be one of them.

Friday: Noticing the God Who Is Near

Yet you are near, Lord, and all your commands are true.
(Psalm 119:151)

GOD HAD PROMISED A SON to Abraham and Sarah, but after ten years they got tired of waiting. They arranged for Abraham to father a child by Hagar, Sarah's servant. Was God pleased by their proactive measures? Not so much.

Whenever we take matters into our own hands instead of waiting on the Lord, bad things happen. So it was in this case. Once Hagar got pregnant, she started looking down her nose at Sarah. Sarah lost her temper, and treated Hagar so roughly that she ran away.

That's when God stepped in. The angel of the Lord visited Hagar as she was weeping alone in the wilderness. God revealed that He had plans for Hagar's son, who would have a multitude of descendants. She was to name him Ishmael, meaning "God hears."

Hagar was an Egyptian and grew up in the middle of pagan idolatry. As a servant of Sarah, she had no doubt heard about this new God who had called Abraham to follow Him into a new land, blessed him abundantly, and made amazing promises about his future. But now, for the first time, deserted and alone, she realized that this God saw her, heard her, and cared for her and her son.

Hagar discovered that this God was not distant and preoccupied with others' lives, but was very near to her in her distress. From now on her life would have plenty of difficulties, but she would never have to face them alone.

Do you realize that God is near to you right where you are?

Saturday: God's Promises Last Forever

Long ago I learned from your statutes that you established them to last forever. (PSALM 119:152)

WHEN YOU BUY FOODS in the supermarket, it's always a good idea to check the expiration date. If you wait too long to eat them, they won't taste so good, and they might even make you sick. They are only good for a certain period of time.

When you buy a new car, new appliances, or new electronic devices, they come with a guarantee. If something goes wrong, you can get them repaired at little or no cost. However, you need to check the length of the guarantee. Once the guarantee expires, you're on your own. (And things usually start to break down just after the guarantee expires.)

It seems that everything in this life is only temporary. Things wear out, break down, and fall apart. This is even true of our bodies. Nothing lasts forever.

Or does it? What about the promises of God? Do they come with an expiration date?

The promises of God are based upon three things:

1) His plans for us.

"The counsel of the LORD stands forever, the plans of his heart to all generations" (PSALM 33:11).

2) His love for us.

"I have loved you with an everlasting love; therefore I have continued my faithfulness to you" (JEREMIAH 31:3).

3) His commitment to us.

"I will never leave you nor forsake you" (HEBREWS 13:5).

God's promises never run out.

The Beauty of Any Day
Is Reflected in Your Heart

Sunday: Hearts That Choose to Rejoice

Rejoice in the Lord always. I will say it again: Rejoice!
(PHILIPPIANS 4:4)

HERE THE APOSTLE PAUL directs us to rejoice. He doesn't say, "If possible, I think it would be a good idea for you to rejoice." This isn't advice. It's a clear command.

If it's a command, then it must be something we can decide to do or not do. Paul is telling us that joy is a choice. We can choose joy.

How is that possible? Sure, it's easy enough to rejoice when our stomachs and pockets are full; when our kids are obedient and well-behaved; when people say nice things to us and about us. But what about when the bills are high and the funds are low; when our kids are in trouble at school or with the law; when people insult and slander us?

These questions miss the point. Paul isn't telling us to rejoice *in the circumstances*. He is telling us to rejoice *in the Lord*. This is something we can do *always*, because no matter how the circumstances change, the Lord remains the same. God is good *all the time*.

And Paul knows what he's talking about. He's writing this letter *from prison*, of all places. If he can rejoice there, then we can rejoice wherever we are right now.

Paul repeats himself, to drive home the point. He is serious about joy, because the joy of the Lord is our strength. If we lose our joy, we lose our strength.

I will say it again: Rejoice!

334

Monday: Be Gentle Today as the Lord Is Near

Let your gentleness be evident to all. The Lord is near.
(PHILIPPIANS 4:5)

GENTLENESS IS IN SHORT SUPPLY these days. Good luck finding any gentleness on Facebook or Twitter. Cruelty rules the day on social media.

Nowadays it's not enough to respectfully disagree with someone. You have to "own" that person, and show how stupid they are for holding that opinion. Celebrities get more fans and politicians get more votes if they show themselves to be tough and unyielding.

Paul gives different counsel. He urges us to show our gentleness. Why?

Because we are supposed to be like Jesus, and Jesus was gentle. Sure, He got angry at times, mainly at people who were failing to be gentle, who were exploiting others for their own gain. But Jesus issued an open invitation to all to come and join Him, describing Himself as "gentle and lowly in heart" (Matthew 11:29).

Jesus was far superior to everyone in status, authority and power. But He chose to treat the people He encountered with gentleness and grace. He had no need to show off, and nothing to prove.

Paul says we should be gentle "to all." Even people of a different race, a different nationality, a different political party? Especially to those people.

Another reason to show our gentleness is because "the Lord is near." This has a double meaning. He is near us at all times, observing our conduct. And His coming is also near, reminding us that we will one day answer to Him for how we treat others today.

Are you known for your gentleness?

Tuesday: Be Calm Today as You Pray

Do not be anxious about anything, but in every situation, by prayer and petition, with thanksgiving, present your requests to God.
(Philippians 4:6)

IT USED TO BE that the most prevalent problem psychologists had to deal with was depression. Now things have changed. The most common psychological ailment today is *anxiety*.

That's no surprise. There's certainly plenty to be anxious about. Satan is real, and this world is filled with physical and spiritual dangers. It is only natural to worry about our families and our futures.

What does Paul say we should worry about? *Nothing.*

Is that really possible? Yes, and here's why: *Worry may be natural, but prayer is supernatural.*

Prayer is the antidote to worry. Here is what Paul is saying: Every time you start to worry about something, pray about it instead. Convert your worries to prayers.

If we turn this into a habit, then Satan will stop trying to make us worry. Because he knows we'll end up praying, and that's the last thing he wants.

Paul reminds us, too, that thanksgiving is a key ingredient in our prayers. The more we thank God for what He has done, the more our anxiety will shrink and the more our faith will grow.

Worry is a waste of time and energy, but prayer is powerful and effective.

Turn your worries into prayers today.

Wednesday: The Beauty of Peace Guarding Hearts and Minds

And the peace of God, which transcends all understanding, will guard your hearts and your minds in Christ Jesus. (PHILIPPIANS 4:7)

THIS VERSE IMMEDIATELY follows yesterday's. It tells us what will happen when we turn our worries into prayers: anxiety will be replaced by peace.

Anxiety and peace are opposites. Yet Paul gives us a magic formula for changing one into the other. Prayer is the catalyst that converts anxiety into peace.

Think of it as a spiritual equation: Anxiety + Prayer = Peace

What kind of peace? A peace that "transcends all understanding." This has a double meaning.

First, this peace does not depend upon our understanding. When some trial comes our way, we immediately want to know why. We want to understand God's purpose in the trial, and how He'll bring us through it. But Paul is telling us we can have the peace of God even when our questions are not answered.

Second, this peace is mysterious. It's a supernatural peace that doesn't make sense on a human level. We don't understand how our anxieties have disappeared, but they have. We are at peace.

This peace guards both our hearts and our minds. Anxiety squeezes the heart in a tight grip, producing apprehension and fear. Anxiety fills the mind with possible scenarios and unanswered questions, with "how's" and "what if's." But the peace of God puts the heart at ease, and frees the mind to dwell on God's grace and goodness.

Thank God for His peace!

Thursday: How to Think

Finally, brothers and sisters, whatever is true, whatever is noble, whatever is right, whatever is pure, whatever is lovely, whatever is admirable—if anything is excellent or praiseworthy—think about such things. (PHILIPPIANS 4:8)

THE DEVIL WANTS TO MESS with your mind.

He has a lot of tools at his disposal for this purpose. He has movies and TV shows to stream into your home, filled with scenes of graphic violence and sinful sex. These images remain long after the show is over.

He has songs playing on the airwaves and on your earphones, with lyrics that spout hate and debase women. The tunes ensure that the words will stay with you.

He has many operatives working on social media. Some post fake news that creates paranoia and hostility toward those who are different from you. Others post comments on your accounts aimed at putting you down and making you feel worthless.

In this polluted climate, you need to exercise discernment. You need to put some filters in place to keep this stuff out of your head.

Don't believe everything you hear or see. The truth is out there, but you have to find it. Don't listen to the loudest voices, but find voices you can trust.

God has filled His world with beauty, and He has many gifted servants who use their talents in music, film, literature, art, etc., to create beautiful things.

Fill your eyes and ears and minds with the good things of God.

Friday: Putting It into Practice

Whatever you have learned or received or heard from me, or seen in me—put it into practice. And the God of peace will be with you. (PHILIPPIANS 4:9)

DAILY BIBLE READING is an essential spiritual discipline. Regular in-depth study is also important, diving deep into the Word. In addition to listening to our local pastor every Sunday, we have an abundance of resources at our fingertips with online podcasts and courses by great teachers.

But all the learning in the world won't do us any good unless we put into practice what we learn. The Word of God isn't just for the head, but for the heart, and for all of life.

Jesus didn't just call His disciples together for special teaching sessions, and then send them home. He trained them by letting them observe His ministry firsthand, and then imitate the things He did.

Even "non-ministry" activities became opportunities for them to learn. Walking along the road from town to town, preparing and eating meals, engaging the people around them—just doing ordinary life together gave them a chance to know Him and pattern their lives after Him.

Paul dares to suggest that people not only listen to his words and read his letters, but to watch his life, and imitate it. With Paul, it wasn't just "do as I say," but "do as I do."

Who are you patterning your life after?

Who is watching and imitating you?

Saturday: A Day of Peace

Whatever you have learned or received or heard from me, or seen in me—put it into practice. And the God of peace will be with you. (PHILIPPIANS 4:9)

PUTTING INTO PRACTICE what we have learned from the Word of God makes all the difference in our lives. Thankfully, we don't have to figure out how to do this on our own. God is with us in all that we do.

Jesus is leading us as our Good Shepherd. The Holy Spirit is working within us to implement the will of God in our lives. As we walk in the Spirit, we are walking with Jesus. We are never alone.

Jesus is our magnificent model, our perfect pattern. But He isn't walking the earth right now. That is why Paul points to himself as a living, breathing, visible example of the Christian life.

God wants all of His people to walk and talk and act like Jesus, so that the world can easily see what He is like. None of us will do this perfectly, not even the Apostle Paul. But by the grace of God upon us and the Spirit of God within us, we can reflect something of the manner and character of Jesus.

Two verses earlier, Paul spoke of the "peace of God." Now he speaks of the "God of peace." God is the source and fount of peace, and we experience His peace because He is with us.

The God of peace is with you today.

Life Is Like Tennis—A Player Who Doesn't Serve Well Often Loses

Sunday: Stand Firm

Therefore, my brothers and sisters, you whom I love and long for, my joy and crown, stand firm in the Lord in this way, dear friends. (PHILIPPIANS 4:1)

WE LIKE TO IMAGINE ourselves doing great exploits for the Lord, advancing the Kingdom, taking new territory in His Name. But more often than not, our calling is simply to stand firm where the Lord has planted us.

We are continuously under attack by the enemies of God and His Kingdom. We are targeted by the devil and his minions, who assail us with a barrage of accusations and lies, intended to intimidate us and push us to the brink of despair. We are also surrounded by a swarm of temptations, striving to lure our hearts away from Christ and fasten our affections on seductive idols.

An image offered by David in Psalm 1 can help us here. He pictures the man or woman of God as a tree planted by streams of water. Through seasonal changes, through storm and wind and drought, the tree remains firmly planted, drawing sustenance from a river that never runs dry.

The key to standing firm is putting down deep roots. These roots are not visible to the world, but they make it possible for the tree to thrive and bear fruit. In another letter Paul says that the believer is "rooted and grounded" in the love of Christ (Ephesians 3:17). Daily spending time in the presence of the Lord, praying and listening and meditating on Scripture—this is what sinks our roots into the abundant flow of Christ's unfathomable love.

Dig deep and stand firm.

Monday: Living with a Servant Heart

I plead with Euodia and I plead with Syntyche to be of the same mind in the Lord. Yes, and I ask you, my true companion, help these women since they have contended at my side in the cause of the gospel, along with Clement and the rest of my co-workers, whose names are in the book of life. (PHILIPPIANS 4:2–3)

PAUL'S WORK FOR THE LORD was never a one-man show. His policy was to travel with a team of co-laborers, all working together and contributing their various talents to the mission.

This was wise policy. A team is much more powerful and effective than an individual. A team means more talents, more energy, more strength, more prayer.

However, a team also means more conflict. Put together several strong-willed men and women who have their own ideas of how things should be done, and disagreement is inevitable.

Euodia and Syntyche are both godly women who have demonstrated strength and courage on behalf of the gospel. But Paul now pleads with them to come together in unity of purpose, and he enlists the help of others to assist them in reaching agreement.

Unity always comes at a cost, but it is well worth paying. The key is to maintain the heart of a servant, with a willingness to set aside our own preferences for the sake of the mission, and to do whatever we can to enable others to fulfill God's calling on their lives.

There is no limit to what you can accomplish if you don't care who gets the credit.

Tuesday: Concern for One Another

I rejoiced greatly in the Lord that at last you renewed your concern for me. Indeed, you were concerned, but you had no opportunity to show it. (PHILIPPIANS 4:10)

PAUL WAS CALLED and sent by God to carry the gospel throughout the regions of the Roman Empire. He realized from the start that this was not a task he could accomplish on his own. He enlisted others to travel with him as co-laborers in the work. In addition, like missionaries today, he had a network of partners who backed him with prayer and financial support.

Foremost among Paul's supporters was the church in Philippi. Paul expresses gratitude for their faithful partnership which commenced from the very founding of the church (Philippians 1:3–5). Time and again, wherever Paul traveled in his mission, messengers from the Philippian church would seek him out and bring him gifts of financial support.

This wasn't always easy to do. Now Paul is imprisoned in Rome, a distance of 700 to 1,200 miles from Philippi, depending on the route taken, by land or by sea. Yet the Philippian church managed to send emissaries with offerings to Paul at least two different times. Paul is moved by this practical expression of concern, and is strengthened and encouraged by their love and support.

What missionary, pastor or ministry leader can you pray for today? Is there a practical way you can show concern for them through a gift, a card or a note?

Wednesday: God Shall Supply

And my God will meet all your needs according to the riches of his glory in Christ Jesus. (PHILIPPIANS 4:19)

THIS IS A VERY POPULAR VERSE, often memorized and frequently quoted. But as with all Scripture, the context of the verse gives deeper insight into its meaning and implications.

Paul has been talking about the financial gift brought to him by an emissary from the Philippian church. Roman prisoners were held in rough conditions, with nothing provided to protect them from the cold, and barely enough to eat to keep them alive. So this donation from his friends would make a huge difference in Paul's daily life.

Paul is extremely grateful, yet also quick to point out that the worth of the gift is not measured in in monetary value, but in the love and concern that motivated it. He calls their gift "a fragrant offering, a sacrifice acceptable and pleasing to God" (Philippians 4:18).

This is very significant. Our financial donations to missionaries and their efforts to promote the spread of the gospel are viewed by God as precious offerings to Him.

Here is where the promise of verse 19 comes in. Because the Philippians have been generous in giving of their resources toward the cause of world evangelism, Paul is confident that God will supply all of their needs.

As for believers who waste their money or rack up credit card debt to satisfy their own desires, the promise may not apply.

Are you a generous giver?

Thursday: The Glory Goes to God

To our God and Father be glory for ever and ever. Amen.
(Philippians 4:20)

PAUL WAS A BOLD MISSIONARY, taking the gospel of salvation across borders, carrying the good news into areas where Christ was not known. He encountered opposition, danger and hardship at every turn. But his pioneer evangelism changed the world.

We are quick to honor Paul for his heroic missionary efforts. Yet in his own thinking, Paul can only marvel at the grace of God in his life.

It was God who mercifully took a zealous persecutor of the church and offered him the privilege of preaching the unsearchable riches of Christ. It was God who brought Paul to testify before governors and kings.

It was God who performed signs and wonders through the hands of Paul. It was God who enabled Paul to endure beatings, shipwreck and imprisonment. And it was God who established new churches throughout Europe and Asia Minor.

For Paul, it was always, "Not I, but Christ" (Galatians 2:20). It was never about what Paul had done for God, but what God had done for him.

Life becomes much easier and much more joyous when we cease striving for our own glory, and simply recognize that all the glory belongs to God.

The heavens declare the glory of God, along with the rest of His creation. But God is most glorified when the people made in His image worship Him, and reflect His glory in their lives.

Let God have His way in your life, so that He may be glorified through you.

Friday: Caring for Your Teammates

Greet all God's people in Christ Jesus. The brothers and sisters who are with me send greetings. All God's people here send you greetings, especially those who belong to Caesar's household.
(PHILIPPIANS 4:21–22)

MOST OF PAUL'S LETTERS in the New Testament are sent to churches and meant to be read in public settings. Yet in all of his letters, Paul takes the time to send personal greetings to the people he is writing, often mentioning individuals by name. Frequently the believers who are with Paul at the time also pass along their greetings as well. These are not businesslike memos, but heart-to-heart messages.

To be sure, Paul's letters address the gamut of theological topics, including salvation, sanctification, the gifts of the Holy Spirit, and the end times. He also deals with major problems that crop up in the churches, including immorality and divisiveness. But Paul never loses sight of the individuals to whom he is writing, and his aim is always to build up their faith and strengthen their interpersonal relationships.

In his efforts to help the church grow, a pastor can get caught up in numbers, counting heads in the pews and dollars in the offering plate. By the same token, church members may begin to see pastors as "professional" ministers always on call and obligated to respond to every need or request.

May the Lord remind us that we all struggle with illness, fatigue, financial problems, family issues, discouragement, and sometimes depression.

We all need to care, and to be cared for.

Saturday: The Grace Be with You as You Serve

The grace of the Lord Jesus Christ be with your spirit. Amen.
(PHILIPPIANS 4:23)

ONE OF THE FUNDAMENTAL TRUTHS of Christianity is that we are saved by grace. There is nothing we can do to earn God's favor or forgiveness. Every blessing from God flows to us in a river of grace. All we have to do is step in.

We do a pretty good job of keeping this straight in our theology. But we don't always remember it when it comes to living the Christian life, or engaging in Christian service.

We may think that after saving us and making us His children, God is now watching us closely to see if we measure up to our new status. Are we virtuous enough to resist the temptations that come our way?

God has called us to serve Him, and to serve one another. But what if He finds out how incompetent we are, how slow to notice and respond to the needs of others? What if He discovers how lazy and self-centered we are? What if He detects our impure motives?

We need to realize that between God and us, it's always grace, all the time, all the way. He gives us grace to cope with our temptations, and grace to lift us up when we fall. He gives us grace to serve, and graciously accepts our feeble efforts when we do.

His grace is sufficient. For you.

The Real Strength of a Person Is Not Physical, But Moral and Spiritual

Sunday: God Preserves a Life

Look on my suffering and deliver me, for I have not forgotten your law. Defend my cause and redeem me; preserve my life according to your promise. (Psalm 119:153–154)

IT'S NOT UNUSUAL for God's people to find themselves in precarious, life-threatening situations. Consider:

- David on the run from Saul's army ...
- Shadrach, Meshach, and Abednego, tossed into the fiery furnace...
- Daniel thrown into a den of lions ...
- Peter locked up in the stocks under guard ...

In every case, all the power of authoritarian governments was deployed against individuals who had no recourse to defend themselves. No attorney to demand respect for their rights. No chance of getting a day in court to argue their case. No hope of deliverance.

But God ...

Two words that change the whole equation. No matter the odds stacked against them, when God enters the picture, inevitable defeat is transformed into certain victory.

Whatever enemies they may face, God's people are never left to fend for themselves.

Here is God's promise: "Call upon me in the day of trouble; I will deliver you, and you shall glorify me" (Psalm 50:15).

God is faithful. God is with us. God is for us.

You may feel as if you're drowning in a sea of troubles, unsure how long you can keep your head above water. Fear not. God Himself is your Life Preserver. He will save you. He will see you through.

348

Monday: Weakness in the Wicked One

Salvation is far from the wicked, for they do not seek out your decrees. (Psalm 119:155)

In the Book of Acts, we meet King Herod Agrippa, grandson of Herod the Great, who slaughtered the male children of Bethlehem in an attempt to kill the baby Jesus.

Herod Agrippa inherited his grandfather's bloodthirsty ways. He initiated severe persecution against the Christians in Jerusalem, targeting the apostles themselves. He went so far as to have James (the brother of John) beheaded. When he saw that the Jewish leaders were pleased with this, he arrested Peter and slated his execution for immediately after the Passover.

God sent an angel to free Peter from his chains and lead him out of prison right under the noses of the guards. This caused quite a stir. Herod was so angry that he had all of the guards put to death for allowing the prisoner to escape.

Leaving behind these troublesome Jews and Christians, Herod headed to Caesarea. There he planned a way to soothe his wounded pride. He held a grand public event where he would dress in his royal robes, mount the throne and deliver a majestic speech. The crowds went wild, declaring him to be a god and not a man.

That was the end of the line for Herod. Because he refused to repent and acknowledge God, the angel of the Lord put him to death then and there. "He was eaten by worms and died" (Acts 12:23).

No power on earth can shield the wicked from the judgment of God.

Tuesday: God's Strong Compassion

Your compassion, Lord, is great; preserve my life according to your laws. (Psalm 119:156)

God met with Moses at the burning bush, and again on Mount Sinai. Moses had a special relationship with God, open and intimate. Because of this, Moses dared to ask God to reveal to him His Glory.

God warned Moses that no man could see His face and live. But God agreed to pass by Moses and proclaim His Name, revealing the essence of His Divine Nature. And what did Moses discover?

"The LORD passed before him and proclaimed, 'The LORD, the LORD, a God merciful and gracious, slow to anger, and abounding in steadfast love and faithfulness'" (Exodus 34:6).

God did not show Moses His power, His wisdom, or His sovereignty. Above all else, God wanted Moses to see His compassion.

It was out of compassion that God delivered the people from bondage in Egypt and brought them into the promised land.

It was out of compassion that God sent judges to Israel again and again to save them from their enemies.

It was out of compassion that God sent prophets to Israel again and again to warn them against the consequences of sin.

It was out of compassion that God came down to live among His people and take their sin and suffering upon Himself.

It was out of compassion that God drew near to us in our sinful state, led us to trust Christ as Savior, forgave us, cleansed us, and made us His children.

Rejoice today in God's great compassion for you.

Wednesday: God's Statutes

Many are the foes who persecute me, but I have not turned from your statutes. (Psalm 119:157)

A society cannot function without laws to regulate behavior. But where do we find the basis for these laws?

God has given every individual a conscience to help us distinguish right from wrong. But our conscience is not infallible, and can be warped by social pressure or personal sin.

In order to provide a foundation for human law and a lasting witness to true morality, God revealed His statutes to Israel, and tasked them with observing and safeguarding these laws. Israel did a better job at remembering and recording God's statutes than obeying them.

God's statutes are precious and beautiful revelations of His will for humanity. They can correct our conscience and call us back to the right road. They can also reveal our faults and failures, and help us to see how far short we fall below God's standards. This is painful, but necessary.

God's statutes cannot save us. Only Christ can save us, for only He lived in perfect obedience to the laws of God. When we are united with Christ by faith, He takes away our sin, and His righteousness becomes ours. His Holy Spirit then lives in us and directs our steps.

"The fruit of the Spirit is love, joy, peace, patience, kindness, goodness, faithfulness, gentleness, self-control; against such things there is no law" (Galatians 5:22–23).

Walk in the Spirit today.

Thursday: Learning from the Faithless Ones

I look on the faithless with loathing, for they do not obey your word. (PSALM 119:158)

THE BIBLE SHOWS human life in all its facets: success and failure, loyalty and betrayal, virtue and vice. We can learn from the examples of the faithful and faithless alike.

Take Samson. Separated from birth and called to the service of the Lord, he was endowed with strength far beyond a normal man. But strong as he was, he never mastered his passions. He failed to maintain his consecration to God, and continually pursued unwise relationships with women. Having lost sight of his calling, he ended up losing both his strength and his vision.

Take Saul. Divinely chosen and anointed to be the first king of Israel, he showed humility and grace at the start of his reign. But he gave in to pride and jealousy, and his lust for power drove him mad. He ended up turning against those loyal to him, and doing great damage to the kingdom.

Take Judas. Privileged to be selected as one of the original twelve disciples, he was also given the role of treasurer, and put in charge of the common purse. But he began to measure everything in terms of its monetary value, and ended up selling out his Master for thirty pieces of silver.

Sex, power and money have been the downfall of many well-known ministers of the gospel, and countless more whose names are unknown.

What is your most vulnerable area of temptation? What measures are you taking to guard your heart?

Friday: Living in Accordance with God's Love

See how I love your precepts; preserve my life, Lord, in accordance with your love. (PSALM 119:159)

How do we know God loves us?

The cross is both the proof and the measure of God's love for us. A cross is not a closed figure. It extends vertically and horizontally with no natural end. No matter how far the vertical and horizontal segments are lengthened, it remains a cross.

The vertical extension shows that there is no limit to how far God descends to demonstrate His love to us. We cannot sink too low for Him to reach us.

"He made himself nothing, taking the form of a servant, being born in the likeness of men. And being found in human form, he humbled himself by becoming obedient to the point of death, even death on a cross" (PHILIPPIANS 2:7–8).

The vertical extension also shows that there is no limit to how high God will lift us. In spite of all our sin, He welcomes us into His family.

"And He has raised us up with Christ and seated us with him in the heavenly places" (EPHESIANS 2:6).

The horizontal extension shows that God's love is wide enough to encompass everyone. Divisions of race and class, rich and poor, beautiful and plain, intelligent and foolish, male and female—all are overcome by the love of God.

"May you have strength to comprehend with all the saints what is the breadth and length and height and depth, and to know the love of Christ that surpasses knowledge" (EPHESIANS 3:18–19).

And may you live today in accordance with that love.

Saturday: The Eternal Perspective

All your words are true; all your righteous laws are eternal.
(PSALM 119:160)

FOOLISHNESS THINKS only of today. Wisdom thinks also of tomorrow.

The human lifespan can be 80, 90, even 100 years. Knowing this, it makes sense to invest 12 to 16 years or more in education and training. This preparation helps us to maximize the potential and productivity of our middle and mature years.

We also know that old age is coming, when our strength and health start to wane. It is wise to think ahead and lay aside resources for the days when our income will shrink or disappear.

But if that's as far as we go, we are fools, indeed.

Our time spent on earth in these bodies is a tiny fraction of the lifespan God has planned for us. According to God's promise, there is an eternal life ahead of us, with resurrected, immortal bodies in a New Heaven and New Earth.

This changes our whole perspective.

It means we can endure pain and loss with patience, for "the sufferings of this present time are not worth comparing with the glory that is to be revealed to us" (Romans 8:18).

It means that instead of grabbing for all we can get now, we lay up treasures in heaven by giving generously and doing good to others.

It means that we make holiness our goal, in preparation for God's Holy Kingdom to come.

Be wise today. Live with an eternal perspective.

At Christmastime Consider Not a Friend's Gift, but the Friendship of the Giver

Sunday: Learning from the Shepherds

And there were shepherds living out in the fields nearby, keeping watch over their flocks at night. (LUKE 2:8)

WHAT IS YOUR FAVORITE PART of the story of Jesus being born on earth? Some people love seeing Christmas musicals where children dress like shepherds. Parents are taking pictures or videoing the entire event. Looking at their daughters and sons on stage dressed up in a church drama is exciting. Especially at Christmas.

If you are accustomed to the story, though, you might ignore the meaning of what all is happening there. Those are shepherds—common, every day people in that culture, just doing their jobs. That is when everything changed. That is when nothing would ever be the same.

We need to learn from those shepherds. They worked, taking care of sheep. Feeding them, protecting them, guiding them. They give themselves to the sheep as they defended them against any other creatures attacking them.

Learning from the shepherds means grasping the importance of a few things:

- Keeping doing what we are here to do.
- Refuse to stop while waiting for a miracle.
- Believe God's miracle will come at God's time in God's way.
- We are important to those we are keeping watch over.

As you live out in your fields nearby, learn today from the shepherds.

Monday: Good News of Great Joy

An angel of the Lord appeared to them, and the glory of the Lord shone around them, and they were terrified. But the angel said to them, "Do not be afraid. I bring you good news that will cause great joy for all the people." (LUKE 2:9–10)

AT CHRISTMASTIME this year, we should consider not so much the gift of a friend, but the friendship of the giver. To help us do that, we need to go back to the original story of Jesus being born on earth.

The shepherds were doing their profession. That normal custom was abruptly interrupted by an angel. Not a typical day on the job. Not a normal time in the field.

Luke describes the scene. As the angel appeared, God's glory was shining all around them.

What do you think that looked like? What do you think it felt like? How would you feel if, as you were working your normal occupation or fulfilling your customary duties, an angel just showed up?

As we can all imagine, the shepherds were terrified. God's works often initially shock us. We might not see His action about to occur. We might not expect an unexpected encounter. Like the shepherds, our nerves might rattle, and our heartbeats might rush.

But when fear began to be obvious, the angel had more words. They were to hear and heed the instructions:

- Do not be afraid.

Reasons were given for the fear to be gone. The angel said this is what he was bringing:

- Good news
- Which will cause great joy
- For all the people.

Don't you love to hear good news? I do! It can bring a smile to our faces. It can bring peace to our spirits. It can bring ambition and hope and assurance and certainty.

Tuesday: A Savior Has Been Born

Today in the town of David a Savior has been born to you; he is the Messiah, the Lord. (LUKE 2:11)

DON'T WE NEED GOOD NEWS these days? Yes, we do.

Listen again to those instructions from an angel to some frightened shepherds: Do not be afraid. Listen again to the reason: Good news is here. That news will cause great joy. It is for all the people.

It is for us today. Good news. Great joy. Today!

The angel offered more details. That day, in the city of David, a Savior had been born. "He is the Messiah, the Lord," said the angel.

As you hurry through all your duties and chores today, can you pause for a few moments to hear again those words? Today. In the town of David. A Savior has been born to you. He is the Messiah. He is the Lord.

The fact that a Savior was born should change all we do and why we do what we do. It should change our perspectives on everything we face in life. It should remind us to be givers not receivers. It should remind us to be friends with God and His people.

Take a moment now to worship and celebrate Jesus. He is the Messiah. He is the Lord. Sing a song to Him. Rejoice and be glad because of Him.

Wednesday: Lying in a Manger

This will be a sign to you: You will find a baby wrapped in cloths and lying in a manger. (LUKE 2:12)

THAT NEWS ABOUT JESUS being born is exciting to us. We sing songs to celebrate. We gather together to rejoice. But think about how the promises from an angel had to shock the shepherds.

We expect the festivities this time of year. They expected just another day.

As more information came, the story became even more peculiar. An angel was there? The angel was talking to shepherds? The angel was promising the coming of the Messiah? All of that was unusual. Look at what the angel alleged next.

"This will be a sign to you," the angel said. "You will find a baby wrapped in cloths and lying in a manger."

Wrapped in swaddling clothes and laying in a manger wasn't the expected location for the birth of a king. A barn around animals was not what the Israelites anticipated for the coming of the Messiah.

But that is how God works. He comes in those unexpected places in unanticipated ways. He shows up around unforeseen people to declare His unusual truth.

Jesus came, lying in a manger. Not on a throne to begin this story.

Believe today Jesus is showing up near you. Believe today Jesus is bringing His love into your story. Believe today that the One who was lying in a manger is the One who is your Lord and your Savior.

Thursday: See What Has Happened

Suddenly a great company of the heavenly host appeared with the angel, praising God and saying, "Glory to God in the highest heaven, and on earth peace to those on whom his favor rests." When the angels had left them and gone into heaven, the shepherds said to one another, "Let's go to Bethlehem and see this thing that has happened, which the Lord has told us about." (LUKE 2:13–15)

I GUESS ONE ANGEL wasn't enough. The story from Luke continues by bringing in "a great company of the heavenly host." We don't know exactly how they looked, but we do know what they were doing:

- Praising God.
- Saying, "Glory to God in the highest heavens."
- Saying, "And on earth peace to those on whom His favor rests."

It probably would be good for us to all do that again today. Praise God, today. State truth, today. Something happens when we choose to praise God and sing His truth aloud.

If we believe in this Christmas story, shouldn't we start singing? Shouldn't we praise the Lord?

Oh, I know we should. And I know what happens when we do.

The angels then left the shepherds alone. Think of those emotions they had to feel. Think of what all they had to be saying to each other—if they had the courage to say anything at all.

Well, when they did talk to each other, this is what they said:

- Let's go to Bethlehem
- And see this thing that has happened
- Which the Lord has told us about.

I guess that could be our assignment for today. Even though we are not where those shepherds were, we can still go. Even though we probably won't travel to Bethlehem, God still has a place for us to go. He wants us to remember what happened and all that He has told us about.

See what has happened. That is our invitation today. Let us not miss it!

Friday: All Were Amazed

So they hurried off and found Mary and Joseph, and the baby, who was lying in the manger. When they had seen him, they spread the word concerning what had been told them about this child, and all who heard it were amazed at what the shepherds said to them. But Mary treasured up all these things and pondered them in her heart.
(LUKE 2:16–19)

THE SHEPHERDS headed out after the angels left them. They traveled with a plan, one plan. They wanted to see Jesus.

Think about your day today. What if that was your main goal: to see Jesus? What if no other priority carried the urgency of this one: to see Jesus?

That is what the shepherds did. They hurried—it was not something to wait on and stall or delay. It was time to find Jesus. It was time to get there then.

They found Jesus and Mary and Joseph. What did they do next? They spread the word concerning what had been told them about the child.

Wouldn't that be another good assignment for Christians today? To spread the word about Jesus? Hurrying toward Jesus, then seeing Jesus, leaves people one real way to respond: Spread the word!

We can't keep it hushed. We can't stay silent about the news. We must go. We must tell.

The people who heard the shepherds were all amazed. We can amaze someone today. Not by getting extravagant or flamboyant or senseless. But by telling them we have seen the Savior.

As the shepherds told the news, look at what Mary did:

· She treasured up all these things.
· She pondered them in her heart.

End today's devotion by doing just what Mary did. Read the story. Treasure it all. Ponder it in your heart.

The world might then be amazed at seeing Jesus through you.

Saturday: All They Had Seen and Heard

The shepherds returned, glorifying and praising God for all the things they had heard and seen, which were just as they had been told. On the eighth day, when it was time to circumcise the child, he was named Jesus, the name the angel had given him before he was conceived. (LUKE 2:20–21)

EACH YEAR CHRISTMAS COMES. Each year Christmas leaves. The songs and decorations and gifts and events. They come. They go. Families travel but return home.

But, like the shepherds, a true experience with Jesus doesn't allow us to return home just the way we left. Those shepherds returned celebrating. Too much good had happened for them to forget it. They were glorifying and praising God for all the things they had seen and heard.

What about you? How has seeing Jesus, knowing Jesus, loving Jesus, changed your life? How has all you've seen and heard from Jesus made you return differently than you were before?

I must tell you this today. Our world is desperate for transformed people. Our culture craves the coming home of shepherds who have seen Jesus. Our society needs a group of folks like you who are willing to see and hear Jesus, then let others know all you have seen and heard.

Can you count on you to do that today? The world is waiting. God is calling. Are you willing to return home and tell them about Jesus?

Do Not Hurry God— He Works Leisurely Because He Has Eternity to Work On

Sunday: Looking into the Future

Look, I am coming soon! My reward is with me, and I will give to each person according to what they have done. (REVELATION 22:12)

GOD WORKS LEISURELY because He has eternity to work on. Therefore, we must not attempt to hurry God. He doesn't go by our clock or our preferences. He sees better and bigger.

If we believe that about God's view of the future, our glance into tomorrow should change. Think about it. If you already know the weather, won't that influence what you wear? If you already know the cost, won't that affect how you save your money? Likewise, looking into a future where we know the results ought to change our glimpse toward tomorrow and our behavior today.

Jesus will give to all who have served Him. What else will really matter in the end? Eternal life in a place of peace and abundance — isn't that what we need?

Knowing such truth about the future, our present situations shouldn't look quite as large as we often let them. Right? We can change that. We can shrink them today. We can see everything better if we remember the Lord's reward is with Him and waiting for us.

That inspires us to conclude this year by thinking of our end on earth as only a new beginning into an eternity with Jesus.

Monday: Remembering God's View

I am the Alpha and the Omega, the First and the Last, the Beginning and the End. (REVELATION 22:13)

So, AS WE TALKED YESTERDAY, the view matters. Instead of our limited vision, the book of Revelation gives us a wider glance. Remembering God's view helps us not try as much to hurry things along.

In Revelation 22 we can listen in to the voice of Jesus. He claims to be the First and the Last, the Beginning and the End. He is the start and the finish. He is now and forever. He is seeing from a glimpse of eternity.

Because of that, our present issues should shift in size. What bothered you the most this year, last month, this week, yesterday? Were those issues worth getting so worked up over? Should you have invested so much energy on them? What if you chose to:

- Remember Jesus is with me.
- Remember Jesus was here before me.
- Remember Jesus will be with me forever.

If those three thoughts covered your mind, you might think differently. If those three beliefs filled your heart, you might respond differently. Small things would be small again. God's things would matter most.

Remembering God's view can change what we do today.

Tuesday: Glancing at the Gates We Will Go Through

Blessed are those who wash their robes, that they may have the right to the tree of life and may go through the gates into the city.
(Revelation 22:14)

You can't get into a locked door without a key or a code. The vehicle won't let you in. The house won't let you in. You might want to go, but you need the right key, or you need to know the correct code to unlock the door and enter.

Thinking about eternal life reminds us about gates to enter "the city." Imagine those gates. Think about those who "have the right to the tree of life and may go through the gates."

That future reality sure can help how we live each day on earth. Maybe today glancing at those gates just might influence:

- Our words
- Our actions
- Our attitudes
- Our dreams
- Our hopes
- Our goals
- Our relationships
- Our priorities
- Our purpose

Look at each of those areas. See how a better view of tomorrow can give you a better perspective for each moment of each day.

Take a glance toward the future. Allow that view to change how you stare at today.

Wednesday: The True Testimony of Us All

I, Jesus, have sent my angel to give you this testimony for the churches. I am the Root and the Offspring of David, and the bright Morning Star. (REVELATION 22:16)

> Although the church has been often defeated, and sometimes appeared to be on the verge of destruction, it has emerged with new life and power. The enemies of Christ nailed Him to a cross, saw His body buried in a tomb, and thought they were rid of Him forever. But on the third day, they were startled by the tidings that He was alive and walking again among men. About the eighteenth century, men like David Hume, the Scottish philosopher and historian, were predicting that Christianity would be dead by the end of the century. But before that century ended, a great revival under Wesley and Whitefield swept over England and America and regions beyond, kindling religious fires that are still burning. In France, Voltaire and his unbelieving associates declared that Christianity was dead and that Christian temples would soon be changed into halls of science. But at that same time William Carey emerged from England and started a missionary movement that was to sweep the entire earth. (BLUEPRINT)

We are a part of that church. We are a part of God's work, the movement that is bringing change in these days.

It helps to remember that Jesus is the root of the church, the offspring of David, the bright Morning Star. He has sent messengers like us to live as testimonies to the church.

Thursday: Cannot Fail

The Spirit and the bride say, "Come!" And let the one who hears say, "Come!" Let the one who is thirsty come; and let the one who wishes take the free gift of the water of life. (REVELATION 22:17)

THERE ARE THOSE TODAY who say the church has failed, and we must look to something else. Many institutions called churches have failed, but the true church of Christ will not fail. Its ultimate victory is assured by several factors.

Christ's church has a divine builder. It was Christ who said, "Upon this rock I will build my church." If it were built by men, it would go down in defeat. But Christ built it, and He built it on a rock that will not crumble. It was said of Abraham that "he looked for a city which hath foundations, whose builder and maker is God" (Hebrews 11:10). That may be said of the church. It has foundations, and its Builder and Maker is Christ.

Yes, some people are still saying, "The church is failing and will pass away." But the living Lord steps into the midst of the doubts and fears and says, "No, the church will not fail. I built it; I know what went into it, and I poured into it the agony and sorrow of Gethsemane, the suffering and death of the cross, the glory of the resurrection, and the power of Pentecost. It will not, it cannot fail." (BLUEPRINT)

Friday: Amen and Amen

He who testifies to these things says, "Yes, I am coming soon." Amen. Come, Lord Jesus. (Revelation 22:20)

YES, THE LORD IS COMING SOON. Not only is another year ending, but the larger end is nearby. Should we live with that perspective? Shouldn't our lives be Amen and Amen?

What happens if we live that way? Here are reminders:

It has divine presence in it. Recall the words of Paul to the church at Corinth: "Know ye not that ye are the temple of God, and that the Spirit of God dwelleth in you?" (1 Corinthians 3:16). This was the assurance of victory that John gave to the church of his day: "Greater is he that is in you, than he that is in the world" (1 John 4:4). With a presence like that within it, the church will not fall before its enemies.

It has a divine promise behind it. It was Jesus Christ our Lord who said, "The gates of Hades shall not prevail against it." That promise of our Lord will not fail. Whatever experiences the church must pass through, and however powerful may be the foes arrayed against it, there will be victory in the end. (BLUEPRINT)

A divine presence and a divine promise. An Amen and an Amen. Those are words for us today. Believe them. Receive them. He is coming soon, so let us live them!

Saturday: Grace for God's People

The grace of the Lord Jesus be with God's people. Amen.
(Revelation 22:21)

In closing this discussion, it is well to emphasize two key points.

Church membership is not to be taken lightly. It means something to be a member of the church of Christ. It carries with it high privileges and holy responsibilities. Those who are members of the church should enter into these privileges and accept these responsibilities.

Some want the privileges of church membership without the responsibilities. They want what the church can give but refuse to carry their part of the load. Others care for neither the privileges nor the responsibilities. Their names are on a church roll, and that is about all that church membership means to them.

There should be deep searching of heart before one unites with the church. It means infinitely more than entering one's name. And the church should exercise more care and watchfulness in receiving members. We need more godly and godward members.

Church membership calls for the best one has. Some seem to think that anything is good enough for the church. They give the church the scraps that are left. They spend their money on luxuries and give a pittance to the church.

A certain business institution had this motto on its walls: "Only the best is good enough." That is truer of the church than any other institution—only the best is good enough for Jesus. (Blueprint)

Conclusion

AS WE CLOSE OUR TIME OF REFLECTION on how to trust God when the world is falling apart, let's conclude this conversation with Scripture we used long ago in week eighteen:

> For this reason, since the day we heard about you, we have not stopped praying for you. We continually ask God to fill you with the knowledge of his will through all the wisdom and understanding that the Spirit gives, so that you may live a life worthy of the Lord and please him in every way: bearing fruit in every good work, growing in the knowledge of God, being strengthened with all power according to his glorious might so that you may have great endurance and patience, and giving joyful thanks to the Father, who has qualified you to share in the inheritance of his holy people in the kingdom of light, for he has rescued us from the dominion of darkness and brought us into the kingdom of the Son he loves, in whom we have redemption, the forgiveness of sins (COLOSSIANS 1:9–14).

Paul had not stopped praying for them. He revealed the specifics of what he was asking God to do. Finishing this book of devotions doesn't mean an ending. I believe this is a new beginning to live out what we have studied. Like Paul, we do not stop. And I ask you, like Paul, to continue praying for others and for yourself. For your friends, your family, for strangers. For people nearby and far away.

Pray for them to be strengthened with all power. Pray that for yourself now, also.

Pray, believing that this power will be coming from God's glorious might. Pray, believing that for yourself now, also.

Pray, that the reasons this is needed are endurance and patience. Pray, believing that you will also have great endurance and patience.

Pray for us to all serve God that way. With His strength. With His power. With His endurance. With His patience.

Throughout this book I have hoped to remind you to think about other people. We must be about our Father's business and His business is serving other people. Treating them right. Showing God's love to them.

However and whenever the results come, we must continue serving. Paul reminds us of a key thought that should keep us trusting in God even when the world is falling apart:

- For He has rescued us
- from the dominion of darkness
- and brought us into the Kingdom
- of the Son He loves.

That thought benefits us in remembering the reason we should serve others. Look at what the Lord has done. He rescued us. From the dominion of darkness, He rescued us. And God brought us into the Kingdom of the Son He loves.

Oh, my friends, shouldn't that change our purpose today? Can't that help us make better decisions with better attitudes, and all for the right reasons?

Yes, it can. Yes, it will.

Please trust God. Please believe that is what He is doing in your life even when the world is falling apart.

And put a smile on your face and joy in your heart as you thank Him. He made this day, so rejoice and be glad!

IF YOU'RE A FAN OF THIS BOOK, HELP ME SPREAD THE WORD

There are several ways you can help get the word out about the message of this book and share in the ministry...

- Post a 5-Star review on Amazon, Goodreads and other places that come to mind.
- Write about the book on your Facebook, Twitter, Instagram, Google+, any social media sites you regularly use.
- If you blog, consider referencing the book, or publishing an excerpt from the book with a link back to our website.
- Take a photo of yourself with your copy of the book. Post it on your social media.
- Share a Facebook Live post on how a particular devotional ministered to you.
- Recommend the book to friends—word of mouth is still the more effective form of advertising.
- When you're in a bookstore, ask if they carry the book. The book is available through all major distributors, so any bookstore that does not have it in stock can easily order it.
- Purchase additional copies to give away as gifts.

You can order additional copies of the book from our website as well as in bookstores by going to livelystone.org. Special bulk quantity discounts are available. https://livelystone.org/

Also available through these fine retailers

amazon BARNES&NOBLE

Be Sure to Order Copies of all 3 Devotionals in the Series!

Trusting God When Your World is Falling Apart is the first of a 3-volume deluxe hardback devotional book set. Be sure to order all three at https://livelystone.org/

Facing Forward
Leading In a Way that Makes Others Want to Follow (Fall 2021)

Growing Together
Experiencing the Joy of a Godly Relationship (Spring 2022)

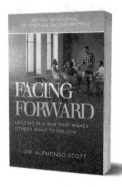

Other Books by Dr. Alphonso Scott

Wisdom Conversations. Church Leaders are facing enormous challenges in their churches and ministries. How do you keep the word from getting lost in today's society reality? This book will calm your soul with conversations regarding leadership in todays model. A great resource read for leaders of any size flock.

Blueprint. This book will give readers a greater understanding of how the New Testament is a handbook for the Church. With a plethora of self-help leadership books by authors who claim to have the answers, this book is a call back to the original source.